The Bible, Mormon Scripture, and the Rhetoric of Allusivity

The Fairleigh Dickinson University Press Mormon Studies Series

The Fairleigh Dickinson University Press Mormon Studies Series is committed to the publication of scholarly works that explore Mormon history, literature, film, biography, and theology, as well as considering how Mormonism has interacted with society, culture, folklore, philosophy, politics, and the arts.

General Editor

Dr. Rachel Cope, Department of Church History and Doctrine,
Brigham Young University

Series Editors

Dr. Andrew Hedges, Associate Professor, Church History and Doctrine,
Brigham Young University
Dr. Susanna Morrill, Department Chair and Associate Professor of Religious Studies,
Lewis and Clark College
Dr. Andrew Skinner, Professor, Ancient Scripture,
Brigham Young University
Dr. John W. Welch, Robert K. Thomas University Professor of Law,
Brigham Young University

Advisory Board

Catherine Brekus (Harvard Divinity School), Richard Bushman (Columbia University), David Campbell (University of Notre Dame), James H. Charlesworth (Princeton Theological Seminary), Terryl Givens (University of Richmond), David Holland (Harvard Divinity School), Kate Holbrook (Church History Library), Laurie Maffly-Kipp (Washington University in St. Louis), Tom Mould (Elon University), and Stephen Webb (Independent Scholar).

Publications in Mormon Studies

Ignacio M. García, *Chicano While Mormon: Activism, War, and Keeping the Faith* (2015)
Mauro Properzi, *Mormonism and the Emotions: An Analysis of LDS Scriptural Texts* (2015)
Adam J. Powell, *Irenaeus, Joseph Smith, and God-making Heresy* (2015)
Nicholas J. Frederick, *The Bible, Mormon Scripture, and the Rhetoric of Allusivity* (2016)

On the Web at http://www.fdu.edu/fdupress

The Bible, Mormon Scripture, and the Rhetoric of Allusivity

Nicholas J. Frederick

FAIRLEIGH DICKINSON UNIVERSITY PRESS
Madison • Teaneck

Published by Fairleigh Dickinson University Press
Copublished by The Rowman & Littlefield Publishing Group, Inc.
4501 Forbes Boulevard, Suite 200, Lanham, Maryland 20706
www.rowman.com

Unit A, Whitacre Mews, 26-34 Stannary Street, London SE11 4AB

British Library Cataloguing in Publication Information Available

Library of Congress Cataloging-in-Publication Data

Names: Frederick, Nicholas J., author.
Title: The Bible, Mormon scripture, and the rhetoric of allusivity / Nicholas J. Frederick.
Description: Madison [New Jersey]; Teaneck : Fairleigh Dickinson University Press | Includes bib-
     liographical references and index.
Identifiers: LCCN 2016006021 (print) | LCCN 2016008221 (ebook) | ISBN 9781611479058 (cloth :
     alk. paper) | ISBN 9781611479065 (electronic)
Subjects: LCSH: Church of Jesus Christ of Latter-day Saints--Sacred books. | Mormon Church--
     Sacred books. | Book of Mormon--Relation to the Bible. | Doctrine and Covenants--Relation to
     the Bible. | Bible. John, I--Criticism, interpretation, etc. | Church of Jesus Christ of Latter-day
     Saints--Doctrines. | Mormon Church--Doctrines.
Classification: LCC BX8622.F74 2016 (print) | LCC BX8622 (ebook) | DDC 289.3/2--dc23
LC record available at http://lccn.loc.gov/2016006021

♾™ The paper used in this publication meets the minimum requirements of American
National Standard for Information Sciences Permanence of Paper for Printed Library
Materials, ANSI/NISO Z39.48-1992.

Printed in the United States of America

Contents

Foreword

Mormon scriptural studies are undergoing something of a Renaissance. The great tradition of close reading and deep analysis characteristic of biblical studies for many centuries is being reborn in and redirected to Mormon texts. The Book of Mormon particularly is being examined with far greater philosophical, theological, and critical acuity than ever before. Earlier scriptural commentaries correlated texts, linked them to authoritative teachings by General Authorities, and embedded them in history. The more recent works open up depths of meaning scarcely glimpsed until now. Works by Joseph Spencer, Grant Hardy, James Faulconer, and Terryl Givens illustrate what I mean.[1]

Nicholas Frederick's study of the uses of the Gospel of John in the Book of Mormon and the Doctrine and Covenants explores another form of literary analysis: intertextuality. During the linguistic turn of the late twentieth century, when the word "theory" came into common usage, intertextuality became a key method for unlocking texts. In its extreme form, the word implied that every text—indeed every person—was but a skein of other texts. Of necessity an author must write in a language, and the words of that language are all resident in countless other texts where they acquire their meanings. When a word or a phrase is put into use it trails all the meanings acquired in these previous texts. Our own personalities, composed largely of the words that we speak and think, likewise are borrowed from other usages by other persons and other texts. We can be thought of a composite of all these previous usages combined into the conglomerate that is each of us. This is intertextuality *in extremis*.

Frederick's work goes nowhere this far. He begins with the simpler fact that lots and lots of biblical phrases occur in the Book of Mormon and the Doctrine and Covenants. For the Book of Mormon, this raises questions. Passages from the Old and New Testaments, from before and after the time when the Book of Mormon text was purportedly written by its ancient authors, turn up in the book's pages. This assimilation of biblical language has been used by its detractors to discredit the Book of Mormon. Critics try to depict the book as a mere pastiche, cobbled together by an author who happened to be steeped in biblical language. Apologists answer that this is not such a simple feat. There is something miraculous about the complexity and depth of the biblical texts woven seamlessly into the Book of Mormon.

Frederick avoids this apologist versus critic debate by examining more closely just exactly how biblical texts function in the Book of Mormon and the Doctrine and Covenants. His aim is not to authenticate the divine origins of either book but to ask how biblical passages work in their pages. Since investigation of all of the biblical intertextuality in Joseph Smith's texts would be a massive and cumbersome undertaking, he has focused on the Book of John which happens to have been plentifully and strategically used in both of Joseph Smith's texts and more particularly the Prologue of John, the first eighteen verses of John's gospel. Well versed in the current scholarship on John's writings, Frederick is in a position to identify distinctive usages in Mormon scripture. What new meanings does Joseph Smith add to the traditional interpretations of John?

An immense effort goes into this kind of close reading. Without electronic search engines, the task would be overwhelming, requiring a lifetime of labor. Besides identifying the Johannine passages in the Book of Mormon and the Doctrine and Covenants, Frederick has read both texts with extreme care to pick out the shades of meaning embedded in their words. The analysis is necessarily technical and detailed, requiring much effort to reach even modest conclusions and much concentration on the part of readers to grasp what has been discovered. The payoff is in the thoroughness. We get to the bottom of things. This is precisely the kind of attention the Bible has received for centuries. It is the labor required now to achieve a comparable level of scrutiny and appreciation of Mormon texts.

Frederick's interpretation of John in Mormon texts will not necessarily coincide with familiar Latter-day Saint understanding of the Johannine passages. Frederick discovers that the textual meanings carried over from the Bible take on new forms in the Book of Mormon and Doctrine and Covenants. Mormon textual usages tug against traditional meanings, straining to say something new and, in places, something theologically radical. Readers must be prepared for new understandings of familiar texts. Intertextuality, it turns out, is not always imitation and repetition. It can also be innovation and revelation.

—Richard Bushman

NOTE

1. Joseph M. Spencer, *An Other Testament: On Typology* (Salem, OR: Salt Press, 2012); Grant Hardy, *Understanding the Book of Mormon: A Reader's Guide* (New York: Oxford University Press, 2010); James Faulconer, *The Life of Holiness: Notes and Reflections on Romans 1, 5–8* (Provo, UT: Neal A. Maxwell Institute for Religious Scholarship, 2012); Terryl L. Givens, *The Book of Mormon: A Very Short Introduction* (New York: Oxford University Press, 2009).

Acknowledgments

This work began as a dissertation written during my time at Claremont Graduate University. It is only due to the effort of a great many people that this project has made it this far. Richard Bushman served as my dissertation advisor during my time at CGU, and it was in his many engaging courses that I developed my love of intertextuality and Mormon scripture. My dissertation committee, Gregory J. Riley, Karen J. Torjesen, and Patrick Q. Mason provided valuable feedback and kept me from biting off more than I could chew. Once I decided to turn the dissertation into a publishable monograph, I received crucial advice and suggestions (and a few much-needed criticisms) from friends and colleagues who took the time to read through various versions of this manuscript: Stephen Robinson, Thomas Wayment, Kerry Hull, Andrew Hedges, Michael MacKay, and Joseph Spencer. My tireless research assistant, Amy Lords, worked hard tracking down obscure articles and checking countless sources. Thanks as well to Rachel Cope and Harry Keyishian at Fairleigh Dickinson University Press, who were so helpful in getting this manuscript published. Of course, none of this would be possible without the support of my wife, Julie, and my children Miranda, Samuel, and Kassandra, who put their lives on hold so I could move us to California, and who continue to be patient with a husband and father who has been blessed with much more than he deserves.

Finally, I must acknowledge the sense of inadequacy I feel about this project. The impetus was an attempt to better understand Joseph Smith and the literary corpus he left behind. I hoped that through the application of a lens such as intertexuality I would come to understand Smith and his work better, or at least in a different way than I already did. In some ways, I believe I do. In other ways, the Book of Mormon and the Doctrine and Covenants have become only more undefinable. There remains a great deal about Smith and his works that lies beyond this type of study. I hope I have made a genuine contribution. All mistakes and errors are, of course, my own.

Introduction

Joseph Smith biographer Richard Bushman has called the Bible "the primary source of his (Smith's) creative energy."[1] Analyses of Smith's use of the Bible in his own corpus have taken many different forms over the years, especially as it pertains to the composition of the Book of Mormon. Some have attempted to psycho-analyze Smith and even find his own childhood within the text of the Book of Mormon.[2] Other studies more favorable toward the historicity of the text have dealt with the problem of authorship by pointing out the remarkable complexities found within the text, or even the possibilities of "Hebraisms," which those same scholars argue is proof of its ancient origins.[3] Furthermore, for over twenty-five years, scholars have been analyzing the earliest versions of the Book of Mormon manuscript as part of a critical text study.[4] The Book of Mormon has also been analyzed through a literary lens,[5] but one particular area of study still remains underdeveloped. Even though Mormon Scripture is filled with chapters and verses from the Bible, there has not been a book length study comparing the text of the Book of Mormon and the Doctrine and Covenants.

The two primary texts produced by Smith, the Book of Mormon and the Doctrine and Covenants, demonstrate a clear dependence on the King James Bible for much of their language and thought. In the course of producing the two texts, the Book of Mormon and the Doctrine and Covenants included thousands of phrases from the King James Bible. These phrases were merged together with nineteenth century vernacular to create modern American scripture—a text that is as authoritative and canonical for Mormons as the Bible is for non-LDS Christians. Reading these texts leaves the impression that Joseph Smith disassembled the Bible, and reconstructed it within the text of the Book of Mormon and the Doctrine and Covenants.[6] It is this amalgamation of ancient and modern scripture that this book attempts to describe.

JOSEPH SMITH AND THE BIBLE

In addition to the Bible, Mormon scripture is largely composed of two texts, the Book of Mormon and the Doctrine and Covenants, as well as a third work, the Pearl of Great Price, which contains some of Smith's biblical revisions, an account of his "first vision," as well as thirteen "articles of faith."[7] The first of these works to be published, the Book of Mormon, was printed in biblical fashion as a collection of books, originally divided into chapters and later into verses. It contained two dozen chapters of material common to the Bible. The subjects of its narrative were originally biblical peoples, many of its episodes paralleled biblical stories, and it purported both to prophesy of the Bible as a book (from a vantage of 600 BC) and to be itself a fulfillment of biblical prophecy. Indeed, the Book of Mormon explicitly identified itself as a companion to the Bible, written as a record of a "remnant of the House of Israel," "to the convincing of the Jew and Gentile that Jesus is the Christ."[8]

Those to whom the book was first shown, while they may have had a variety of reactions as to the legitimacy of its origins, noted the strong similarities between the two texts:

> Contemporaries thought of the book as a "bible," and that may be the best one-word description. Martin Harris referred to the manuscript as the "Mormon Bible" when he was negotiating with the printer. Newspapers derisively called it the "Gold Bible." Eber D. Howe, the Painesville, Ohio, editor who took an interest in Mormonism, described the recovery of the *Book of Mormon* as "a pretended discovery of a new Bible, in the bowels of the earth." The literary historian Lawrence Buell, after describing the desire of New England authors to write books with the authority of the Bible, notes that "the new Bible did not get written, unless one counts the *Book of Mormon*."[9]

The Doctrine and Covenants, while having its origins in the nineteenth century, also relies heavily upon the Bible. This text purports to be largely a collection of revelations received by Smith from God, and unsurprisingly the revelations were recorded in King James English.[10] Thus, readers of the Doctrine and Covenants will find that "Biblical expressions from the Authorized Version are sprinkled throughout," and that "the revelation's ideas are sometimes biblical even when the language is less exactly parallel to the King James text."[11] Joseph Smith lived in a time replete with religious inspiration and revelation, with other visionaries such as Ann Lee and Ellen G. White also laying claim to being recipients of a divine message. Within such a religiously charged environment, Joseph Smith's revelations opened space because they "sounded like scripture" and "were immediately treated like the Bible, a status that no other contemporary visionary writings achieved."[12]

THE "RHETORIC OF ALLUSIVITY" AND MORMON SCRIPTURE

Like Smith's culturally ingrained language of the Bible, the language of revelation was a shared concept that allowed Smith's modern scripture to seem as if it was part of the Bible.[13] In some places, Mormon scripture appropriates entire verses or chapters and inserts them wholesale into the text. In other places, this appropriation takes the form of small phrases or sentences, which are then woven together to form larger blocks of writing. While a great deal of research performed on Mormon scripture has been done with the intent of identifying *where* the Book of Mormon and the Doctrine and Covenants[14] borrow language from the Bible, not enough has been done in regards to exploring *why* or *how* so much biblical language appears throughout Mormon scripture.[15] The premise of this work is that Mormon scripture's explicit and provocative use of the language of the King James Bible can better be understood through the lens of *allusivity*. At the basic literary level, allusivity can be understood as presupposing "the existence of a semantic code, a particular body of common language and interpersonal relationships. It is created through widely understood associative or contextual semantics."[16] For writers of Jewish and Christian literature, particularly between 300 BC and 100 AD, scriptural text provided the "semantic code" used throughout documents within the Hebrew Bible, the Dead Sea Scrolls, the Jewish "Pseudepigrapha," and several of the Christian documents that became the New Testament.

The utilization of allusivity within pseudepigraphic literature is particularly noteworthy. "Pseudepigrapha," like "midrash," is a term that has been used in a number of different contexts and subsequently has lost a lot of its value. Moshe J. Bernstein offers a useful definition: "Originally, 'pseudepigrapha' was used to describe texts falsely ascribed to an author (usually of great antiquity) in order to enhance their authority and validity. Gradually, the connotation of this word was expanded to include a collection of Jewish and Christian writings dating from the last centuries BCE to the first centuries CE which did not become part of the canon in either religion."[17] Exclusion from the Jewish or Christian canon ought not, however, to diminish the value of many of these texts, especially when their interaction with the books that were canonized as scripture are considered. As James Charlesworth observes, "the Pseudepigrapha were often produced within the crucible of biblical interpretation . . . to speak to the curiosities and needs of a later time the stories needed to be retold and completed with details. All the evidence seems to suggest that what we call additional facts and details were considered by the early Jews who revered these Pseudepigrapha to be part of the true story. Now they were revealed to serve the curiosities and needs of later generations."[18] Charlesworth prefers the phrase "pneumatic exegesis" as a means of describing the manner and method of pseudepigraphic composition: "Like the Dead Sea Scrolls and the documents collected into the New Testament, the Pseudepigrapha tend to treat the Tanach in ways that are shockingly cavalier to modern biblical critics. It seems obvious that the text was considered divine, but the spirit for interpretation allowed the Jewish exegete to alter, ignore, expand, and even rewrite the sacred Scripture."[19]

One of the significant observations that has emerged from a study of pseudepigraphic literature is the myriad of ways authors of such texts attempted to position their texts as authoritative. James A. Sanders writes of the Jewish and Christian texts that emerged from roughly 250 BC to 200 AD that "All of the literature of the period was written Scripturally in one sense or another, and to one degree or another. The depth and extent of Scriptural intertextuality in this literature is perhaps its most marked common feature. Not only is most of it attributed to great names in Scripture, but it was variously composed in the manner of and in the light of various parts of Scripture."[20] Faced with the passing of time and the shifting of circumstance, authors penned texts that relied upon the language of texts such as the Torah, Psalms, or Isaiah and "re-wrote" them in a manner that rendered them contemporarily applicable. Sanders elaborates on how authors composed their texts, in terms quite reminiscent of Joseph Smith's corpus: "they were so convinced of what they felt they had been given to say that they wrote it in scriptural phrases, shapes, tones and cadences. There are clear citations of the Hebrew Bible or Septuagint, uncounted paraphrases and weavings of scriptural phrases into the fabric of the newer compositions, many allusions to passages, figures and episodes, and untold echoes of Scripture passages in various combinations; *and through them all there was the desire as well to write scripturally in form and structure.*"[21]

One of the crucial elements commonly employed in the composition of these texts, as Sanders notes, was the usage of *allusivity*, which we will define as "the transformative reproduction of language, phrases, texts, or stories from one text that allows them to be part of a new text while still maintaining a link with their source text."[22] The biblical text provided a rich vocabulary and a powerful paradigmatic force from which to draw upon, one that would evoke powerful images and meaning in the minds of readers. By adopting the rhetoric of allusivity, authors intentionally link themselves to earlier texts. Reasons for this may vary, but "by acknowledging a predecessor, an author may seek to gain entry into a canon; through allusion the poet avows, 'This work is worth reading, just as its predecessors were.' In such a case, allusion represents an attempt to bolster the authority of the work."[23] For example, in the case of a text such as *Jubilees*, which presents a different account (one delivered by an angel to Moses) of the events in Genesis and Exodus with a hyper-sensitivity to legal concerns, "Verbal echoes of the older scriptures would probably have facilitated acceptance of *Jubilees* as a credible account of Sinaitic revelation."[24] In this case, the rhetoric of allusivity provides the foundation of textual authority for Jubilees. However, while allusivity may serve to tether two texts together, it also paradoxically "can distance the new work from the old, since it is precisely when one juxtaposes two works (as one is forced to do by allusion) that one notices their differences." This allows "the new text to achieve a distinct identity in opposition to the older work."[25] Thus allusivity can illustrate both the dependent nature and independent function of a text, a key component for understanding Mormon scripture.

An additional key facet undergirding the motivations for producing writings that relied upon the language and imagery of a previous work was the recognition of the author(s) that certain texts may have outlived some of their usefulness and needed to be "re-interpreted" or "re-written" to serve the needs of contemporary believers. The author of Deutero-Isaiah appropriated content from Jeremiah and First Isaiah, and "he reformulated single lines and whole sections from the work of his predecessors" in order to help the Jews make sense of the Babylonian captivity.[26] Deuteronomy is the product of a radical reworking of the Covenant Code, a "deliberate attempt to rework prestigious texts in light of the innovation of centralization."[27] Part of the reasoning behind this re-working of scripture likely stemmed from a belief that inspiration had not ceased. For example, the covenanters at Qumran "considered biblical literature a living matter, and participated in the ongoing process of its creation," as can be seen from works such as the Temple Scroll.[28]

However, it is also important to note that writers of literature both canonical and non-canonical did not necessarily intend their texts to replace the Bible. In his analysis of *Jubilees,* James VanderKam observes that "*Jubilees* does not replace Genesis; it uses and supplements it, adding clarification and reinforcing lessons to be learned from it."[29] One possible reason for this desire to stand alongside the Bible may be that the authors faced a dilemma similar to that of Joseph Smith; while the borders of canon may not have been firmly set by the second century BC, they were beginning to be, and any tampering of texts recognized as authoritative, especially the Pentateuch, would have likely been viewed as a violation.[30] Perhaps more importantly, however, "some authors call attention to their own allusivity; they seem to insist on their relation to earlier texts,"[31] and without the Bible their allusions would fall upon deaf ears.

In a similar fashion, the Christian New Testament also made great and diverse use of the rhetoric of allusivity. Readers of the New Testament, in particular the Gospel of Matthew, encounter a text replete with quotations from the Hebrew Bible which are often re-integrated into new contexts that provided a self-understanding for the nascent Christian church.[32] The Book of Revelation has been mined for its frequent allusivity to the Hebrew Bible.[33] Thanks to the pioneering work of Richard Hays, a recent trend in Pauline studies has been to examine how Paul integrates the Hebrew Bible into his epistles.[34] Recent scholarship on this topic has debated how best to label Paul's usages (Quotation? Allusion? Echo?) as well as the criteria that ought to be considered when identifying potential references by Paul to the Hebrew Bible. Authors have engaged various issues such as Paul's respect (or lack thereof) for the context of his quotations,[35] his audience's ability to discern the quotations or allusions,[36] or whether or not a consideration of the context of a quotation, allusion, or echo should be a significant feature of a hermeneutical lens into the Pauline corpus.[37]

The employment of the rhetoric of allusivity can be seen in two Christian texts which today are considered deutero-Pauline. The first, the epistle to the Hebrews, is a text that borrows a number of phrases and words from the recognized Pauline corpus yet in "a patently derivative context."[38] However, the author may have adopted this means "as a method of extending Paul's corpus through allusion to his letters thereby accessing new revelation."[39] Thus for the author of Hebrews "scripture—including Paul's writings—functioned as pliant material from which to create new, openly derivative yet distinctive, inspired teachings."[40] Through the use of allusivity, the author appropriated the authority of Paul while at the same time crafting an epistle that had contemporary relevance for a specific Christian community. The author of the epistle to the Laodiceans employs the same method as Hebrew's author, although with far less-successful result. Barely a page long in the English translation, Laodiceans is best described as a pastiche of phrases from various Pauline epistles clumsily stitched together and thus lacking a central focus. The function of the letter appears to be largely ideological: "the author enlists the powerfully persuasive character of Paul—the Paul who suffers and perseveres—in order to promote his vision of orthodoxy and morality."[41] Both Hebrews and Laodiceans demonstrate that in the battlegrounds of early Christianity "old revelation is plumbed as the richest and most reliable source for the invention of new revelation."[42]

Joseph Smith faced the dilemma of introducing additional chapters of the larger sacred narrative of God's interaction with his children into a culture where violations of the canonical borders would not be easily dismissed, where theological innovation, particularly innovation claiming a divine provenance, would be met with skepticism.[43] Locating a new text within the larger biblical narrative "can and will continue, but now only under the biblical *model,* and not in the biblical *mode* . . . it is now a process that is *extrinsic* to the biblical text and corpus. It cannot follow the biblical mode and become part of the text or corpus itself."[44] The close textual relationship between the Bible and Mormon scripture suggests that Smith's response to this dilemma was to do to the Bible what ancient authors encountering similar circumstances had done, namely appropriate its language (although not necessarily its characters) in a manner that maintained links with the biblical text while also redefining the biblical text in a way that rendered the newer text culturally relevant.[45] Historian Jan Shipps has famously noted Joseph Smith's positioning of Mormonism as the "new Israel," and nowhere is that more apparent than the Mormon scripture Smith produced.[46] Speaking of the Qumran community, Jewish sectarians who also produced a number of innovative scriptural texts, George Brooke wrote "The place of scripture in the community's own sectarian compositions may be read in one way as an insistence on looking at themselves as continuous with Israel's earlier experiences, but from another angle it is closer to an appropriation of language from another time so that the community's contemporary experiences are biblicised."[47] The Book of Mormon and the Doctrine and Covenants had the same effect upon the Mormon Church, entrenching them in the biblical world not just through a similarity in language or narrative, but in the method of textual composition.

In this regard, by creating a corpus of scripture so closely tethered to the Bible Smith did what many Americans had done, namely to produce "pseudo-biblical" literature that helped Americans situate themselves historically through application and exegesis of the biblical text. Eran Shalev has studied pseudo-biblical literature produced during the eighteenth and nineteenth century and concluded that, while the language of the King James Bible "was as strange and foreign to late eighteenth-century and nineteenth-century Anglophones as it is to twenty-first-century English-speakers," the Bible and especially the language of King James provided a medium for self-contexualization.[48] According to Shalev, "generations of Americans reverted to that language and its accompanying structures and forms to discuss their difficulties and represent their achievements, past and present . . . American authors and commentators used this ontologically privileged language as a means to establish their claims for truth, as well as their authority and legitimacy in public discourse."[49]

Much like those authors of Jewish and Christian texts who relied upon the "rhetoric of allusivity" to instill authority in literary works intended to establish a continuity with an earlier era and make the word of God relevant for their contemporary audiences, Smith, who unabashedly proclaimed that the "it is high time for a christian world to awake out of sleep and cry mightely to that God day and night whose anger we have Justly incured,"[50] understood how to carry the Bible into the nineteenth-century in order to stave off God's anger. Shalev notes that "Through pseudo-biblicism the Bible became a living text, an ongoing scriptural venture which complemented and fortified notions of national chosenness and mission."[51] Smith's corpus of scripture represents a pinnacle of this biblical growth. Both the Book of Mormon and the Doctrine and Covenants trumpet the divine future of the Americas, a "promised land" that God had begun constructing twenty-five hundred years earlier. The authors of the Book of Mormon demonstrate a hyper-awareness for their nineteenth-century audience, with one author stating that "Behold, I speak unto you as if ye were present—and yet ye are not—but behold, Jesus Christ hath shewn you unto me, and I know your doing" (Morm. 8:35). The Book of Mormon even predicts that it and the Bible "shall grow together unto the confounding of false doctrines and laying down of contentions . . ." (2 Nephi 3:12).

One of the notable facets of Smith's scriptural corpus is that his appropriation of biblical verse is not uniform in its activity. In some places,
Mormon scripture simply "echoes" the Bible, desiring to be seen as an
equal. Yet in other places Mormon scripture "expands" upon the context
or meaning of the biblical verse, building upon its biblical antecedent in
ways that reflect an evolution of the biblical text. The purpose of this
work is to explore how the Bible is both *deconstructed* and *reconstructed* in
the course of composing the Mormon scriptural corpus. Because an examination of every biblical phrase found in Mormon scripture would be
unwieldy and time-consuming, this work will focus strictly upon the
eighteen verses that compose the Prologue of John's gospel. Focusing on
these eighteen verses will allow for a full evaluation of three crucial contentions: First, that Mormon scripture employs the rhetoric of allusivity
as a means of juxtaposition with the Bible in order to procure literary
authority with a nineteenth-century audience. Second, that through the
rhetoric of allusivity Joseph Smith initiated a lengthy and complex discourse between the Prologue of John and Mormon scripture. Third, that
four different strata or levels of discourse within this larger Johannine
discourse can be identified and analyzed.

These four "levels of discourse" become an important tool for analyzing Mormon scripture due to the complexity of the biblical appropriation. Because of this complex interaction, simply searching for strings of consecutive words proves an inadequate measure for how and where the
Bible appears in Mormon scripture. Additionally, for reasons that will be
discussed below, popular terms such as "quotation," "allusion," and
"echo" become problematic, unless they are defined much more precisely. In order to obtain a clearer understanding of how biblical phrases are
being used by Joseph Smith, factors such as biblical context, Mormon
scriptural context, and word alterations all need to be considered for each
phrase. This can become a very time consuming process, but a necessary
one. After having carefully studied each phrase from the Johnnine Prologue in Mormon scripture, there appears to be four specific types of
ways in which Mormon scripture has deconstructed and reconstructed
these phrases:

1. *Johannine Echo:* There are several places where the Book of Mormon
   or the Doctrine and Covenants appropriates a phrase from the
   Prologue of John where the biblical context plays very little role in
   the Mormon scripture context. This lack of contextual continuity
   suggests that the primary function of the phrase in the Mormon
   text is *rhetorical,* intended to *echo* the Bible in the minds of readers
   without actually performing a transferal of meaning. Thus, "Johannine echo" would include places in Mormon scripture where small
   pieces of biblical verse have been woven through Joseph Smith's
   corpus in a way that does not suggest an explicit connection be-

tween the two texts. In respect to the Johannine Prologue, this trend seems most apparent in the Book of Mormon but can still be found in the Doctrine and Covenants. In these cases, the use of Johannine language is largely authoritative[52] and does not seem intended to create any significant "subtext" or dialogue between Mormon scripture and the Gospel of John, although one may be implicitly present. Again, the clearest way to make this determination is to carefully consider the context of how the phrase is used in both the Gospel of John and Mormon scripture.

2. *Johannine Allusion:* There are several instances where not only the *language,* but also the *context* of John's Prologue is carried over into Mormon scripture. This allows for the context or the theology of the Johannine text to become valuable interpretive elements for Mormon scriptural text. Due to the duplication of the Johannine theology or context, the theological or contextual interpretation of the Mormon scriptural text can be understood on a broader level. In other words, the context or theology of a Johannine phrase used in Mormon scripture closely matches or mirrors the Johannine context or theology of that phrase. This is not to say that the intent of Joseph Smith was to create a significant subtext or active dialogue between the two texts, but due to the similarity in contexts a subtext or dialogue has been initiated. This category is prominent in the Book of Mormon as well as some of the early revelations from the Doctrine and Covenants.

3. *Johannine Expansion:* Often a phrase from the Prologue of John has been re-cast in Mormon scripture in a manner that suggests Mormon scripture is building or *expanding* upon the Johannine context, taking the meaning of the Johannine phrase beyond its use or application in the Prologue. This expansion tends to be performed in one of two ways: 1) The language of the Johannine passage is altered, either through the addition or subtraction of words; and 2) The Johannine context of the phrase has been broadened or expanded through the way in which it has been woven into the Mormon scriptural text. Thus the Johannine text and meaning are expanded, explored, and manipulated beyond the context or meaning of the Johannine text. This type of dialogue can be seen on a few occasions in the Book of Mormon as well as in several instances in the later revelations in the Doctrine and Covenants.

4. *Johannine Inversion:* Finally, there is at least one instance where a phrase from the Johannine Prologue has been adopted and adapted by Mormon scripture in a manner that has *inverted* or *reversed* the Johannine context of the phrase. This category is similar to "Johannine Expansion," in that the Johannine context has been broadened, but in the case of "Johannine Inversion" the specific result is a reversal in context. This category perhaps demon-

strates most fully how Mormon scripture creatively "deconstructs" and "reconstructs" biblical texts to form an innovative and unique theology that is counter-intuitive to the biblical verse upon which it is constructed. Doctrine and Covenants 93 represents the only example of this category as it relates to the Prologue of John.[53] As with "Johannine Expansion," the value of this category comes not simply from noting the correlation between the two texts, but from evaluating and analyzing how the original text has been "inverted" into something new.[54]

THE PROLOGUE OF JOHN

The reason for choosing to center this study on phrases from the Prologue of John is due in large part to both its versatility and its uniqueness. Throughout these eighteen verses such themes as light and darkness, reception and rejection, life and glory are woven into the tale of the descent of the λόγος to earth and signify the divine beginnings of Christ's earthly ministry. In a way, the Prologue represents an encapsulation of the entire Gospel, "that in the life and ministry of Jesus of Nazareth the glory of God was uniquely and perfectly disclosed."[55] In the Prologue, much of the Christology of the primitive church is revealed, including the pre-existent nature of the λόγος, the creative capacity of the λόγος, Jesus Christ as an incarnate, divine figure, and the possibility of divine filiation. The Prologue is, in the words of Raymond Brown, "a description of the history of salvation in hymnic form."[56] Köstenberger, expanding upon Brown, writes of the Prologue that:

> Unlike the Synoptics, John supplies neither a genealogy nor a birth narrative of Jesus. Rather, he reaches back all the way to eternity past, prior to creation. By linking Jesus' coming into the world to its creation, John signals that the incarnation of the Word culminates a stream of salvation-historical events that command humanity's utmost attention. Thus the evangelist shows the progression from preexistence to creation, the time subsequent to creation but prior to the incarnation, the Baptist, and the incarnation and its results and benefits.[57]

The Johannine Prologue is also an ideal text due to the uniqueness of its language. In order for the study to succeed, the source of the phrase or sentence needs to be determined in order to contextualize it properly. Thus phrases such as "the power of God" or "the remission of sins" are of little help, as they occur too frequently to adequately determine the provenance even when they occur in both the Bible and Mormon scripture. Additionally, exploring phrases from the Synoptic gospels become problematic due to the difficulty of deciphering the distinct voices of Matthew, Mark, and Luke. However, phrases such as "born of God," "only begotten of the Father," "full of grace and truth," "grace for grace," "bosom of the Father," "sons of God," and "believe on his name," as well as longer clauses such as "the light shineth in the darkness" and "he came unto his own" are phrases that are specific to the Johannine Prologue, but also appear again and again throughout Mormon scripture and thus are phrases that can be identified as allusions to the Fourth Gospel.[58] If a study of the relationship between Mormon scripture and John's Prologue yields no useful results, it is unlikely that any other biblical text would.[59]

The value of the Prologue for a study such as this comes from its depth and breadth, from the unique language and theology that emerges from such a unique literary composition.[60]

METHODOLOGY

It has become fashionable in the last two decades to employ the term "intertextuality" when speaking about how biblical texts interact with one another. At its base, "Intertextuality" is simply "the literal presence (more or less literal, whether integral or not) of one text within another."[61] Although intertextuality has largely been used as a method of literary criticism applied to more creative works, following the lead of Julia Kristeva, Mikhail Bahktin, and Michel Foucault,[62] it should not be seen as reserved specifically for a certain type of literature. In the field of biblical studies, it has become common to speak of the literary relationship between the Old and New Testament as intertextuality, due primarily to the work of Richard Hays and G. K. Beale.[63]

Hays's works, *Echoes of Scripture in the Letters of Paul* and more recently *The Conversion of the Imagination: Paul as Interpreter of Israel's Scripture*, laid the groundwork for the technical evaluation of a New Testament text based upon its use of Old Testament quotations or allusions.[64] Hays studied the letters of Paul and observed what he termed "echoes," phrases that were constructed by Paul but contained within them vague references to Old Testament texts. Hays saw meaning in the Pauline echoes, writing that "When a literary echo links the text in which it occurs to an earlier text, the figurative effect of the echo can lie in the unstated or suppressed (transumed) points of resonance between the two texts. . . . Allusive echo functions to suggest to the reader that text B should be understood in light of a broad interplay with text A, encompassing aspects of A beyond those explicitly echoed."[65] Critical to his study were seven criteria Hays identified for determining the validity of an "echo."[66] Once these "echoes" have been identified, then "The result is that the interpretation of a metalepsis requires the reader to recover unstated or suppressed correspondences between the two texts . . . we must go back and examine the wider contexts in the scriptural precursors to understand the figurative effects produced by the intertextual connections."[67]

This dialogic relationship between author and reader noted by Hays plays a significant role in understanding Mormon scripture. While Kristeva was generally uninterested in the role of the reader in the intertextual process, focusing primarily on how the writer read other works intertextually and is subsequently influenced by them, Bahktin and Barthes understood the process as more dialogic, with the reader of a text playing a pivotal role. Barthes has famously written: "The reader is the space on which all the quotations that make up a writing are inscribed without any of them being lost; a text's unity lies not in its origin but in its destination. Yet this destination cannot any longer be personal: the reader . . . is simply that *someone* who holds together in a single field all the traces by which the written text is constituted."[68] While Barthes's description of an author's "death" may be overstated, his focus upon the role of the reader, especially the expectations placed upon the reader who recognizes the literary allusions made by the author, is a significant step in understanding Joseph Smith, for whom the Bible presented an engrained mosaic ready to be exploited and utilized in drawing the reader into a modern biblical world.[69]

However, the notable production of intertextual analyses that have arisen since Hays's work has not been without difficulties.[70] Michael Fishbane specifically avoided the term "intertextuality" in his seminal work *Biblical Interpretation in Ancient Israel*, preferring instead "inner-biblical exegesis" as a way of describing the interaction between the authors of the Hebrew Bible. Ellen van Wolde charged scholars to avoid "trendy" intertextuality that "does not contribute much to bible exegesis when it uses literary theory merely to supply labels." Intertextuality "becomes significant only when it causes a change in our understanding of texts."[71] More recently, Russell L. Meek has issued a corrective to the methodology, stating that "Given the vast amount of literature that has distinguished between these three methodologies (intertextuality, inner-biblical exegesis, inner-biblical allusion) over the past forty years, it is no longer viable—and indeed is misleading and unethical—to employ the language of intertextuality when attempting to demonstrate—or presupposing—an intentional, historical relationship between texts."[72]

Unfortunately, neither "inner-biblical exegesis/allusion" nor "intertextuality" adequately describe the methodology needed to explore Mormon scripture and its relationship to the Bible.[73] "Inner-biblical exegesis/allusion" is useful in orienting readers diachronically, as Mormon scripture clearly emerges at a later point in history than does the Bible, but Mormon scripture is not "inner-biblical." On the other hand, "intertextuality" allows us to view the Bible and Mormon scripture synchronically, but lacks the historical awareness necessary for this type of analysis.[74] Both diachrony and synchrony are needed. Instead, we have chosen "allusivity" or the "rhetoric of allusivity" as a way of describing the interactions between the Gospel of John and Mormon scripture, aware that this language does not fully encapsulate the engagement at work between the two texts.[75] Additionally, we will not be employing the tripartite breakdown of "quotation," "allusion," or "echo" that has become popular in these types of studies.[76] The majority of phrases from the Prologue of John in Mormon scripture are implicit citations that lack formal markers and thus negate the need for "quotation." We will therefore use the unqualified term "allusion" to refer throughout the work to a passage in Mormon scripture that actively or explicitly directs readers toward a biblical passage. Furthermore, we will use "Johannine echo" or "Johannine allusion" as specific categories of allusivity and as a means of explicating their *function* within the text. Such usages are limited to the descriptions and definitions given above and in their respective analyses and nothing more should be read into them.

With this in mind, this work will proceed in the following manner. Each verse of Mormon scripture containing a type of allusivity to the Prologue of John will be isolated and evaluated in three respects:

1. The *Text:* The immediate context of the verse—what are the circumstances under which this verse appears?[77]
2. The *Intertext:* The Johannine context of the verse in question—how is this phrase used in the Prologue of John? Is there a difference of opinion among scholars regarding interpretation?[78]
3. The *Subtext:* Isolating and analyzing the dialogue between Mormon scripture and John—this section will consider how much of a dialogue is at work between the Mormon scriptural text and its Johannine subtext. Does the allusion to John matter? Does understanding a Johannine context add anything to a reading of the text? Does the context and usage of the restoration text equate with the context and meaning of the Johannine subtext, or are there layers of dissonance? If so, why?[79]

MORMON SCRIPTURE

In addition to the Bible, the corpus of Mormon scripture is composed of three works: the Book of Mormon, the Doctrine and Covenants, and the Pearl of Great Price. The first of these, the Book of Mormon, was published in New York in March of 1830 and "occupies a position of major importance in both the religious and intellectual history of the United States."[80] The book presents itself as "an abridgment of the record of the people of Nephi, and also of the Lamanites" and is addressed to these same Lamanites, "which are a remnant of the house of Israel, and also to Jew and Gentile."[81] The "author" of this text was a young farmer named Joseph Smith, born in Vermont in 1805. Smith claimed that the provenance of the Book of Mormon lay in a set of "gold plates" that had been buried in a local hill almost 1,500 years earlier by a Nephite general named Moroni. According to Smith, this same Moroni had appeared to him numerous times in a vision and had revealed to him the location of these plates. While he saw the plates for the first time in 1823 as a seventeen-year-old, Joseph Smith was not allowed to take possession of them until 1827, four years after having first seen them.[82] After a few delays, Smith began in earnest a "translation" of these plates in the spring of 1829.[83] Smith, with the aid of five scribes, dictated and recorded a 588-page book between the spring of 1828 and the summer of 1829.[84]

The Book of Mormon weaves together the tragic tale of the Nephites, descendants of a Jewish refugee named Lehi who managed to escape from Judaea prior to the fall of Jerusalem in 586 BC Following the arrival in America and Lehi's death, the party split into two groups. One of these groups became the Nephites (named after Nephi, the son of Lehi), who for the next millennium would encounter periods of prosperity, in large part due to righteous behavior, and periods of apostasy, in large part due to pride and disobedience. The main antagonists of the Nephites were the Lamanites (named for the eldest son of Lehi), who chose to rebel against God and as a result became "cursed" by God (2 Nephi 5:22). Much of the narrative is occupied by the often violent contests between the Nephites and Lamanites as well as the struggles of the Nephites to maintain their own state of righteousness when faced with challenges from within their own ranks. The highpoint of the narrative involves a visitation by the resurrected Jesus to the Nephites in the days following his crucifixion and resurrection. Here Jesus gives instructions reminiscent of Matthew's Sermon on the Mount and leaves the Nephites only after having organized a church. The book ends tragically four centuries later with the annihilation of the Nephite society and the final victory of the Lamanites.

Various accounts exist describing how the Book of Mormon was written, with the general consensus being that Joseph Smith appeared to read the text of the Book of Mormon off of a seer stone he placed in a hat.[85] Smith's wife Emma stated that he "dictated each sentence, word for word, and when he came to proper names he could not pronounce, or long words, he spelled them out, and while I was writing them, if I made a mistake in spelling, he would stop me and correct my spelling, although it was impossible for him to see how I was writing them down at the time."[86] A close friend of Smith's, Joseph Knight, Sr., stated that after Smith put his head in a hat a sentence would appear on the stone in "Brite Roman Letters" and that "if it was not spelt rite it would not go away till it was rite so we see it was marvelous."[87] Another associate of Smith's, David Whitmer, wrote that: "Joseph Smith would put the seer stone into a hat, and put his face in the hat, drawing it closely around his face to exclude the light; and in the darkness the spiritual light would shine. A piece of something resembling parchment would appear, and on that appeared the writing. One character at a time would appear, and under it was the interpretation in English. Brother Joseph would read off the English to Oliver Cowdery, who was his principal scribe, and when it was written down and repeated to Brother Joseph to see if it was correct, then it would disappear, and another character with the interpretation would appear. Thus the Book of Mormon was translated by the gift and power of God, and not by any power of man."[88] Unfortunately, Joseph Smith himself remained largely silent on this issue, stating only that the translation was accomplished "by the gift and power of God."[89]

The fact remains that there is the clear and undeniable presence of the Bible in the Book of Mormon. It seems highly unlikely that the close linguistic relationship between the two texts can be anything other than intentional on the part of the Book of Mormon. As one scholar notes, "Even a cursory glance reveals that the Book of Mormon wants to be seen as a companion to the Bible. It is divided into books named after prophets; biblical phrases[90] and even chapter-length quotations are scattered throughout; and it is written in the diction of the Authorized Version, including the general use of archaic words such as *thou, doth, hath,* and all manner of verbs ending in *–eth.*"[91]

The second major work of Mormon scripture, the *Doctrine and Covenants,* defines itself as "a collection of divine revelations and inspired declarations given for the establishment and regulation of the kingdom of God on the earth in the last days."[92] The primary recipient of these "revelations" was also Joseph Smith. Although he would claim to have received angelic visitors as early as 1823, the revelations, direct messages from God, would begin in earnest for Joseph Smith in the summer of 1828. These revelations were not limited in topic or scope, including everything from the practicalities of missionary calls to visions of the heavenly abode of God himself. Arranged roughly in chronological order, this collection "was a melange much like the Bible: unsystematic, concrete, sometimes sweeping, other times pedestrian, both effulgent and spare."[93] Some were short, only a few verses long, while others occupy several pages. Some are full of compliments and encouragement, while others express criticism, often of Joseph Smith himself. Some are addressed to individuals, others to the church as a whole. The overriding tone of most of the revelations is that of eschatological optimism, one where the prior age has ended and the heavens are bursting forth once more, introducing a wondrous new era where the traditions of both Jews and Christians will find their true realization upon the American continent.[94]

One crucial aspect of the revelations becomes immediately apparent to readers. First, the voice is not that of Joseph Smith but of Jesus Christ himself, who consistently speaks of himself through the first-person "I." As Richard Bushman has noted, "The striking feature of Joseph Smith's revelations is the purity of God's voice coming out of the heavens and demanding our attention . . . the Lord alone is speaking, and all readers and hearers are called upon to give heed. *Listen, hearken,* and *hear* are the words with which the classic revelations typically open, and then the voice of God comes right out of the heavens into our ears. From the first word, a relationship is put in place: God speaks to command or inform; we listen."[95]

Much like the process by which the Book of Mormon was translated, the manner of Joseph's revelatory process remains obscure.[96] Was Joseph, like Homer and Hesiod, "invoking" the voice of the divine and allowing it to speak directly through him? Did he receive some sort of "inspiration," a heavenly "nudging" to which he gave a voice and a verbalization? Or was Joseph Smith actually an instrument, a receptacle through which God could make known his will? One contemporary of Joseph Smith's, Parley P. Pratt, wrote of the revelatory process:

> After we had joined in prayer in his translating room, he dictated in our presence the following revelation: "Each sentence was uttered slowly and very distinctly, and with a pause between each, sufficiently long for it to be recorded, by an ordinary writer, in long hand. This was the manner in which all his written revelations were dictated and written. There was never any hesitation, reviewing, or reading back, in order to keep the run of the subject; neither did any of these communications undergo revisions, interlinings, or corrections. As he dictated them so they stood, so far as I have witnessed; and I was present to witness the dictation of several communications of several pages each."[97]

Another contemporary, William E. McClellin, who served at one time as Smith's scribe, wrote:

> I, as scribe, have written revelations from the mouth of [the Prophet]. And I have been present many times when others wrote for Joseph; therefore I speak as one having experience. The scribe seats himself at a desk or table, with pen, ink and paper. The subject of enquiry being understood, the Prophet and Revelator enquires of God. He spiritually sees, hears and feels, and then speaks as he is moved upon by the Holy Ghost, the "thus saith the Lord," sentence after sentence, and waits for his amanuenses to write and then read aloud each sentence. Thus they proceed until the revelator says Amen, at the close of what is then communicated. I have known [Joseph], without premeditation, to thus deliver off in broken sentences, some of the most sublime pieces of composition which I ever perused in any book.[98]

Unfortunately, neither statement satisfactorily explicates the *source* of the revelations. While Joseph Smith "spoke the words as if God were speaking to him, the divine voice was apparently not audible to others present when Smith received them,"[99] thus leaving unanswered the question of whether the revelations were "word-for-word" statements by God, or how much Joseph himself added to them. Many modern Mormons likely prefer the former, believing that the revelations represent an exact transcription of a message relayed directly from God. Others, however, are more cautious, and perhaps the best statement on this question has been provided by Robert J. Woodford:

> Various means were used to impart these revelations to Joseph Smith. He communed in open vision with both God and Jesus Christ (that is, the First Vision). The ancient Book of Mormon prophet Moroni person-ally guided him over an almost seven-year period in translating the Book of Mormon. Other angelic messengers came to him (see D&C 27, for example) and to both him and Oliver Cowdery (D&C 13 and 110). Together with Sidney Rigdon, he saw a vision of the future state of mankind after this life (D&C 76). Others were in the room with them at the time, and at least one of them reported he "saw the glory and felt the power, but did not see the vision." Joseph Smith's prophecy on war was given him by an audible voice (D&C 131:12–13), and he received at least six revelations (D&C 3, 6, 7, 11, 14, and 17) through divine instru-ments such as the Nephite interpreters and the seer stone that he had in his possession. However, the great majority of the revelations were given to him through inspiration to his mind, and it was left to him to write them so others could also obtain the same message.[100]

The second trait of the revelations that is immediately noticeable is the presence and prominence of the King James Bible. Philip Barlow has observed how Joseph Smith's nineteenth-century revelations "remained intimately linked to the Bible. Some dealt directly with biblical themes, and quoted or closely paraphrased traditional scripture. All were saturat-ed with KJV words, phrases, and concepts: for every two verses of the revelations recorded in the Doctrine and Covenants, approximately three phrases or clauses parallel some KJV phrase or clause."[101] Much like the Book of Mormon, the Doctrine and Covenants appropriated the language and tone of the Bible, sanctifying the latter-day narrative by adopting the tongue of its spiritual predecessor. One explanation for the choice of King James English for the language of God is given in D&C 1:24: "Behold I am God & have spoken it these commandments are of me, & were given unto my Servants in their weakness after the manner of their language that they might come to understanding." This verse suggests that the revelatory process is best understood as God directly speaking through Joseph Smith, and that he chose King James English as a method of "ac-commodation." However, Joseph likely considered the revelations sacred and the decision to give them a King James voice may have been his own, a way of lending them weight. This idea is supported by the claims of another contemporary of Smith's, Orson Pratt, who wrote that "Jo-seph . . . received the ideas from God, but clothed those ideas with such words as came to his mind."[102] Like the Book of Mormon, the revelations rely upon the "rhetoric of allusivity" to claim for themselves the author-ity bestowed upon the Bible. Much as the Book of Mormon is the result of a "deconstructing" and "reconstructing" of scripture, the "weaving" to-gether of bits and pieces borrowed from the King James Bible, the revelations also demonstrate a clear reliance upon biblical verse, as if the words and phrases of the Bible were "building blocks" that could be used to create a modern spiritual mosaic. Yet it would be unfair and inaccurate to claim that the author of the revelations merely borrowed the words or diction of the King James Bible. Like the Book of Mormon, the revelations contain different methods of employing that allusivity, whether through echo, allusion, expansion, or inversion.

NOTES

1. Richard Lyman Bushman, *Joseph Smith: Rough Stone Rolling* (New York: Alfred A. Knopf, 2005), 66.

2. Fawn M. Brodie, *No Man Knows My History: The Life of Joseph Smith* (New York: Vintage Books, 1995); Dan Vogel, *Joseph Smith: The Making of a Prophet* (Salt Lake City: Signature Books, 2004).

3. This apologetic approach to the Book of Mormon was popular up through the 1990s but has been more tempered in recent works on the text. See, for example, John A. Tvedtnes, "The Hebrew Background of the Book of Mormon," in *Rediscovering the Book of Mormon*, ed. John L. Sorenson and Melvin J. Thorne (Salt Lake City and Provo: Deseret Book and Foundation for Ancient Research and Mormon Studies, 1991), 77–91. See also Paul C. Gutjahr, *The Book of Mormon: A Biography* (Princeton: Princeton University Press, 2012), 137–52; and Terryl L. Givens, *The Book of Mormon: A Very Short Introduction* (Oxford: Oxford University Press, 2009), 112–22.

4. Royal Skousen, ed., *The Book of Mormon: The Earliest Text* (Yale: Yale University Press, 2009). For technical comparisons of changes in the Book of Mormon over time, see Royal Skousen, ed., *Analysis of Textual Variants of the Book of Mormon*, 6 vols. (Provo: Foundation for Ancient Research and Mormon Studies, 2004–2009).

5. Grant Hardy, *Understanding the Book of Mormon: A Reader's Guide* (New York: Oxford University Press, 2010); Richard Dilworth Rust, *Feasting on the Word: The Literary Testimony of the Book of Mormon* (Salt Lake City: Deseret Book, 1997).

6. In a book discussing the use of Old Testament quotations by Paul in his epistles, Christopher D. Stanley writes that "Although it appears that the quoting author is momentarily stepping aside and letting the source text speak for itself, the author's act of selecting and embedding a quotation into a new rhetorical context actually amounts *to a substantial deconstruction and reconstruction of the original text*" (Christopher D. Stanley, *Arguing with Scripture: The Rhetoric of Quotations in the Letters of Paul* [New York: T&T Clark International, 2004], 34). Italics mine.

7. Due to the ambiguous origins and function of Joseph Smith's biblical translation project, only the Book of Mormon and the Doctrine and Covenants will be considered in this work.

8. Philip Barlow, *Mormons and the Bible: The Place of the Latter-day Saints in American Religion*, 2nd ed. (Oxford: Oxford University Press, 2013), 27.

9. Bushman, *Rough Stone Rolling*, 85.

10. Regarding the influence of the King James Bible upon a nineteenth-century audience, David Holland has noted that "The King James Version of the Bible remained the United States' dominant biblical text throughout the 1800s, just as it had for the previous century. The version was so deeply interwoven with the religious idiom of the day that even some who acceded to its errors nonetheless felt as though the introduction of a new version would do irreparable damage to religious stability in the Anglophonic world" (David Holland, *Sacred Borders: Continuing Revelation and Canonical Restraint in Early America* [Oxford: Oxford University Press, 2011], 112).

11. Barlow, *Mormons and the Bible*, 23.

12. Bushman, *Rough Stone Rolling*, 128.

13. In a debate that closely mirrors that of the provenance of Mormon scripture, examiners of Mormonism tend to vary widely in their opinion of Joseph Smith's direct familiarity with the Bible. Joseph's mother, Lucy Mack Smith, wrote that at the age "16 (19) yars of age [Joseph] had never read the Bible through by course in his life for Joseph was less inclined to the study of books than any child we had but much more given to reflection and deep study" (Lucy Mack Smith, *History, 1844–1845*, bk. 4, p. 1, The Joseph Smith Papers, accessed 11 Mar. 2016, josephsmithpapers.org/paper summary/lucy-mark-smith-history-1844-1845). David Whitmer, one of the founding members of the Mormon church, stated that in respect to translation Joseph "was illiterate and but little versed in biblical lore, was oftentimes compelled to spell the words out, not knowing the correct pronunciation" (Lyndon W. Cook, ed., *David Whitmer Interviews: A Restoration Witness* [Orem: Grandin Book Co., 1991], 174). Even Joseph's own wife, Emma Hale Smith, was skeptical regarding his knowledge of the Bible: "He could not pronounce the word 'Sariah.' And one time while translating, where it speaks of the walls of Jerusalem, he stopped and said, 'Emma, did Jerusalem have walls surrounding it?' When I informed him it had, he replied, 'O, I thought I was deceived'" (Cook, *David Whitmer Interviews*, 126–27). However, in one of Smith's earliest attempts to pen a history, he acknowledged a clear biblical awareness: "At about the age of twelve years my mind become seriously imprest with regard to the all importent concerns for the wellfare of my immortal Soul which led me to searching the scriptures believeing as I was taught, that they contained the word of God thus applying myself to them and my intimate acquaintance with those of differant denominations led me to marvel excedingly for I discovered that they did not adorn their profession by a holy walk and Godly conversation agreeable to what I found contained in that sacred depository . . ." (Karen Lynn Davidson, et. al, *The Joseph Smith Papers: Histories, vol. 1* [Salt Lake City: The Church Historian's Press, 2012] 11). Lavina Fielding Anderson believes that Joseph Smith could have been astutely familiar with the language of the Bible, if not the text itself: "I argue that the Smith family's oral culture was so thoroughly imbued with biblical language, both the Old and New Testaments, that its use was fluent, easy, and familiar. When they reached for a colorful phrase, searched for a simile, or stressed a point, the vocabulary that their minds offered readily was an appropriate and often vivid phrase from the Bible. Seldom did the context of secondary use relate to the biblical context. It also seems likely that this easy familiarity with KJV language made it possible for them to quickly adopt and incorporate images and phrasing from specifically Mormon scriptures" ("Mother Tongue: KJV Language in Smith Family Discourse," *MHA* Address, 2009. Quoted in Brant Gardner, *The Gift and Power of God: Translating the Book of Mormon* [Salt Lake City: Greg Kofford Books, 2011], 302).

14. The two studies in regards to the Doctrine and Covenants were Master's theses written at Brigham Young University: Ellis J. Rasmussen, "Textual Parallels to the Doctrine and Covenants and Book of Commandments as Found in the Bible" (Master's Thesis, Brigham Young University, 1951), and Lois Jean Smutz, "Textual Parallels to the Doctrine and Covenants (Sections 65–133) as Found in the Bible" (Master's Thesis, Brigham Young University, 1971).

15. Notable studies done on exploring *how* the Bible functions within Mormon scripture include Barlow, *Mormons and the Bible* and Brant Gardner, who offered his own take on Joseph Smith's employment of King James English: "King James Version style appears in the Book of Mormon because Joseph could not escape it. I doubt that it was a conscious decision to imitate that style. It was a decision that had already been made by the cultural expectation that this was the way scripture should sound" (Gardner, *Translating the Book of Mormon*, 302). Especially noteworthy is the work of David P. Wright, "In Plain Terms that We May Understand: Joseph Smith's Transformation of Hebrews in Alma 12–13," in *New Approaches to the Book of Mormon*, ed. Brent Lee Metcalfe (Salt Lake City: Signature Books, 1993), 165–229. Wright's work perhaps comes closest to what this work is attempting to accomplish, namely the in-depth analysis and categorization of how a portion of the Bible is used within Mormon

scripture. Wright's examination of how the epistle to the Hebrews functioned in Alma 12–13 led him to describe Smith's use of the Bible as textual conservation, problem solving, midrashic expansion, and a recontextualization. Wright wrote that "Such classification provides a basis for further study" (Wright, "In Plain Terms," 208). Although my scope and methodology, and thus my categorization, differ from his, I view this work as part of the "further study" Wright intended.

16. Jacek Dabala, *Mystery and Suspense in Creative Writing*, International Studies in Hermeneutics and Phenomenology vol. 7 (LIT Verlag: Munster, 2012), 46.

17. Moshe J. Bernstein, "Pseudepigraphy in the Qumran Scrolls: Categories and Functions," in *Pseudepigraphic Perspectives: The Apocrypha and Pseudepigrapha in Light of the Dead Sea Scrolls*, eds. Esther G. Chazon and Michael Stone (Leiden: E. J. Brill, 1999), 1.

18. James H. Charlesworth, "In the Crucible: The Pseudepigrapha as Biblical Interpretation," in *The Pseudepigrapha and Early Biblical Interpretation*, eds. James H. Charlesworth and Craig A. Evans JSPSup 14 (Sheffield: Sheffield Academic Press, 1993), 39. Especially useful for this discussion is the work of David G. Meade, *Pseudonymity and Canon: An Investigation into the Relationship of Authorship and Authority in Jewish and Earliest Christian Tradition* (Grand Rapids: William B. Eerdmans Publishing Company, 1986), 1–16.

19. Charlesworth, "In the Crucible," 39.

20. James A. Sanders, "Why the Pseudepigrapha?" in *The Pseudepigrapha and Early Biblical Interpretation*, eds. James H. Charlesworth and Craig A. Evans JSPSup 14 (Sheffield: Sheffield Academic Press, 1993), 15.

21. Sanders, "Why the Pseudepigrapha?," 15. Italics added. This is not to say that all authors of Psedepigraphic works had the same motivations. As Outi Leppä explains, "The motives for producing pseudepigraphic works were various. When the libraries in the Museum of Alexandria and in Pergamum were enlarged, it is said that gold was promised to people who were able to present a book of an ancient author and thus pseudepigraphic writings were also composed out of the desire for financial gain. Sometimes authors sought to defame, like for example Diotimus, who produced fifty letters of low value as if they were written by Epicurus. Much more often than malice, the motive was respect and innocent admiration which influenced the formation of pseudonymous works. For example, the Neo-Pythagoreans so respected Pythagoras, the founder of the philosophical school, that they attributed their treatises to him. One reason for this habit was the modesty of the disciples against presenting under their own name the ideas which they conceived to be their masters" (*The Making of Colossians: A Study on the Formation and Purpose of a Deutero-Pauline Letter* [Vandenhoeck & Ruprecht in Göttingen: The Finnish Exegetical Society, 2003], 11).

22. Clare K. Rothschild, in her treatment of Pseudepigraphy in the epistle to the Hebrews, defines what she calls the "rhetoric of allusion" as a "recognition that a literary work or corpus of a single writer both *repeats* and *develops* previously published concepts, theories, values and ideals—and the manner in which they are expressed" (*Hebrews as Pseudepigraphon: The History and Significance of the Pauline Attribution of Hebrews* [Tübingen: Mohr Siebeck: 2009], 120).

23. Benjamin D. Sommer, *A Prophet Reads Scripture: Allusion in Isaiah 40–66* (Stanford: Stanford University Press, 1998), 18. Michael Segal adds: "The dependence upon biblical compositions in the process of creating new works is a product of the author's desire to impute authority to his work; by associating his composition with the holiest of texts, the new work is also granted the same stamp of authority. The author's worldview and his interpretation of biblical passages are not presented as revolutionary ideas, created ex nihilo by the writer. The inclusion of this material within the framework of the biblical passages under interpretation transforms the ideas of the later writer into authoritative and accepted beliefs. They are no longer new ideas, but are found in ancient texts alongside accepted notions" ("Between Bible and Rewritten Bible," in *Biblical Interpretation at Qumran*, ed. Matthias Henze [Grand Rapids: William B. Eerdmans Publishing Company, 2005], 11).

24. John J. Collins, "Changing Scripture," in *Changes in Scripture: Rewriting and Interpreting Authoritative Traditions in the Second Temple Period*, eds. Hanne von Weissenberg, Juha Pakkala, and Marko Marttila (Berlin: Walter de Gruyter, 2011), 36.

25. Sommer, *Prophet Reads Scripture*, 19.

26. Sommer, *Prophet Reads Scripture*, 3.

27. Bernard M. Levinson, *Deuteronomy and the Hermeneutics of Legal Innovation* (Oxford: Oxford University Press, 1997), 6.

28. Shemaryahu Talmon, "The Textual Study of the Bible—A New Outlook," in *Qumran and the History of the Biblical Text*, eds. F. M. Cross and S. Talmon (Cambridge: Harvard University Press, 1975), 379. Of the Temple Scroll's usage of the Old Testament, John Collins remarks: "The fact that it uses language familiar from the traditional Torah would probably make it easier to accept as the authentic revelation on Sinai" (Collins, "Changing Scripture," 39).

29. VanderKam "Moses Trumping Moses: Making the Book of *Jubilees*," in *The Dead Sea Scrolls: Transmission of Traditions and Production of Texts*, eds. Sarianna Metso, Hindy Najman, and Eileen Schuller (Leiden: E. J. Brill, 2010), 37.

30. "By the mid-second century BCE, any major, sectarian tampering with the Pentateuch would surely have been a controversial undertaking; its text was simply too widely known, and its study too well entrenched, across the spectrum of Jewish groups" (James Kugel, "On the Interpolations in the Book of Jubilees," *RevQ* 24 [2009]: 271).

31. Sommer, *A Prophet Reads Scripture*, 9.

32. See the lengthy study edited by G. K. Beale and D. A. Carson, *Commentary on the New Testament Use of the Old Testament* (Grand Rapids: Baker Academic Press, 2007).

33. See Steve Moyise, *The Old Testament in the Book of Revelation* JSNTSup 115 (Sheffield: Sheffield Academic Press, 1995), and David Mathewson, *A New Heaven and a New Earth: The Meaning and Function of the Old Testament in Revelation 21.1–22.5* JSNTSup 238 (Sheffield: Sheffield Academic Press, 2003).

34. See Richard B. Hays, *Echoes of Scripture in the Letters of Paul* (New Haven: Yale University Press, 1989). One subsequent works on this topic acknowledged the debt to Hays, ironically enough, through allusion: Christopher A. Beetham, *Echoes of Scripture in the Letter of Paul to the Colossians* BIS 96 (Leiden: E. J. Brill, 2008).

35. See, for example, Steve Moyise, "Does Paul Respect the Context of His Quotations," in Christopher D. Stanley, ed., *Paul and Scripture: Extending the Conversation* (Atlanta: Society of Biblical Literature, 2012), 97–114. This particular discussion has reached the point where even the meaning of the term "respect" has been closely analyzed. See Mitchell Kim, "Respect for Context and Authorial Intention: Setting the Epistemological Bar," in Christopher D. Stanley, ed., *Paul and Scripture: Extending the Conversation* (Atlanta: Society of Biblical Literature, 2012), 115–29.

36. See, for example, Christopher D. Stanley, "'Pearls Before Swine': Did Paul's Audience Understand his Biblical Quotations?" *NovT* 41 (1999): 122–44.

37. This inquiry into Paul's usage of scripture recently culminated in the publication of two ground-breaking monographs resulting from six years of SBL meetings: Stanley E. Porter and Christopher D. Stanley, eds., *As it is Written: Studying Paul's Use of Scripture* (Atlanta: Society of Biblical Literature, 2008), and Christopher D. Stanley, ed., *Paul and Scripture: Extending the Conversation* (Atlanta: Society of Biblical Literature, 2012).

38. Rothschild, *Hebrews*, 132.

39. Rothschild, *Hebrews*, 133.

40. Rothschild, *Hebrews*, 133.

41. Mark Harding, "Disputed and Undisputed Letters of Paul," in Stanley E. Porter, ed., *The Pauline Canon* (Leiden: E. J. Brill, 2004), 139.

42. Rothschild, *Hebrews*, 135. The rhetoric of allusivity was a widely-spread practice in the early Christian centuries. According to Everett Ferguson, "We find that Clement of Rome, Ignatius, and Polycarp made extensive use of Paul's letters and drew on them as authoritative. . . . More significant overall is the overwhelming use Polycarp

and others made of New Testament writings. Polycarp wove the phraseology of Paul's letters together with 1 Peter and 1–2 John for his own letter to the Philippians." Ferguson further observes that "Both *Barnabas* (4.14) and *2 Clement* (2.4) quote Matthew. . . . It may be argued that the authority is the Lord and not a written document, but his words are found in a writing, and they are quoted from this writing in a manner that puts it on the same level with the Old Testament" ("Factors Leading to the Selection and Closure of the New Testament Canon," in *The Canon Debate,* eds. Lee Martin McDonald and James A. Sanders [Peabody: Hendrickson Publishers, 2002], 297–298).

43. David Holland has written "To American observers, this heedless Mormon commitment to ongoing revelations was precisely what made the movement so menacing" (Holland, *Sacred Borders,* 150). It is also important to distinguish between Joseph Smith's "authorial motives" and his "communicative intentions." According to Stephen Fowl, the former could be defined as "a desire for fame and fortune, hopes of acquiring tenure, a deep psychological need for self-expression, and so forth" (Stephen Fowl, "The Use of Scripture in Philippians," in Christopher D. Stanley, ed., *Paul and Scripture: Extending the Conversation* [Atlanta: Society of Biblical Literature, 2012], 166–67). Dan Vogel's recent biography of Joseph Smith is an example of a work seeking to explore "authorial motives." More important for this work is the concept of "communicative intentions," which "requires attention to matters of semantics, of linguistic conventions operative at the time, and of implication and inference, among other factors . . . attention to these matters is inescapably historical." This work is not intended to take us further inside the mind of Joseph Smith, but to explore how the Mormon scripture produced by Smith found expression and relevance in nineteenth century America (Fowl, "The Use of Scripture in Philippians," 167).

44. Meade, *Pseudonymity and Canon,* 217–18.

45. This work is not the first to link Joseph Smith with pseudepigraphy. In an insightful 2002 article, Robert M. Price wrote that "Joseph Smith seems to have created new holy fictions by running the old ones through the shredder and reassembling the shreds in wholly new combinations. His method appears to be precisely that of the old rabbis and of the New Testament evangelists" ("Joseph Smith: Inspired Author of the Book of Mormon," in *American Apocrypha: Essays on the Book of Mormon,* eds. Dan Vogel and Brent Lee Metcalfe [Salt Lake City: Signature Books, 2002], 347). In a recent monograph, David Bokovoy applied the Higher Critical method used in Torah studies to the Book of Moses, the Book of Abraham, and the Book of Mormon. He observed: ". . . Joseph was doing the very thing that the ancient authors of the Hebrew Bible did by taking a previous source and making it relevant for a contemporary audience. Nephi, Mormon, Moroni, and Joseph Smith were all continuing the tradition of using archaic sources to create new scripture" (David Bokovoy, *Authoring the Old Testament: Genesis-Deuteronomy* [Salt Lake City: Greg Kofford Books, 2014], 213). This work attempts to build and expand upon Price's and Bokovoy's work through a careful study of a New Testament text, the Prologue of John, as it appears in the Book of Mormon and the Doctrine and Covenants.

46. Jan Shipps, *Mormonism: The Story of a New Religious Tradition* (Chicago: University of Illinois Press, 1987), 67–85.

47. George J. Brooke, "Between Authority and Canon: The Significance of Reworking the Bible for Understanding the Canonical Process," in *Reworking the Bible: Apocryphal and Related Texts at Qumran,* eds. Esther G. Chazon, Devorah Dimant, and Ruth A. Clements (Leiden: E. J. Brill, 2005), 99.

48. Eran Shalev, "Written in the Style of Antiquity: Pseudo-Biblicism and the Early American Republic, 1770–1830," *Church History* 79.4 (December 2010): 801.

49. Shalev, "Written in the Style of Antiquity," 801.

50. Matthew C. Godfrey, et al., eds., *The Joseph Smith Papers: Documents, vol. 2* (Salt Lake City: Church Historians Press, 2013), 351.

51. Shalev, "Written in the Style of Antiquity," 812. One result of the contemporalization of the Bible through the Book of Mormon has been noted by Timothy L. Smith: "the Book of Mormon also helped bring to fruition the movement, rooted in puritan,

pietist, Quaker, and Wesleyan experience, to restore to prominence the doctrine of the presence of the Holy Spirit in the lives of God's people and in the testimony of his witnesses. That the prophecy of Isaiah and Acts were so central in the Book of Mormon encouraged this result" ("The Book of Mormon in a Biblical Culture," *JMH* 7 [1980]) 15–16.

52. "By claiming the voice of Scripture as one's own, a speaker/author can increase the chances that an audience of Christians or Jews will adopt or reject the set of beliefs and/or practices that the speaker/author recommends or opposes" (Stanley, *Arguing with Scripture*, 27).

53. Beale refers to this method as "Ironic or Inverted Use of the Old Testament," and writes that this trend is present in passages from the New Testament where "Clear OT allusions are used but with the opposite meaning from the OT. . . . At first sight one might think that these are wrong uses of the OT, but upon further reflection, an intentionally inverted use can be perceived." He gives as an example of this the question "Who is like the beast" from Revelation 13:4, an "inversion" of Exodus 15:11, "Who is like you . . . O LORD?" (G. K. Beale, *Handbook on the New Testament Use of the Old Testament* [Grand Rapids: Baker, 2012], 92). One could also point to Paul's quotation from Habakkuk 2:4, "Behold, his soul which is lifted up is not upright in him: but the just shall live by his faith," in Galatians 3:11: "But that no man is justified by the law in the sight of God, it is evident: for, The just shall live by faith." Habakkuk 2:4 emphasizes that life comes through faithfulness to the Law of Moses, yet Paul inverts this passage in Galatians 3:11 to suggest that faith in Jesus Christ is superior to living the Law of Moses. A similar argument could also be made for Paul's use of Deuteronomy 27:26 in Galatians 3:10. In a phrase that would be equally true of Joseph Smith, Barnabas Lindars has observed that when Paul quoted from the Old Testament "he always strongly impressed it with his own creative ability" (Barnabas Lindars, *New Testament Apologetic: The Doctrinal Significance of the Old Testament Quotations* [London: SCM Press Ltd., 1961], 222).

54. It is important to note that, as far as these four "strata" or "categories" go, there is no scientific way to quantify what phrases belong to which categories. A similar issue occupies those who seek to understand how the Hebrew Bible functions in the New Testament, and the solution is often to look for strings of consecutive words. However, due to the different ways Mormon scripture "reconstructs" the Bible, counting up consecutive words is not very efficient. Another scholar may read the Book of Mormon or the Doctrine and Covenants and argue that what this study has labeled "Echo" is better classified as "Allusion," or that an "Expansion" really ought to be an "Inversion." This type of disagreement would not be a sign of problematic categorization but a welcome progress in advancing the study of the interaction between the Bible and Mormon scripture.

55. F. F. Bruce, *The Gospel of John* (Grand Rapids: William B. Eerdmans Publishing Company, 1994), 28.

56. Raymond B. Brown, *The Gospel According to John* (Garden City: Doubleday and Company, Inc., 1966), 1:23–24. However, it would be a disservice to the Prologue to imply that it can be easily interpreted. As Thomas A. Wayment has noted, "One of the most remarkable aspects of the Prologue has been its enduring ability to defy a unique and precise interpretation" ("The Logos Incarnate and the Journey of the Soul: A New Paradigm for Interpreting the Prologue of John" Ph.D. Dissertation, Claremont Graduate University, 2000, 31).

57. Andreas J. Köstenberger, *John* (Grand Rapids: Baker Academic Press, 2004), 19.

58. An additional reason for choosing the Gospel of John for this examination is that Joseph Smith was clearly familiar with it, providing viable points of contact. Smith mentions discussing it as early as April 1829 (see Michael Hubbard MacKay, et al., *The Joseph Smith Papers: Documents, vol. 1: July 1828–June 1831* [Salt Lake City: Church Historian's Press, 2013], 47), and a reading of John 5 prompted the reception of a vision recorded in D&C 76 (see Godfrey, et al., *Documents*, 179).

59. It should be noted that this work, while discussing extensively the Johannine Prologue, will not attempt to offer conclusions on how verses from John 1:1–18 or the Prologue as a whole ought to be interpreted. On the contrary, one of the values of an intertextual study is utilizing different interpretations in examining the degree to which there exists an intertextual dialogue.

60. There is an inherent danger within comparative studies, namely the subjective nature of what is being compared. William E. Paden writes: "Comparison can create error and distortion as well as insight and knowledge, and this is noticeably so in the area of religion. Religious phenomena have been compared for centuries, but not necessarily in the pursuit of fair description or accurate understanding. Comparison is most often a function of self-interest. It gets used to illustrate one's own ideology. It easily becomes an instrument of judgment, a device for approval or condemnation" (*Religious Worlds: The Comparative Study of Religion* [Boston: Beacon Press, 1988], 2). Biblical scholars have also noted a penchant among some for "parallelomania," namely the attempt to give validity to a modern source based upon the discovery of several "parallels" in the ancient world. The classic study remains Samuel Sandmel, "Parallelomania," *JBL* 81 (1962): 2–13.

61. Gerard Genette, *The Architext: An Introduction,* trans. Jane E. Lewin (Berkeley: University of California Press, 1992), 81–82. As G. K. Beale has noted, the term "intertextuality" when used to refer to a method of biblical criticism is somewhat problematic, as "intertextuality" usually refers to two different texts that have a common point of interaction. Beale writes that in biblical studies "'intertextuality' is sometimes used merely to refer to the procedure by which a later biblical text refers to an earlier text, how that earlier text enhances the meaning of the later one, and how the later one creatively develops the earlier meaning. In this respect, 'intertextuality' may be seen as a procedure of inner-biblical or intrabiblical exegesis, which is crucial to doing biblical theology and for understanding the relation of the OT to the NT." Beale suggests that "inner-biblical exegesis" or "inner-biblical allusion" may be more appropriate terms, but the idea of "biblical intertextuality" has become common enough that it is unlikely to be changed in the near future (Beale, *Handbook,* 40). Beale is building upon the work of Michael Fishbane, whose work *Biblical Interpretation in Ancient Israel* (Oxford: Clarendon Press, 1985), looked at how various authors of the Hebrew Bible interpreted other biblical texts. Also useful in this context is the work of Daniel Boyarin, who examines biblical intertextuality in rabbinic Midrash (*Intertextuality and Midrash* [Bloomington: Indiana University Press, 1990]). However, unlike the works of Richard Hays and his successors, Fishbane and Boyarin limit themselves to direct quotations.

62. It was in Kristeva's ground-breaking work *Semiotike: Recherchés pour une semanalyse* (Collections Tel Quel; Paris: Le Seuil, 1969), that notions of "Intertextuality" began to develop. Kristeva argued that all texts share links between them that "intersect and neutralize one another" (*Desire in Language: A Semiotic Approach to Literature and Art,* ed. Leon S. Roudiez [New York: Columbia University Press, 1980], 36). This led to Kristeva's well-known statement that every text is a "mosaic of quotations" ("Word, Dialog and Novel," ed. Toril Moi, *The Kristeva Reader* [New York: Columbia University Press, 1986], 37). However, as Clayton and Rothstein have noted, "Kristeva does not discuss what happens to a fragment of the social text when it is 'absorbed' and 'transformed' by literature, nor does she account for how specific social texts are chosen for 'absorption'" (Jay Clayton and Eric Rothstein, "Figures in the Corpus: Theories of Influence and Intertextuality," in Jay Clayton and Eric Rothstein, eds., *Influence and Intertextuality in Literary History* [Madison: University of Wisconsin Press, 1991], 20). Two other notable critiques of Kristeva's work are those of James H. Charlesworth, "Intertextuality: Isaiah 40.3 and the Serek Ha-Yahad," in *The Quest for Context and Meaning: Studies in Biblical Intertextuality in Honor of James A. Sanders,* eds. Craig A. Evans and Shemaryahu Talmon (Leiden: E. J. Brill, 1997), 197–224, and Jonathan Culler, *The Pursuit of Signs: Semiotics, Literature, Deconstruction* (Ithaca: Cornell University Press, 1981).

63. The potential of intertextual study of the Bible has been most fully realized to this point in G. K. Beale's and D. A. Carson's massive work, *Commentary on the New Testament Use of the Old Testament* (Grand Rapids: Baker Academic Press, 2007).

64. Prior to Hays, others had noted these quotations but had not examined them as minutely or as technically as Hays would. Old Testament quotations were first organized by J. Rendel Harris in his two volumes entitled *Testimonies* (Cambridge: Cambridge University Press, 1916–1920). Subsequent analysis of those quotations, looking at context, comparison, and methodology, has been performed by scholars such as C. H. Dodd, *According to Scriptures: The Sub-Structure of New Testament Theology* (London: Nisbet, 1952); E. Earle Ellis, *St. Paul's Use of the Old Testament* (London: Oliver and Body, 1957); Krister Stendahl, *The School of St. Matthew and its Use of the Old Testament* (Philadelphia: Fortress Press, 1968); Lindars, *New Testament Apologetic*; and F. F. Bruce, *New Testament Development of Old Testament Themes* (Grand Rapids: William B. Eerdmans Publishing Company, 1968). Dodd's work was especially significant for later intertextual studies, as he concluded that "very often a quotation is intended to evoke the whole passage from which it has been selected" (Lindars, *New Testament Apologetic*, 14).

65. Hays, *Echoes*, 20.

66. 1) Availability, 2) volume, 3) recurrence, 4) thematic cohesion, 5) historical plausibility, 6) history of interpretation, and 7) satisfaction (Hays, *Echoes*, 29–32). More recently, Michael Thompson has further broken Hays's seven categories down into eleven: 1) Verbal Agreement, 2) Conceptual agreement, 3) Formal agreement, 4) Place of the Gospel saying in the tradition, 5) Common motivation, rationale, 6) Dissimilarity to Graeco-Roman and Jewish traditions, 7) Presence of dominical indicators, 8) Presence of tradition indicators, 9) Presence of other dominical echoes or word/concept clusters in the immediate context, 10) Likelihood the author knew the saying, and 11) Exegetical Value (Michael Thompson, *Clothed with Christ: The Example and Teaching of Jesus in Romans 12:1–15:13* JSNTSup 59 [Sheffield: JSOT Press, 1991], 31–36). Thompson does recognize, as did Hays, that "Criteria such as these cannot be expected to *prove* dependence in a mathematical way. . . . Their value lies in assisting the judgment of relative probability" (Thompson, *Clothed with Christ*, 36). On the other hand, Robert L. Brawley (*Text to Text Pours Forth Speech: Voices of Scripture in Luke-Acts* [Bloomington: Indiana University Press, 1995), finds only two of Hays's categories, "availability" and "volume," to be worth consideration in identifying echoes.

67. Richard Hays, *The Conversion of the Imagination: Paul as Interpreter of Israel's Scripture* (Grand Rapids: William B. Eerdmans Publishing Company, 2005), 2–3. Hays believes that these "unstated or suppressed correspondences" should not be strictly located within the author's mind, the reader's mind, or the text itself, preferring instead to see a "creative tension" existing between all three. (Hays, *Echoes*, 27). Hays himself states "The hermeneutical event occurs in my reading of the text, but my reading always proceeds within a community of interpretation, whose hermeneutical conventions inform my reading. Prominent among these conventions are the convictions that a proposed interpretation must be justified with reference to evidence provided both by the text's rhetorical structure and by what can be known through critical investigation about the author and original readers. Any interpretation must respect these constraints in order to be persuasive within my reading community. Claims about intertextual meaning effects are strongest where it can credibly be demonstrated that they occur within the literary structure of the text and that they can plausibly be ascribed to the intention of the author and the competence of the original readers" (Hays, *Echoes*, 28).

68. Roland Barthes, "The Death of the Author," in *Image-Music-Text*, trans. Stephen Heath (London: Fontana, 1977), 148. For Bakhtin's discussion of dialogic, see "Discourse in the Novel," in *The Dialogic Imagination: Four Essays by M. M. Bakhtin*, ed. Michael Holquist (Austin and London: University of Texas Press, 1981), 259–422. James A. Sanders has provided two useful, more contemporary definitions of intertextuality that build off of both Kristeva and Barthes: intertextuality is both the "recogni-

tion that all literature is made up of previous literature and reflects the earlier, through citation, allusion, use of phrases and paraphrases of older literature to create newer references to earlier literary episodes, even echoes of earlier familiar literature in the construction of the later," and "recognition that the reader is also a text and that reading is in essence an encounter between texts. The reader is a bundle of hermeneutics, as it were, engaging a text that is itself a bundle of hermeneutics" ("Intertextuality and Dialogue: New Approaches to the Scriptural Canon," in *Canon vs. Culture: Reflections on the Current Debate*, ed. Jan Gorak [New York: Garland Publishing, Inc., 2001], 180).

69. See Terryl L. Givens, *By the Hand of Mormon: The American Scripture that Launched a New World Religion* (New York: Oxford University Press, 2002), 62–88, 218–39.

70. "It is important to realize that the term *intertextuality* is actually a 'grab bag' concept which embraces a broad range of literary phenomena, including genre, motif, formulae, type-scenes and parallel accounts, allusion, quotation and hypertextual commentary" (Cynthia Edenburg, "Intertextuality, Literary Competence and the Question of Readership: Some Preliminary Observations," *JSOT* 35.2 [2010]: 137).

71. Ellen van Wolde, "Trendy Intertextuality?" in Sipke Draisma, ed., *Intertextuality in Biblical Writings: Essays in Honour of Bas van Iersel* (Kampen, Netherlands: Uitgeversmaatschappij J. H. Kok, 1989), 43.

72. Russell L. Meek, "Intertextuality, Inner-Biblical Exegesis, and Inner-Biblical Allusion: The Ethics of a Methodology," *Biblica* 95.2 (2014): 291.

73. "It is not recommended to make a clear distinction between allusion (echo) and exegesis on the one hand, and intertextuality on the other . . . however, scholars often cross the border between these approaches" (Karl William Weyde, "Inner-Biblical Interpretation: Methodological Reflections on the Relationship between Texts in the Hebrew Bible," *SEA* 70 [2005]: 300).

74. For more on this tricky issue, see Geoffrey D. Miller, "Intertextuality in Old Testament Research," *Currents in Biblical Research* 9.283 (2011): 283–309.

75. I borrow the phrase "rhetoric of allusivity" from Clare K. Rothschild, who speaks of "pseudonymity" as a "rhetoric of allusion" (*Hebrews as Pseudepigraphon*, 132).

76. It was Richard Hays who defined "quotation," "allusion," and "echo" as "points along a spectrum of intertextual reference, moving from the explicit to the subliminal" (*Echoes*, 23).

77. To put it simply, a "text" is "evidence of an attempt by a producer (speaker/writer) to communicate his message to a recipient (hearer/reader)" (Gillian Brown and G. Yule, *Discourse Analysis* [London: Cambridge University Press, 1983], 24).

78. An "intertext" is the "text-within-a-text." As Michel Foucault has observed, "The frontiers of a book are never clear-cut: beyond the title, the first lines, and the last full stop, beyond its internal configuration and its autonomous form, it is caught up in a system of references to other books, other texts, other sentences: it is a node within a network" (*The Archaeology of Knowledge and the Discourse on Language*, trans. A. M. S. Smith [New York: Pantheon, 1972], 165).

79. When the "text" is understood within the context of the "intertext," then the "subtext" is revealed: "Through its subtext, therefore, a text reveals its possibilities of meaning, possibilities which may be denied by what it appears to communicate. . . . It is as if the text reveals fault lines, fissures on its surface which, if traced to the centre, illuminate the subtext lying beneath its surface. Where these fault lines appear—at these points of disjunction, rupture, and stress—the inconsistencies, contradictions, evasions, and obfuscations of the text show themselves, however unwillingly, as clues to a meaning which the text forbids itself, at least on its surface" (W. John Harker, "Framing the Text: The Year 2000 in British Columbia," *Canadian Journal of Education* 17:1 [1992], 3). Those who advocate this type of intertextual approach, who attempt to uncover a "subtext" within a "text," often run into questions such as "Did the author intend for that subtext to be relayed" or "Would a reader have picked-up on the allusion?" However, as W. K. Wimsatt and Monroe Beardsley famously noted, the text itself is the only true source of meaning. Terry Eagleton adds that "a text which runs

within it, visible at certain 'symptomatic' points of ambiguity, evasion or overemphasis, and which we as readers are able to 'write' even if the novel itself does not" (*Literary Theory* [Oxford: Blackwell, 1983], 178). In a statement more directly related to biblical studies, Christopher A. Beetham has written of allusions in the writings of Paul that "Even if Paul only unconsciously echoed a text simply out of his saturation with Scripture, we can still speak of Paul 'doing' something as an author with and in the words he wrote. In such a case, Paul still expressed himself with phraseology whose language stems from a particular text that he had read on a previous occasion, whether he himself was aware that he was doing it or not" (*Echoes of Scripture in the Letter of Paul to the Colossians*, BIS 96 [Leiden: E. J. Brill, 2008], 13–14).

80. Jan Shipps, "The Prophet Puzzle: Suggestions Leading Toward a More-Comprehensive Interpretation of Joseph Smith," *Journal of Mormon History* 1 (1974): 11.

81. Book of Mormon Title Page.

82. Joseph Smith, History, Vol. A-1, 9.

83. MacKay, et al., *Documents, vol. 1*, xxviii–xxxii; See also John W. Welch, "The Miraculous Translation of the Book of Mormon," in *Opening the Heavens: Accounts of Divine Manifestations, 1820–1844*, ed. John W. Welch with Erick B. Carlson (Provo and Salt Lake City: Brigham Young University Press and Deseret Book, 2005), 82–98; Royal Skousen, "Translating the Book of Mormon: Evidence from the Original Manuscript," in *Book of Mormon Authorship Revisited: The Evidence for Ancient Origins*, ed. Noel B. Reynolds (Provo, Utah: Foundation for Ancient Research and Mormon Studies, 1997), 61–93.

84. See Bushman, *Rough Stone Rolling*, 48–52; See also Gardner, *Translating the Book of Mormon*, 65–90, 259–77; Givens, *By the Hand of Mormon*, 16, 25, 32–34; D. Michael Quinn, *Early Mormonism and the Magic World View* (Salt Lake City: Signature Books, 1988), 40–65, 169–77; Welch, "Miraculous Translation," 87. Robert V. Remini, *Joseph Smith* (New York: Viking/Penguin Putnam, Inc., 2002), 16; Shipps, *Mormonism*, 10–11.

85. For a very useful discussion of the translation process, including Smith's use of seer stones, see MacKay, et al., *Documents, vol. 1*, xxix–xxxii.

86. "Emma Smith Bidamon Interview with Edmund C. Briggs, 1856" in *Early Mormon Documents*, ed. Dan Vogel (Salt Lake City: Signature Books, 1996), 1:530.

87. Joseph Knight Sr., Reminiscences, as cited in MacKay, et al., *Documents, vol. 1*, xxx–xxxi.

88. David Whitmer, *An Address to all believers in Christ*, 1887 in Vogel, *EMD*, 5:196–97.

89. Book of Mormon Title Page.

90. Philip Barlow writes of biblical phrases in the Book of Mormon that "More than fifty thousand phrases of three or more words, excluding definite and indefinite articles, are common to the Bible and the Book of Mormon," and that "Sometimes the Book of Mormon employs KJV phrases far more frequently than the KJV itself," even though "the Book of Mormon is only one-third the volume of the Bible." Barlow sees the relationship between the Book of Mormon and the language of the Bible as a complementary one, noting that "biblical phrases constitute the vocabulary building blocks of much of the Book of Mormon narrative, yet that narrative maintains an independent coherence" (Barlow, *Mormons and the Bible*, 28–29).

91. Grant Hardy, *Understanding the Book of Mormon*, 5–6.

92. Doctrine and Covenants, "Explanatory Introduction."

93. Bushman, *Rough Stone Rolling*, 172.

94. See Grant Underwood, *The Millenarian World of Early Mormonism* (Chicago: University of Illinois Press, 1993).

95. Richard Bushman, "The 'Little, Narrow Prison' of Language: The Rhetoric of Revelation," in *Believing History: Latter-day Saint Essays*, ed. Reid L. Neilson and Jed Woodworth (New York: Columbia University Press, 2004), 253.

96. The problem is summed up well by H. Michael Marquardt: "While Smith did not comment on the manner in which he perceived God's mind, the linguistic idiosyncracies are assumed to be his own. Whether he believed that the ideas or the words

themselves were God's is not completely understood" (H. Michael Marquardt, *The Joseph Smith Revelations: Text and commentary* [Salt Lake City: Signature Books, 1999], xiii). Further complicating the question is the fact that Joseph Smith often altered the language of the revelations, which may suggest that he understood himself as having some role in the reception of the revelations beyond a passive receptacle. However, Smith also envisioned himself as God's Prophet and thus may have felt it was his privilege to alter or "expand upon" the words of God.

97. Parley P. Pratt, Jr., *Autobiography of Parley P. Pratt* (Salt Lake City: Deseret Book, 2000), 72.

98. William E. McClellin, "Revelations," *Ensign of Liberty, of the Church of Christ* (Kirtland, Ohio), 1, no. 7 (August 1849): 98–99.

99. MacKay, et al., *Documents, vol. 1*, xxxiii.

100. Robert J. Woodford, "Joseph Smith and the Revelations: From Manuscripts to Publication," *MHS* (Fall 2005): 137. See also MacKay et al., *Documents, vol. 1*, xxix–xxxiv.

101. Barlow, *Mormons and the Bible*, 68. Additionally, "The revelations often incorporated phrases, ideas, and terms found in the King James Version of the Bible and in the Book of Mormon" (MacKay, et al, *Documents, vol. 1*, xxvii).

102. Minutes of the School of Prophets, Salt Lake Stake, 9 Dec. 1872, Church Historical Department Archives. Family and Church History Department, The Church of Jesus Christ of Latter-day Saints, Salt Lake City, Utah.

ONE

Mormon Scripture and the Echo of John

In his intertextual study of Jeremiah and Second Isaiah, Benjamin J. Sommer presented a methodology in which he attempted to distinguish between allusion and echo. Following the work of Ziva Ben-Porat, Sommer argued that the point of demarcation between allusion and echo occurs when meaning is transferred from one text to the other.[1] While both allusion and echo demonstrate a dependence upon an earlier text, only in the case of allusion will a knowledge of the source material affect interpretations of the newer text.[2] The presence of a literary echo in a text enables a reader to "recognize the markers (the many words borrowed from the source) and identify the source, but doing so does not lead the reader to change his or her interpretation. . . ." D. L. Peterson, in his intertextual study of Zechariah, comes to a similar conclusion: "the presence of echo in the derivative text does not constitute a consequential reuse of the earlier text. It is more of a literary fossil than a living entity in the new text."[3] This does not mean, however, that echo does not have a function within a text beyond recognition. Speaking of echoes of the biblical book of Numbers in Psalms 4 and 67, Sommer writes: "the reuse of the vocabulary may represent a claim to authority by the psalms or an attempt by them to reinforce the authority of the ancient benediction."[4] Thus echo serves two important functions: first, it directs the attention of the reader back to an earlier text without the expectation that the original context or meaning of the echoed text will alter the interpretation of the echoing text. Second, through the employment of echo the echoing text often asserts a "claim to authority" on the earlier text.

This utilization of a recognized text as a means of establishing a "claim to authority" becomes especially pertinent to studies of Mormonism. In an age of Enlightenment, early converts to Mormonism largely

1

consisted of contemplative readers of the Bible who relied upon popular "common sense" rationality when evaluating spiritual concepts. The close linking of Bible and Book of Mormon provided the empirical evidence needed to sway them toward accepting the new text. According to Timothy L. Smith, ". . . it seems evident also that Joseph Smith and the early apostles relied upon the Bible to establish the credibility of both the Book of Mormon and the revelations recorded in his Doctrine and Covenants."[5] Historian Steven C. Harper has noted how some early converts to the movement, after a thorough investigation of the Book of Mormon, would note how the Book of Mormon "corresponded" to or "corroborate[d]" with the Bible in a reciprocal fashion, providing some of the "infallible proofs" that led to their baptisms.[6] Philip Barlow elaborates on what form these "infallible proofs" may have taken: "The new 'gold bible' would have been incomprehensible apart from a biblical context. It was printed in biblical fashion as a collection of books, originally divided into chapters and later into verses. It contained two dozen chapters of material common to the Bible. The subjects of its narrative were originally biblical peoples, many of its episodes paralleled biblical stories, and it purported both to prophesy of the Bible as a book and to be itself a fulfillment of biblical prophecy. Indeed, the Book of Mormon explicitly identified itself as a companion to the Bible."[7]

In his literary-oriented analysis of the Book of Mormon, Terryl Givens, following Mikhail Bahktin, discussed how certain elements of Smith's Book of Mormon narrative, such as the use of seer stones for translation, provided Smith with a means of validity extending beyond his own claims. This "authoritative discourse" is "quite independent of any power it might have to persuade us internally; we encounter it with authority already fused to it."[8] The result is a text that "is so wedded to an authoritative source that we find it difficult or impossible to assess the content as content."[9] Through the use of Johannine echo in the Book of Mormon and the Doctrine and Covenants, Smith will do precisely this: tether the language of John so closely to his own composition that "it stands and falls together with that authority."[10] The result of this "authoritative discourse" is that to resist or ignore Joseph Smith is to resist or ignore John. The purpose of this chapter will be to study four occasions where an "echo" from the Prologue of John can be found in Mormon scripture, one rather lengthy (3 Nephi 9:15–18) and three rather brief (2 Nephi 9:24, D&C 42:52, D&C 20:29) where the function of the language appears primarily to be the assertion of authority through the use of allusivity rather than any transference of meaning from the source text.[11]

In 3 Nephi 9, the Book of Mormon claims that the resurrected Jesus appeared to a group of Nephites following his crucifixion. According to Mormon, the narrator of the text, the Nephites first heard the voice of Jesus pronouncing condemnation upon the wicked Nephites. Jesus then introduced himself and left the Nephites in silence for several hours.

Subsequently, the Nephites saw Jesus descend down from heaven while another voice witnessed to the identity of his "Beloved Son, in whom I am well pleased, in whom I have glorified my name" (3 Nephi 11:7). Finally, Jesus introduced himself in a lengthy statement consisting primarily of phrases borrowed from the Prologue of John. The following paragraph presents this Nephite introduction, with the Johannine language italicized:

> Behold, *I am Jesus Christ the Son of God. I created the heavens and the earth and all things that in them is* (John 1:3). *I was with the Father from the beginning* (John 1:2). *I am in the Father and the Father in me* (John 14:10); *and in me hath the Father glorified his name* (John 17:1). *I came unto my own, and my own received me not* (John 1:11); and the scriptures concerning my coming are fulfilled. *And as many as have received me, to them have I given to become the sons of God* (John 1:12). *And even so will I to as many as shall believe on my name* (John 1:12). For behold, by me redemption cometh, and *in me is the law of Moses fulfilled* (John 1:17). *I am the light and the life of the world* (John 1:4). I am Alpha and Omega, the beginning and the end (Rev. 18:11).[12]

Immediately apparent is the similarity between Jesus' words and John's Prologue in a way that moves beyond the inclusion of lengthy segments of the Bible, such as chapters from Isaiah or Matthew's Sermon on the Mount.[13] 3 Nephi 9:15–18 seems to be a conscious attempt by the Nephite Jesus to imitate the Prologue, down to both order and language, in his introduction, without necessarily quoting it verbatim. For example, the *pericope* begins with echoes of John 1:2–3 before echoing phrases from John 14 and 17. The speaker then returns to the Prologue, with echoes from John 1:11 and John 1:12, followed by an echo of John 1:17. It is only with the last of the Prologue echoes, "I am the light and the life of the world," from John 1:4, that this trend diverges. This consistency could be attributed to the logical order by which the Prologue unfolds, going from pre-mortal λόγος to incarnate Christ, or it could suggest that the author of the verses was himself familiar with the Prologue and was relying upon his audience being likewise familiar.

This clever re-working of the Johannine prologue can be seen even more clearly at the phrasal level. The Book of Mormon Jesus opens his introduction with the declaratory statement "Behold, I am Jesus Christ the Son of God," before directly engaging the Prologue with a description of his role as creator, stating: "I created the heavens and the earth and all things that in them is." This statement echoes John 1:3, where John says of Jesus that "All things were made by him; and without him was not anything made that was made." The phrase "all things" serves to link the two, but the same point is driven home in both verses—nothing was done without Jesus, neither in Heaven nor on Earth. He is the supreme creator. If readers wanted to take this imagery a step further, John 1:1, "In the beginning was the Word" links the Johannine Prologue with Genesis 1:1, "In the beginning God created the heaven and the earth," a connection demonstrating that a new phase of creation is being undertaken with the incarnation of the Word. The Book of Mormon attempts a similar maneuver though appropriating the phrase "the heavens and the earth" from Genesis 1:1 and merging it with John 1:3 and its reference to "all things." Through this double allusion the Book of Mormon subtly claims for itself the authority of both the Old and the New Testaments, arguing that, like links in a grand literary chain, it warrants a place alongside the biblical texts.

The Book of Mormon continues its adoption of Johannine language through the statement of Jesus that "I was with the Father from the beginning." This verse echoes John 1:1–2, where one of the purposes was to emphasize the pre-mortal existence of the Son. The use of "from the beginning" suggests a co-eternality as well, although it is unclear whether Jesus is talking about the beginning of time or the beginning of the creation of the world. Once again, the strong sense of unity between Father and Son is underscored, yet there is also a striving for individuality in this statement, as Jesus says he was "with the Father" rather than "is the Father," as he does in other places in the Book of Mormon. Curiously, the phrase from John 1:1 that "the Word was God" is missing.[14] For all the emphasis in the Book of Mormon upon the unity between Father and Son and how Jesus is both Father and Son, this statement, which would have supported that claim, is now notably absent. One other significant difference is the repeated use of "I." In John's gospel, it is the "he" or "him" that refers to Jesus, yet the Jesus who appears to the Nephites makes it clear that he himself, "I," is a creator, that "I" was around "from the Beginning." The Jesus of the Book of Mormon has taken the Prologue of John and personalized it, using it as a means of relating to a Nephite audience.

At this point, the Book of Mormon Jesus makes a statement that is Johannine but not necessarily reflective of the Prologue: "I am in the Father and the Father in me," an allusion to John 14:10: "Believest thou not that I am in the Father, and the Father in me? the words that I speak unto you I speak not of myself: but the Father that dwelleth in me, he doeth the works." If the point of using John 1:1–2 in the previous clause was to obtain some sort of distinction or demarcation between deities, this verse muddies up the waters again by emphasizing the absolute closeness and unity of the Father and Son, down to the point that they are "in" each other. The presence of this clause in 3 Nephi 9 is somewhat curious for an additional reason. In John 14, Philip inquired of Jesus about the Father, leading to Jesus' response, namely that "he that hath seen me hath seen the Father" (John 14:9). So why is Jesus' answer to Philip repeated here, completely removed from the context of Philip's question? How does this help the Nephites?

Now, we begin to more fully understand the rhetorical strategy of the Book of Mormon, how it has employed the "rhetoric of allusivity." While the allusion to John 14 and Jesus' answer to Philip's question does work within the narrative developed by the Book of Mormon, serving to further blur the lines between Yahweh and the Messiah and taking the attention of the Nephites back to the "Father/Son" theology of Abinadi, the more likely reason for its inclusion in 3 Nephi is that the primary audience for the Book of Mormon was nineteenth-century Christians. Through the employment of a familiar verse such as John 14:10 the Book of Mormon speaks in a language that it is not simply recognizable to a nineteenth-century audience but a language that carries with it the authority of the Bible. Would the Book of Mormon Nephites have noticed that Jesus was alluding to a verse from the Gospel of John, a text which hadn't even been written at the time when the Book of Mormon claims Jesus appeared to the Nephites? Certainly not. But would nineteenth-century readers of the Book of Mormon? Most likely. And even if they didn't recognize the exact verse, they would have recognized the words of the Book of Mormon Jesus as biblical. Joseph Smith may have included this phrase for the benefit of his audience who would have recognized in the "new" Book of Mormon the old familiar voice of the Johannine Jesus. It is not so much *what* Jesus says, but *where* what he says originates, that is of primary importance.

The subsequent clause again alludes to a Johannine passage not found in the Prologue: "and in me hath the Father glorified his name," in this case an allusion to John 17:1–6, where John records Jesus' intercessory prayer, specifically entreating the Father to "glorify thy Son, that thy Son also may glorify thee. . . . I have manifested thy name unto the men which thou gavest me" (John 17:1, 6). Again, we must ask ourselves: are Jesus' words meant to be heard by a Nephite audience or a nineteenth-century American audience? Later on in 3 Nephi the Book of Mormon Jesus will deliver a lengthy variation of the intercessory prayer in 3 Nephi 19, with verses 28–29 alluding in particular to John 17:

> Father, I thank thee that thou hast purified these which I have chosen because of their faith. And I pray for them and also for them which shall believe on their words, that they may be purified in me through faith on their words, even as they are purified in me. Father, I pray not for the world but for them which thou hast given unto me out of the world because of their faith, that they may be purified in me, that I may be in them as thou Father art in me, that we may be one, that I may be glorified in them. (3 Nephi 19:28–29)

Significantly, following the deliverance of the prayer Jesus states to the Nephites that "Verily I say unto you: There are none of them (i.e., the Jews) that have seen so great things as ye have seen, neither have they heard so great things as ye have heard" (3 Nephi 19:36). The "rhetoric of allusivity" once again is subtle but present in this Johannine echo: Jesus' words to the Nephites hint at a superiority of the Book of Mormon apostles and people as a whole to those of the Old World, and by extension the superiority of the Book of Mormon to the Bible. The echo of John 17 in 3 Nephi 9:15 prepares the reader for what is to follow, ensuring that they don't overlook the allusivity present in the text.

In the following statement, the Book of Mormon Jesus returns to the wording of the Prologue "I came unto my own and my own received me not," an allusion to John 1:11. In the context of the Johannine Prologue, Jesus was likely alluding to his rejection and execution by the Jews, those who were "his own." In an earlier Book of Mormon passage, 3 Nephi 1:14, the pre-mortal Jesus proclaimed that "Behold, I come unto my own." The statement in 3 Nephi 9:16 brings readers of the Book of Mormon full circle, and in this sense Jesus' statement may have meaning within the Book of Mormon narrative. However, the allusion to John seems more likely to be directed at a nineteenth-century audience, who would recognize the allusion to John and understand Jesus' statement in 3 Nephi as another attempt to link themselves with the Book of Mormon, claiming both as covenant people. This verse becomes the ideal example, then, of a clause that attempts to work within the larger narrative while resonating more fully with a nineteenth-century audience, suggesting again a deliberate, intentional use of Johannine language by Joseph Smith.

Subsequent echoes of the Prologue of John in the Book of Mormon, "And as many as have received me, to them have I given to become the sons of God," "And even so will I to as many as shall believe on my name," and "I am the light and the life of the world" appear to serve a similar function to the phrases discussed above. All three phrases can function within the Book of Mormon narrative, but no meaning is carried over from the Bible to the Book of Mormon from a hermeneutical perspective because the Nephites could not have understood the source material and its significance. In the time frame laid out by the Book of Mormon, the Gospel of John did not yet exist. For this reason we must seek an audience for whom the language of John would have been meaningful, an audience for whom the "echo" would have actually signified something, in this case the nineteenth century readers of the Book of Mormon.

This focus by the Book of Mormon upon a nineteenth-century audience can most clearly be demonstrated in the final clause of the *pericope*, 3 Nephi 9:18, where Jesus follows "I am the light and the life of the world" with "I am Alpha and Omega, the beginning and the end." While this phrase is not from the Prologue of John or even the Gospel of John itself, its usage by Jesus is germane to this discussion because it is clearly a phrase originating in the Bible (Revelation 1:8, 11; 21:6; 22:13)[15] and as such requires an awareness of the Greek alphabet to understand.[16] Without a knowledge of the Greek alphabet, a merism constructed around the first and last letters of the Greek alphabet is anachronistic and nonsensi-cal.[17] Additionally, it is not simply a matter of ignorance regarding the Greek meaning of "Alpha and Omega," but the idea that this clause is an echo of the biblical Book of Revelation that is significant as well. As with the echoes of the Gospel of John, an echo of the Book of Revelation would have had meaning only for an audience familiar with the Book of Revela-tion. The presence of verbiage from such a well-known text tethers both Bible and Book of Mormon together through the rhetoric of allusivity.

The presence of biblical language strewn through the Book of Mor-mon can likely be attributed to the text's numerous claims for nineteenth-century relevance. From the opening pages of the text various authors speak to a future audience. The early Nephite prophet, Nephi, in the course of an apocalyptic vision, witnesses the coming forth of the Book of Mormon (1 Ne. 13:39). While Nephi preserves lengthy portions of Isaiah for his people, his own midrashic writings, beginning in 2 Nephi 25 and continuing through the end of 2 Nephi, reveal that Nephi began " to suspect that he will eventually have a broader readership consisting of not only the descendants of Lehi in the last days but also Jews and Gen-tiles."[18] According to Grant Hardy, the references to a people of Nephi "in the last days" is a significant one, as it represents "his first acknowl-edgement that his prophecies will be more intelligible to a distantly re-moved audience, who will eventually become his primary readership."[19] Because this "primary readership" would only emerge after the Book of Mormon had come forth in English (i.e., the nineteenth century), readers should expect the text to speak to them in their own religious language, the language of the King James Bible.

Perhaps the author who demonstrates the most awareness of a nine-teenth-century audience is the text's final author, Moroni. The title page of the Book of Mormon, which the text attributes to Moroni, identifies the intended audience of the text as "the Lamanites, who are a remnant of the house of Israel" as well as to the "Jew" and the "Gentile." In the course of completing his father's own short record, Moroni writes:

> Behold, the Lord hath shewn unto me great and marvelous things con-cerning that which must shortly come, at that day when these things shall come forth among you. Behold, I speak unto you as if ye were present—and yet ye are not—but behold, Jesus Christ hath shewn you unto me, and I know your doing. (Morm. 8:34–35)

Here Moroni explicitly claims that he witnessed firsthand the events and people of the nineteenth century, and that he is speaking to them "as if (they) were present." As Grant Hardy notes, Moroni "knows his core audience intimately; beginning with his first chapter he speaks regularly and explicitly to latter-day Gentiles."[20] For a text that has as its intended audience nineteenth-century Gentiles and demonstrates an acute aware-ness of nineteenth-century concerns, the language of the King James Bible becomes crucial to finding a receptive audience. Additionally, the Prologue of John, with its memorable language and remarkable imagery, as well as phrases from John 14 and 17 and the Book of Revelation, becomes an ideal manner of crafting a record of a visitation of Jesus Christ in a way that would resonate with readers living in the nineteenth century.

In order to demonstrate the rhetorical function played by weaving language from the Prologue of John throughout the Book of Mormon, it might be useful to examine an additional passage, although one that is significantly shorter than 3 Nephi 9:15–18. 2 Nephi 9–10 preserves one of the most important sermons in all the Book of Mormon. In these two chapters, Jacob, the son of Lehi and brother of Nephi, attempts to answer the question of "how does salvation work?" The answer to this question will allow him to expand upon the nature of covenants, atonement, sin, death, and agency. Paramount for Jacob is developing a high Christology for Jesus.[21] First, he states that "But behold, the righteous, the saints of the Holy One of Israel, they which have believed in the Holy One of Israel, they which have endured the crosses of the world and despised the shame of it, they shall inherit the kingdom of God, which was prepared for them from the foundation of the world; and their joy shall be full forever" (2 Nephi 9:18). This verse relays the temporal extensiveness of the "kingdom of God," which was in existence from the "foundation of the world" and those who participate in it shall experience joy "forever." Second, Jacob notes the omnipotence of the Son in 2 Nephi 9:19: "O the greatness of the mercy of our God, the Holy One of Israel! For he delivereth his saints from that awful monster, the devil and death and hell and that lake of fire and brimstone which is endless torment." In the following verse, Jacob praises the omniscience of the Son: "O how great the holiness of our God! For he knoweth all things, and there is not any thing save he know it." Jesus is all-powerful, all-knowing, and the plan for his kingdom has been in place from the beginning and will extend forever. There is no limit to Jesus, even 600 years prior to his birth. This *pericope* provides an example of a phenomenon in the Book of Mormon that could be termed "realized messialogy," namely that the life, character, and mission of Jesus Christ were explicitly understood by the Book of Mormon authors, even those who lived centuries before Jesus' birth.[22] They teach and preach as if the coming of Jesus has already occurred and the requirements for becoming a "Christian" have already been established, concepts that would have been familiar to a nineteenth-century audience but stand out somewhat anachronistically in the pages of the Book of Mormon.

Having established the eternal nature and power of Jesus Christ, 2 Nephi 9:23–24 elaborates on the qualifications one must have in order to participate in the atonement process. According to 2 Nephi 9:23, "And he commandeth all men that they must repent and be baptized in his name, having perfect faith in the Holy One of Israel, or they cannot be saved in the kingdom of God." Thus the requirements are repentance, baptism, and faith. Yet in verse 24, Jacob adds a further requirement: "And if they will not repent and *believe in his name* and be baptized in his name and endure to the end, they must be damned, for the Lord God, the Holy One of Israel, hath spoken it." This addition, "believe in his name," as well as be baptized "in his name," directs the attention of the reader back to John 1:11, where John states that "But as many as received him, to them gave he power to become the sons of God, even to them that believe on his name." This pairing of "repent" and "believe in his name" is found seven times in Mormon scripture, but not anywhere in the Bible, although biblical writers would likely not have seen the two concepts as mutually exclusive.[23] Furthermore, the exact phrase "baptized in his name" is also unique to Mormon scripture and is not found in the Bible.[24]

What is most curious, especially for readers of John's gospel, is the placing of the phrase "believe in his name" inside of a larger list of requirements for believers. For John, belief is of paramount importance. Those who recognize who Jesus is will receive salvation, while those who can't recognize him won't. According to John 1:12, power was given to those who proclaimed belief, not to those who were baptized. Additionally, John 1:12–13 signified that belief generates a spiritual "birth." The focus of the belief was upon "his name." It was very much a binary—one either believes and is saved or one doesn't believe and is not saved. It is this point that is obscured in Jacob's sermon. Instead of the polarity of do/ don't found in John 1, readers of the Book of Mormon are now told that in addition to expression of belief "in his name," one must also repent, be baptized, and endure to the end, or else they face damnation and lose out on a place and role in the kingdom of God. Jacob appears to be expanding on "believe on his name" to include repentance, baptism, and endurance.

How close are John and Jacob in agreement on this issue? Would John concede that belief "in his name" would also include baptism or enduring "to the end?" Johannine scholar C. K. Barrett writes that when speaking of "believing on his name," the use of τὸ ὄνομα "is not enough to suggest that John has baptism in mind. He mentions only faith, not knowledge, as the means of life and regeneration."[25] However, Barrett notes that the combination of the accusative object τὸ ὄνομα with the preposition εἰς suggests more than just assent, rather it carries with it the sense of allegiance as well.[26] Perhaps this allegiance could be expressed through the idea of repentance and baptism, in which case Jacob is just expanding explicitly on what John is saying implicitly, but that interpretation seems to be a stretch. From a Johannine perspective, Jacob appears to be misapplying the phrase "believe in his name," while from a Book of Mormon perspective his use of the phrase will greatly differ from how it is used by later authors.[27] It is difficult to see any attempt to engage the Gospel of John in this verse or the verses surrounding it beyond the repetition of its language, indicating that the presence of an allusion from John 1:12 in 2 Nephi 9:24 primarily serves a rhetorical function, namely to "echo" the text of the Bible for the benefit of a nineteenth-century audience.

As with the text of the Book of Mormon, the primary function of the Johannine echo in the Doctrine and Covenants was to establish a textual legitimacy through the repetition of a recognized, authoritative text.[28] Its presence serves largely a rhetorical function, without attempting any interpretive moves. In order to demonstrate this, the presence of Johannine language in two documents, D&C 42 and D&C 20, will be examined. The first of these, D&C 42, was written down following an earlier injunction to gather to Ohio, on 9 February 1831.[29] Presented as a series of answers to questions posed to Joseph Smith by twelve elders, the revelation (actually a combination of five separate ones) lays out how the Lord wants his kingdom to be administered. There are no longer a series of Mormon groups, but now one "people" who should "hearken" to the Lord. In many ways, this revelation encapsulates how the restored church appropriated both the heritage of Judaism and Christianity, both the Old Testament and the New, in the construction of a "new Israel." As historian Jan Shipps has noted, Mormonism, with its blend of authority and faith, scripture and revelation, high priests and apostles, was a religious movement "in which leader and followers were together living through—recapitulating—the stories of Israel and early Christianity."[30] Thus the reader of D&C 42 finds passages alluding to the Old Testament as well as the New Testament. Mormons are referred to as "my covenant people" (D&C 42:36), tasked to build "the new Jerusalem" (D&C 42:35). The first word of the revelation is "hearken," bringing to mind the sacred *shema* of Deuteronomy 6:5. Many of the Ten Commandments are repeated, along with the proper procedure for dealing with violators. Of this Mormon synthesis of the Judaic covenant, Mark L. Staker wrote: "The law as received in Kirtland reordered and repeated the commandments given to ancient Israel, expanding and providing further details on some, repeating others, barely touching on still others, and remaining silent on a few."[31] Yet this revelation is clearly addressed to a Christian church. The speaker of the revelation identifies himself as "Jesus Christ the Son of the living God the Saveiour of the world" (D&C 42:1). Terms such as "faith" (D&C 42:48–52), "repent" (D&C 42:7, 23–25), and "baptizing" (D&C 42:7) appear throughout. An economic system of consecration, similar to that mentioned in Acts 2 and 4, is outlined (D&C 42:30–35). Finally, in the midst of all this Old and New Testament language, one encounters the names of ninteenth-century Americans: Joseph Smith, Sidney Rigdon, and Edward Partridge. This revelation takes the three worlds of Joseph Smith—Judaism, Christianity, and Mormonism—and seamlessly syncretizes them so that all three converge in one place (Kirtland, Ohio) at one time (9 February 1831).

It is this effort to syncretize the Old Testament, the New Testament, and nineteenth-century American Christianity that may assist readers in understanding the first of the passages that adopt the language of the Johannine Prologue. D&C 42:1 reads "Hearken oh! ye Elders of my Church who have assembled yourselves together in my name even Jesus Christ the Son of the living God the Saveiour of the world in as much as they believe on my name and keep my commandments." The important clause is the final one. "In as much as they believe on my name" is an echo of John 1:12 and signifies the New Testament church. "Keep my Commandments" is an injunction encountered frequently in the Old Testament, in particular the Book of Deuteronomy, where the Lord elaborates on his law prior to the death of Moses and the entrance of the Israelites into the Promised Land. [32] In Kirtland, Ohio in February of 1831, the Lord again gathers his people and reveals his law to them: "again I say unto you hearken and hear and obey the laws which I Shall give unto you" (D&C 42:2). It is not surprising to see the phrase "Keep my Commandments" used in a revelation that, like Deuteronomy, contains the law of the Lord. What D&C 42:1 does, then, is encapsulate in one clause the theme of the entire revelation. The phrase "in as much as they believe on my name" alludes to the New Testament, Christian church. The phrase "Keep my commandments" alludes to the Old Testament, Jewish church. The phrase itself is spoken by Joseph Smith, again forming a convergence of Judaism, Christianity, and Mormonism. As with the Book of Mormon, it is not *what* these phrases teach, but *where* the phrases are drawn from that matters. For this particular passage from John, the exact context is not important. What is important is that when Joseph Smith seeks a phrase that will summarize what it means to belong to the Church of Christ, he chooses this passage from John. Just as "keep the commandments" signifies the requirements for a devoted Jew, "believe on my name" signifies the requirements of a faithful Christian, even if the rest of the revelation, with its emphasis upon law and commandments, may be somewhat counter-intuitive to the context of John 1:12.

The rhetorical function of this Johannine phrase becomes clear when we look at a second Johannine phrase found further on in D&C 42. Verse 52 states: "and they that have not faith to do these things but believe in me hath power to become my sons and in as much as they break not my Laws thou Shalt bear their infirmities." Careful readers will note that the phrase "power to become my sons" is the phrase that immediately precedes "believe on his name" in John 1:12. As with D&C 42:1, this verse presents something of an intertextual curiosity. From the context, it appears that Joseph Smith is establishing a hierarchy of belief. In D&C 42:48–51 he states that "and again it shall come to pass that he that hath faith in me to be healed and is not appointed unto death shall be healed he that hath faith to see shall see he that hath faith to hear shall hear the Lame that have faith to leep shall leep." Thus faith is a requirement for those who seek to be healed, an idea consistent with the New Testament. The curiosity is the next verse: "and they that have not faith to do these things but believe in me hath power to become my sons and in as much as they break not my Laws thou Shalt bear their infirmities" (D&C 42:52). The implication is that "belief" is something of a "second-tier" or "watered-down" version of faith. The truly devoted will have faith, while those who cannot quite muster enough devotion for faith can at least achieve "belief." Steven Harper writes of this verse that "Those who have faith to see, hear, or leap will do so, and those without such faith who still choose to believe have power to become sons and daughters of Jesus Christ if they do not break his laws."[33] The concept that "faith" is a superior form of "belief" is perhaps acceptable, but the language used in the D&C 42:52 to construct this idea is clearly Johannine. Compare the two:

- But as many as received him, to them gave he *power to become the sons of God*, even to them that *believe on his name*. (John 1:12)
- and they that have not faith to do these things but *believe in me* hath *power to become my sons* and in asmuch as they break not my Laws thou Shalt bear their infirmities. (D&C 42:52)

The contextual problem is that in the Fourth Gospel only the truly faithful were given the power "to become the Sons of God." In D&C 42 the implication is that this "power" is available to even those who fall short of true faith. In John "belief on his name" was the hallmark of a true disciple, not a sub-standard version of faith. In this instance, Joseph Smith has appropriated the language of John but misapplied the original meaning of the verse. These are John's words, but not John's meaning. This reading conflicts with the earlier passage in D&C 42:1, where Joseph had used John 1:12 as a signifier for his amalgamation of Judaism and Christianity. Smith may have stated in verse one that "belief" was necessary, but the revelation itself suggests the opposite. As with the Book of Mormon, Joseph Smith demonstrates in D&C 42 that he is becoming more and more comfortable in adopting the language of the Bible in a way that has little use for context outside of the fact that it is biblical language he is using. Smith seems to view the scriptures as sacred, but he also views himself as a prophet, a man who can cross back and forth between the sacred and the profane.[34] Thus, although the words of John may be sacred, they are not etched in stone. As he begins to solidify his church and grow more confident in his mission, Joseph Smith will continue to test the elasticity of scripture, contorting it, reshaping it, and even rewriting it.

This re-writing of scripture, the "deconstruction" and "reconstruction" of the word of God, can be seen even more clearly in D&C 20:29, another location where John 1:12 appears: "And we know that all men must *repent and believe on the name of Jesus Christ*, and *worship the Father in his name,* and endure in *faith on his name* to the end, or they cannot be saved in the kingdom of God." This verse presents readers with a slightly different perspective on how Joseph Smith views biblical verse, namely how extremely malleable he regards it, as if these biblical phrases were pieces he could arrange and re-arrange. D&C 20:29 contains three variations on the Johannine "believe on his name."

1. Repent and Believe on the Name of Jesus Christ

This clause is the truest to its Johannine origins as far as preservation of language goes, but the combination of "repent" and "believe on/in his name" cannot be found in the Gospel of John. They do occur together three times in the Book of Mormon:

1. And if they will not *repent and believe in his name* and be baptized in his name and endure to the end, they must be damned, for the Lord God, the Holy One of Israel, hath spoken it. (2 Nephi 9:24)
2. And thus the work of the Lord did commence among the Lamanites. Thus the Lord did begin to pour out his Spirit upon them. And we see that his arm is extended to all people who will *repent and believe on his name.* (Alma 19:36)
3. Now, have we not reason to rejoice? Yea, I say unto you: There never was men that had so great reason to rejoice as we since the world began. Yea, and my joy is carried away, even unto boasting in my God. For he has all power, all wisdom, and all understanding; he comprehendeth all things, and he is a merciful Being, even unto salvation to those who will *repent and believe on his name.* (Alma 26:35)

2. Worship the Father in his name

This phrase is likely building upon John 1:12 (and may be alluding to John 2:23), and even the theology of the Fourth Gospel is present in that Jesus acts as the agent of the Father, and thus one worships the Father through Jesus. While the title "Father" appears 124 times in the three Synoptic Gospels, it occurs 116 times in the Fourth Gospel alone. The phrase itself is not found in John, but is found in two verses from the Book of Mormon. The first, 2 Nephi 25:16, states:

> And after that they have been scattered and the Lord God hath scourged them by other nations for the space of many generations— yea, even down from generation to generation until they shall be persuaded to believe in Christ the Son of God and the atonement, which is infinite for all mankind—and when that day shall come that they shall believe in Christ and *worship the Father in his name* with pure hearts and clean hands and look not forward any more for another Messiah—and

then at that time the day will come that it must needs be expedient that they should believe these things—

The second is Jacob 4:5, where the phrase "worship/ed the Father in his name" appears twice:

Behold, they believed in Christ and *worshiped the Father in his name*; and also we *worship the Father in his name*. And for this intent we keep the law of Moses, it pointing our souls to him. And for this cause it is sanctified unto us for righteousness, even as it was accounted unto Abraham in the wilderness to be obedient unto the commands of God in offering up his son Isaac, which was a similitude of God and his Only Begotten Son.

Note that the idea of "believing in Christ" is present both in Jacob 4:5 and D&C 20:29.

3. *Endure in* Faith on his Name *to the End*

This clause is a slight variation on the phrase, "faith *in* his name," which is found once in the New Testament, Acts 3:16. This same phrase is found in the Book of Mormon two times: Moroni 7:26, 38. The exact phrase "faith on his name" is not found in the Bible, but is found five times in the Book of Mormon:

And lo, he cometh unto his own that salvation might come unto the children of men, even through *faith on his name*. And even after all this, they shall consider him as a man and say that he hath a devil, and shall scourge him and shall crucify him. (Mos. 3:9)

And now because of the covenant which ye have made, ye shall be called the children of Christ, his sons and his daughters; for behold, this day he hath spiritually begotten you, for ye say that your hearts are changed through *faith on his name*; therefore ye are born of him and have become his sons and his daughters. (Mos. 5:7)

And behold, he cometh to redeem those who will be baptized unto repentance through *faith on his name*. (Alma 9:27)

In the name of Jesus Christ, I ordain you to be a priest—or if he be a teacher, I ordain you to be a teacher—to preach repentance and remission of sins through Jesus Christ by the endurance of *faith on his name* to the end. Amen. (Mor. 3:3)

I am mindful of you always in my prayers, continually praying unto God the Father in the name of his Holy Child Jesus that he through his infinite goodness and grace will keep you through the endurance of *faith on his name* to the end. (Mor. 8:3)

Notably, these last two verses, Moroni 3:3 and 8:3, also contain the more elaborate phrase "the endurance of faith on his name to the end," very similar to D&C 20:29 "endure in faith on his name to the end." Furthermore, the phrase "faith in his name" is found in one other place in the Doctrine and Covenants, in D&C 3:20:

> and that the Lamanites might come to the knowledge of their Fathers and that they may know the Promises of the Lord that they may believe the Gospel and rely upon the merits of Jesus Christ and that they might be glorified through *faith in his name* and that they might repent and be Saved Amen.

Likewise, other than D&C 20:29, the phrase "faith on his name" is found in only one other revelation as well, D&C 29:42:

> But Behold I say unto you that I the Lord God gave unto Adam and unto his seed that they should not Die as to the temporal death untill I the Lord God should send forth Angels to declare unto them Repentance and redemption through *faith on the name* of mine only begotten Son.

In the case of the phrase "repent and believe on his name," these echoes appear to be primarily rhetorical in function, signifying the language of the Bible without any attempts to signify John or his theology in general. In the case of the other two phrases, "worship the Father in his name" and "endure in faith on his name," both stress what John 1:12 does, namely the crucial importance of the name of Jesus as a requirement for salvation—He is the only way to the Father, and his name brings eternal life. Yet while Joseph Smith demonstrates creativity in how he combines words and phrases in the construction of the language that forms these verses, there is still the sense that their primary purpose for being placed in the text is rhetorical rather than theological. The Johannine echoes serve to textually unify the revelations to the Bible in the minds of readers and listeners, re-enforcing a link between Mormonism and the ancient Christian church. Joseph Smith captures the language of John, altering the order of the words and substituting additional terminology, but the primary purpose seems to be an attempt to direct the minds of readers to the Bible in general and John in particular, with little or no expectation that the context of the Johannine phrases should have any relevance in the interpretive process.

At the beginning of this chapter, we noted that an "echo" serves two primary functions: it directs the attention of the reader back to an earlier text without the expectation that the original context or meaning of the echoed text will alter the interpretation of the echoing text, and through the employment of echo the echoing text often asserts a "claim to authority" through the earlier text. As to the first point, the examples of 3 Nephi 9:15–18, 2 Nephi 9:24, D&C 42:52, and D&C 20:29 demonstrate that their function within the text was to signify the biblical text, not engage in an extended dialogue with it or to apply the biblical context to the Mormon scriptural context. These passages reflect the language of the Bible, but they serve little function in the text beyond simply *being* text. As to the second, it is this desire noted by Barlow that the Book of Mormon longs to be "explicitly identified as a companion to the Bible," and by extension to assume the authority of the biblical text, that best encapsulates the function of "echo" in the Book of Mormon and by extension the Doctrine and Covenants.

NOTES

1. The work of Ziva Ben-Porat and the Israeli school which she represents has become a pivotal feature of biblical intertextual studies. See "The Poetics of Literary Allusion," *PTL: A Journal for Descriptive Poetics and Theory of Literature* 1 (1976): 105–28.

2. "Ben-Porat stresses that a text which allows the reader to note the marker and to identify the source is not an allusion. Only with the fuller interpretation of the alluding text which occurs in the third stage is it possible to assert the presence of an allusion" (Sommer, *Prophet Reads Scripture*, 15).

3. D. L. Peterson, "Zechariah 9–14: Methodological Reflections," in *Bringing out the Treasure: Inner Biblical Allusion in Zechariah 9–14*, eds. Mark J. Boda and Michael Floyd JSOTSup 370 (London: Sheffield Academic Press, 2003), 212. See also Susan Hylen, *Allusion and Meaning in John 6* (Berlin: Walter de Gruyter, 2005), 52–53.

4. Sommer, *Prophet Reads Scripture*, 31. In her study of the Book of Revelation, Elisabeth Schüssler Fiorenza makes a similar observation about how the author of the Apocalypse integrates the Hebrew Bible into his own text: "Therefore Rev. does not even once quote the OT. John uses OT texts as he uses Jewish apocalyptic, pagan mythological, or early Christian materials in an allusive 'anthological' way. He does not interpret the OT but uses its words, images, phrases, and patterns as a language arsenal in order to make his own theological statement or express his own prophetic vision. He adapts or borrows whole OT text sequences as patterns for his own original compositions but never refers to the OT as authoritative Scripture" (*The Book of Revelation: Justice and Judgment* [Minneapolis: Augsburg Fortress Press, 1998], 135).

5. Smith, "The Book of Mormon," 18.

6. Steven C. Harper, "'Infallible Proofs, Both Human and Divine:' The Persuasiveness of Mormonism for Early Converts," *RAC* 10.1 (Winter 2000): 105–108. Timothy Smith adds: "The first impact of the Book of Mormon upon readers thus seems in many cases . . . to have been to confirm or authenticate their belief in the old scriptures" (Smith, "Book of Mormon," 9).

7. Barlow, *Mormons and the Bible*, 27.

8. Mikhail Bakhtin, "Discourse in the Novel," 42, as cited in Givens, *By the Hand of Mormon*, 80.

9. Givens, *By the Hand of Mormon*, 80.

10. Mikhail Bakhtin, "Discourse in the Novel," 47, as cited in Givens, *By the Hand of Mormon*, 81.

11. This is not to say that the only function of allusivity is the assertion of authority. In the case of "Echo," the function could also be viewed as one of recognition, where the reader recognizes the source-text behind the echo and briefly stops to ponder its meaning and place within the subtext. The result of this is that the reader is more actively involved in the text, an involvement facilitated by allusivity. According to Michael C. J. Putnam, "Allusivity, like apostrophe, is by nature an anti-narrative gesture. It forces the reader to linger and gain a frisson of pleasure, in epic's case, not from description of the excited propulsion of events but from an act of intellectual recognition and inner reflection. We take a moment to watch the mirroring of one previous poetic context upon another subsequent to it which compounds the latter's importance and signification" ("The Lyric Genius of the 'Aeneid,'" *Arion: A Journal of Hu-*

manities and the Classics, 3.2/3 [Fall 1995–Winter 1996]: 81). However, the fact that the text being echoed is from the Bible, an authoritative source, should still be recognized.

12. All quotations from the Book of Mormon are taken from *The Book of Mormon: The Earliest Text*, ed. Royal Skousen (Yale: Yale University Press, 2009).

13. This type of lengthy appropriation that one finds in 3 Nephi 9:15–18 is by no means unique to the Book of Mormon, and there is certainly biblical precedent. Sommer notes that "It is also possible for a new work to borrow whole sections word for word from an older text, so that the new text does not merely allude to scattered material but incorporates whole sections of an older work." Sommer uses as an example the book of Chronicles, which composes its history largely through the repetition of lengthy segments from the texts of Samuel and Kings. As for small nuances or meanings that may be added to the alluding text, Sommer continues: "In cases of inclusion, the new work may make small but highly significant changes in the reused material, but this does not change the *formal* status of the borrowing . . ." (Sommer, *Prophet Reads Scripture*, 22).

14. This clause from John 1:1 will also be noticeably absent from D&C 93.

15. The connection with John would come from a shared authorship of the Gospel and the Book of Revelation, assuming the claims of the New Testament texts claiming Johannine authorship are valid.

16. Even Latter-day Saint authors writing from a faithful perspective find this passage troubling. Mormon author Brant Gardner writes: "This particular Book of Mormon phrase is obviously Joseph Smith's translation of the concept using familiar New Testament language" (Brant Gardner, *Analytical and Contextual Commentary on the Book of Mormon*, 6 vols. [Salt Lake City: Greg Kofford Books, 2007–2011], 5:319). Monte S. Nyman, adds that: "Christ's use of the Greek *Alpha* and *Omega* to identify himself to the Nephites was probably intended as a confirmation of the New Testament designation for the latter-day reader" (Monte S. Nyman, "The Designations Jesus Gives Himself in 3 Nephi," in *3 Nephi: This Is My Gospel*, eds. Monte S. Nyman and Charles D. Tate [Provo: Religious Studies Center, 1993], 53).

17. This style of speech—using polar opposites to express the expansive nature of God's power—was common in Semitic language: "The use of the first and last letters of the alphabet was typical of the ancients in expressing merisms. Jews could, for instance, refer thus, using the Hebrew alphabet, to the whole law, saying that it should be kept 'from *aleph* to *tau*'" (G. K. Beale, *The Book of Revelation*, 199). One could thus view the "Gold Plates" containing some sort of merism, such as "aleph and tau" that becomes the more familiar "alpha and omega" in the translated Book of Mormon.

18. Hardy, *Understanding the Book of Mormon*, 221.

19. Hardy, *Understanding the Book of Mormon*, 78. The primary editor of the Large Plates, the Nephite general Mormon, senses this as well. 3 Nephi concludes with a warning aimed specifically at "ye Gentiles," who are strongly urged to "turn . . . from your wicked ways" if they desire to "be numbered with my people who are of the house of Israel" (3 Nephi 30:2).

20. Hardy, *Understanding the Book of Mormon*, 221.

21. "Scholars distinguish different kinds of Christology. 'Low christology' covers evaluation of him in terms that do not *necessarily* include divinity, e.g., Messiah, Rabbi, Prophet, High Priest, Savior, Master. 'High christology' covers the evaluation of Jesus in terms that include *an aspect of* divinity, e.g., Lord, Son of God, God" (Raymond Brown, *An Introduction to New Testament Christology* [Mahwah: Paulist Press, 1994], 4). Normally the Gospel of Mark is cited as the prime example of the former, with the Gospel of John the prime example of the latter.

22. This idea of "realized messialogy" could be viewed as another Johannine parallel. One of the features of John's Gospel is "realized eschatology," meaning that the gospel unfolds as if the final kingdom of God has been established already prior to the crucifixion. Raymond Brown writes that "John is the best example in the NT of realized eschatology. God has revealed Himself in Jesus in a definitive form, and seemingly no more can be asked" (Raymond Brown, *The Gospel According to John* [Garden City:

Doubleday and Company, Inc., 1966], 1: cxvii). Brown points specifically to John 3:18–19 as an example. The Book of Mormon's "realized messialogy" begins very explicitly in 1 Nephi 10 and continues throughout the text.

23. See, for example, Peter's Pentecost injunction to "Repent, and be baptized every one of you in the name of Jesus Christ for the remission of sins, and ye shall receive the gift of the Holy Ghost" (Acts 2:38). See also Alma 19:34, 26:35, Helaman 14:13, and D&C 20:29.

24. In addition to 2 Nephi 9:23–24, the phrase "baptized in his name" occurs, sometimes with slight variation, in Mosiah 18:10; 3 Nephi 11:23; 21:6; D&C 20:27; 76:51; and Moses 6:52. This continues a trend of adding the Johannine phrase "in/on his name" to other spiritual activities such as "faith" or "baptism." Although the phrase "believe in his name" is not present in the Bible, variations such as "Lest any should say that I had baptized in mine own name" (1 Cor. 1:15) and "For as yet he was fallen upon none of them: only they were baptized in the name of the Lord Jesus" (Acts 8:16) are present.

25. C. K. Barrett, *The Gospel According to St. John, Second Edition: An Introduction with Commentary and Notes on the Greek Text* (Philadelphia: The Westminster Press, 1978), 164. The significance and function of baptism within the theology of the Gospel of John is difficult to pin down and has been the subject of much speculation. See Raymond Brown, *The Gospel According to John*, 1:141–45 and Rudolf Bultmann, *The Gospel of John: A Commentary* (Philadelphia: The Westminster Press, 1971), 138 fn. 3.

26. "Allegiance as well as assent is intended" (Barrett, *The Gospel According to St. John*, 164).

27. See, for example, Alma 34:14–15, where Amulek teaches: "And behold, this is the whole meaning of the law, every whit pointing to that great and last sacrifice; and that great and last sacrifice will be the Son of God, yea, infinite and eternal. And thus he shall bring salvation to all those who shall *believe on his name*; this being the intent of this last sacrifice, to bring about the bowels of mercy, which overpowereth justice, and bringeth about means unto men that they may have faith unto repentance." This use of "believe on his name" is close to that of John 1:12.

28. All quotations from the Doctrine and Covenants come from the earliest extant manuscripts published in *The Joseph Smith Papers*.

29. MacKay, et al., *The Joseph Smith Papers: Documents, vol. 1*, 246. The importance of the 9 February 1831 revelation can be gleaned from the fact that while few extant manuscript copies exist for many of Joseph Smith's early revelations, no fewer than five manuscript copies exist and it was one of the earliest revelations to be published, printed in two Ohio newspapers shortly after its reception. See MacKay, et al., *The Joseph Smith Papers: Documents, vol. 1*, 246–47.

30. Shipps, *Mormonism*, 38. As with many of Smith's religious ideas, this blending of ancient Israel and modern American Christianity was not necessarily unique. Many Americans, both religious and secular, found themselves identifying with biblical events and people. See, for example, Conrad Cherry's *God's New Israel: Religious Interpretations of American Destiny* (Chapel Hill: University of North Carolina Press, 1998), or, more recently, Bruce Ellis's *America's Prophet: Moses and the American Story* (New York: HarperCollins, 2009). Perhaps what made Smith's vision unique was that he did not view his movement as one that held points in common with ancient Israel or Christianity. Mormonism was not an imitation or an homage. Rather Smith saw Mormonism as the fulfillment or culmination of those religions, almost as if he had gone back in time and brought both Judaism and Christianity, in their perfect, uncorrupted states, forward into the nineteenth century.

31. Mark L. Staker, *Hearken O Ye People: The Historical Setting of Joseph Smith's Ohio Revelations* (Salt Lake City: Greg Kofford Books, 2009), 104.

32. The phrase "keep my commandments" and variations of it occur forty-four times in the Bible. It occurs thirty-nine times in the Old Testament (Exod. 15:26; 16:28; Lev. 22:31; Deut. 4:2, 40; 6:2, 17; 7:9, 11; 8:2, 6; 10:13; 11:1, 8, 22; 13:4, 18; 19:9; 26:17–18; 27:1; 28:9, 45; 30:10, 16; Jos. 22:5; 1 Kings 2:3; 8:61; 2 Kings 17:13; 23:3; 1 Chr. 28:8; 29:19; 2 Chr. 34:31; Neh. 1:9; Psalms 78:7; 119:115; Prov. 7:2; Eccl. 12:13; Dan. 9:4) and five

times in the New Testament (Matt. 19:17; I John 5:2–3; Rev. 12:17; 14:12). Of the thirty-nine occurrences in the Old Testament, twenty-two of those are found in Deuteronomy.

33. Steven C. Harper, *Making Sense of the Doctrine and Covenants* (Salt Lake City: Deseret Book, 2008), 142.

34. Perhaps the best example of this sense of prophethood (outside of the production of the Book of Mormon) can be seen in Smith's 4 January 1833 letter to Rochester Newspaper editor Noah C. Saxton. See Godfrey, et al., *The Joseph Smith Papers: Documents, vol. 2*, 348–55.

TWO

Mormon Scripture and the Allusion of John

As opposed to "echo," the purpose of which is to signify an earlier text without a transference of meaning from the source text, "allusion" occurs when a later text utilizes the language of an earlier text not simply to signify the earlier text (as echo does) but also to allow for the application of context or meaning from the original text to the alluding text. Allusion thus strengthens the rhetorical impact of the biblical language by introducing *directional* meaning. Simply put, once it is recognized that some of the usage of biblical verse in the Book of Mormon or the Doctrine and Covenants exceeds simple rhetorical echo, the effect is that "an intertextual reference can enhance the meaning of the text that *makes the allusion.*"[1] Theoretically, the scholarship and tradition-history surrounding John 1:13 can be brought to bear in an interpretation of Alma 36:5 and could even guide how Alma 36:5 ought to be interpreted.

To put it another way, as readers of Mormon scripture recognize the language of the Johannine Prologue within its pages, they can consider the Johannine context and meaning of the phrase being alluded to by Mormon scripture. They can then apply that context and meaning to the passage in the Book of Mormon or the Doctrine and Covenants. Allusion, then, at this point becomes a form of exegesis as the reader derives meaning from the source text in order to draw meaning out of the alluding text.[2] Benjamin Sommer, again following Ben-Porat, states of allusion: "The reader brings certain elements of the evoked text or the marked to bear on the alluding text, and these alter the reader's construal of meaning of the sign in the alluding text."[3] Cynthia Edenburg provides a very useful definition of allusion:

> In allusion, one text constructs a covert level of significance by indirect-
> ly invoking another text. For allusion to fulfill its purpose as a signify-
> ing device, it must be accompanied by textual markers that alert the
> audience to an underlying significance. The marker is an element that
> is "borrowed" from another context where it is at home, and then
> planted in a new, foreign context. The foreignness of the marker ham-
> pers superficial comprehension of the text's overt significance, and inti-
> mates that full comprehension of the text will be attained only after
> identifying the function and significance of the marker in its original
> textual context. Thus, in order to attain full comprehension of the text,
> one must decode the markers and identify the allusions, thereby re-
> creating the links between the host and the alluded texts.[4]

The purpose of this chapter is to locate and examine instances in the Book
of Mormon and the Doctrine and Covenants of Johannine "allusion."
With allusion, the rhetoric of allusivity is still very much present, but the
level of interaction between the two texts has changed. Instead of utilizing Johannine language primarily as a means of drawing upon the *authority* of the Bible, Johannine "allusion" draws both authority and *meaning*
from the biblical text. In order to fully explore the dimensions of this type
of dialogue, this chapter will examine three specific phrases from the
Prologue of John present within the Book of Mormon: 1) "the light and
the life of the world;" 2) "born of God;" and 3) "Only Begotten Son," and
three specific phrases in the Doctrine and Covenants, 4) "Only Begotten
Son;" 5) "And the light shineth in darkness; and the darkness comprehended it not," and 6) "He came unto his own, and his own received him
not."

1. THE LIGHT AND THE LIFE OF THE WORLD

An example of Johannine allusion within the Book of Mormon comes
when the Nephite prophet Abinadi states that Jesus ". . . is the light and
the life of the world, yea, a light that is endless that can never be darkened; yea, and also a life which is endless, that there can be no more
death" (Mosiah 16:9). The crux of Abinadi's multi-layered *apologia* is that
salvation comes only in and through the sacrifice of Jesus Christ, a curious assertion considering that Abinadi lived about 150 years prior to the
birth of Jesus. Yet for Abinadi, the sacrifice of Jesus is a *sine qua non* for
salvation and the event towards which the Law of Moses points, a primary point of contention between Abinadi and the Law of Moses-abiding
Nephite priests. Abinadi emphasizes that "if Christ had not come into the
world—speaking of things to come as though they had already come—
there could have been no redemption. And if Christ had not risen from
the dead or broken the bands of death—that the grave should have no
victory and that death should have no sting—there could have been no
resurrection" (Mos. 16:6–7). Thus mortals become absolutely dependent

upon Jesus—there is no other way by which death and the grave can be avoided. He concludes his discourse by returning to this idea of the exclusivity of Jesus Christ: "And now had ye not ought to tremble and repent of your sins?—and remember, only in and through Christ ye can be saved" (Mos. 16:13).

Because the specific title "the light and the life of the world" is not found anywhere in the King James Bible (although it will appear numerous times in the writings of Joseph Smith), Abinadi's statement presents readers of the Book of Mormon with something of a novelty. The phrase appears to be an allusion to John 1:4, "In him was life; and the life was the light of men," or possibly John 8:12, which reads "Then spake Jesus again unto them, saying, I am the light of the world: he that followeth me shall not walk in darkness, but shall have the light of life." (There may also be influence from John 11:25: "I am the resurrection, and the life"). These are the only places in the Bible where the two words—light and life—occur in any manner similar to the verse in Mosiah 16:9. However, the fact that the title "the light and the life of the world" often appears in conjunction with other verses in Mormon scripture that directly quote from or allude to the Johannine Prologue suggests John 1:4 as a likely origin.[5]

Identifying the origin of the allusion as John 1:4 is important, as that verse is a crucial part of the Prologue. In John 1:4 the Evangelist expounds upon the pivotal relationship between Jesus/λόγος and humanity. While the role of Jesus as God and creator had been established in verses 1–3, in verse 4 John states that the "life" that was "in" Jesus is the "light of men." It is here that for the first time the divine λόγος and humanity intersect. A clear sense develops that without Jesus, the "life" and the "light," humanity would find only death and darkness. Something inherent within Jesus, something only he can offer, is crucial for the salvation of humankind. These two words will continue to play a prominent role throughout the Fourth Gospel. John will return again and again to the contrast between "light" and "dark,"[6] while "life" occurs in the Fourth Gospel a total of 36 times,[7] including Jesus' words following the resurrection of Lazarus that "I am the resurrection, and the life: he that believeth in me, though he were dead, yet shall he live" (John 11:25). Thus the use of terms like "light" and "life" become crucial in understanding Jesus' salvific role,[8] as light "is part and parcel of the life that is in the Word, and therefore eternal."[9]

This demarcation of Jesus as the sole pathway to salvation is a prominent theme running throughout the Gospel of John. In John, more than in any of the Gospels, the emphasis is placed upon Jesus as the only true "door" through which all who enter "will be saved," a point that is irrefutable and non-negotiable. Only those who "believe on his name" will receive from Jesus "the power to become the sons of God." While this exclusivity can be seen to run through much of the New Testament, it appears most explicitly in John's Gospel. Without the "light," there is only darkness. Without the "shepherd," the sheep are lost. Without the "life," there is only death. In this way, the Prologue "serves to orient the reader to the rest of the Gospel," [10] planting the seeds for ideas that will later come to fruition.

With this Johannine emphasis in mind, Abinadi's claim that "He is the light and the life of the world" fits well within the context of Mosiah 16. Abinadi's overall argument is that without Jesus salvation is impossible. The Law of Moses, which the priests of king Noah offer as the pathway to salvation, has no salvific affect but is merely a "shadow" (Mos. 16:14) of the true act of atonement that Jesus himself will perform. The emphasis must be placed upon Jesus, and it is only because Jesus is the "light" and the "life" that are "endless" that death can be overcome, thus mortality leads to immortality, corruption to incorruption. This employment of the Prologue serves as more than an echo of the biblical text. Joseph Smith has borrowed language from the Prologue and astutely employed it as part of a well-developed argument regarding the necessity of Jesus' sacrifice within his own text. The use of the "life" and "light" imagery, especially when paired with the similarly Johannine terms "darkened" and "death" in the second half of Mosiah 16:9, drives home the point that ultimately salvation comes through Jesus Christ. Thus "light" and "life" fill a similar role in the Book of Mormon to what they fill in the Gospel of John, namely highlighting this exclusivity and directing the focus of redemption onto Jesus Christ himself. Joseph Smith's literary protagonist could have made his point to the priests of king Noah without using the phrase "light and life of the world." But the presence of a Johannine phrase grounds his discussion of a pre-Christian Jesus in the Bible, specifically the New Testament, demonstrating a "realized messialogy" similar to that of Jacob in 2 Nephi 9:23–24.

In the pages of the Book of Mormon, the title "the light and the life of the world" appears next in the midst of Moroni's editorial work on the Jaredite plates. At one point, Moroni pauses his account of the Jaredite exodus in order to offer his ruminations regarding the future of the Book of Mormon. He tells the reader that some will believe on it, and some will not, writing "And whatsoever thing persuadeth men to do good is of me, for good cometh of none save it be of me. I am the same that leadeth men to all good. He that will not believe my words will not believe me, that I am. And he that will not believe me will not believe the Father, which sent me. For behold, I am the Father. I am the light and the life and the truth of the world" (Ether 4:12).

As we saw, Abinadi employed the title "the light and the life of the world" in a way that corresponded to the language of John, one that reflected a sense of necessity and need for a redeeming Savior. The question for readers of Ether 4 is determining whether the statement made by Jesus that "I am the light and the life and the truth of the world" has a similar function. The next four verses, Ether 4:13–16, suggest that it does:

Come unto me, O ye Gentiles, and I will shew unto you the greater things, the knowledge which is hid up because of unbelief. Come unto me, O ye house of Israel, and it shall be made manifest unto you how great things the Father hath laid up for you from the foundation of the world; and it hath not come unto you, because of unbelief. Behold, when ye shall rend that veil of unbelief which doth cause you to remain in your awful state of wickedness and hardness of heart and blindness of mind, then shall the great and marvelous things which have been hid up from the foundation of the world from you—yea, when ye shall call upon the Father in my name with a broken heart and a contrite spirit—then shall ye know that the Father hath remembered the cove-nant which he made unto your fathers, O house of Israel. And then shall my revelations which I have caused to be written by my servant John be unfolded in the eyes of all the people. Remember, when ye see these things, ye shall know that the time is at hand that they shall be made manifest in very deed.

The language in these verses demonstrates a subtle awareness of how Jesus is the "light" and "life." Jesus referred to himself in Ether 4:12 as "the light and the life and the truth of the world." He then proceeds to use words like "show," "hid up," "manifest," "rend that veil," "blindness of mind," "unfolded in the eyes," and "manifest in very deed." All these words or phrases signify either a lack of "light" (hid up, blindness of mind) or the presence and benefits of light (show, manifest, rend the veil, unfolded in the eyes, etc.). Through this language, Jesus literally (and literarily) reveals himself as the "light." Thus the title "I am the light and the life and the truth of the world" is not an allusion that has simply been inserted into a larger speech, but one of the pivotal ideas upon which the speech is fashioned. Its presence within Ether 4 is crucial for understand-ing what Jesus is saying. Just as the Gospel of John employed contrasting images of "light/dark," "sight/blind," and "day/night,"[11] so too does the Book of Mormon Jesus use contrasting imagery in Ether 4 with the result that readers are left with the message that all who choose not to align themselves with him, to "believe on his name," are left to fend for them-selves in a state of spiritual blindness and darkness. This phrase is far more than just an echo; rather it describes *who* Jesus is, while the follow-ing verses describe *how* and *why* he is.[12]

As with 3 Nephi 9:15–18, the placement of language from the English translation of the Johannine Prologue into a character who supposedly lived prior to the time in which the Greek text of John was written (Abi-nadi) or directed toward a Nephite who lacked knowledge of both Greek or English (Moroni) strongly indicates that the primary audience of Mo-siah 16:9 and Ether 4:12 was nineteenth-century readers.[13] The claim for a nineteenth-century audience is strengthened by the appearance of the phrase "the light and the life of the world" in literature roughly contem-porary with Joseph Smith. The origin of the title dates back to at least

1660, when it was used in a text by Obadiah Sedgwick.[14] Shortly there-
after the Quaker George Whitehead wrote a small treatise entitled "The
Light and Life of Christ Within," and the work was popular enough to be
reprinted during the 1820s.[15] The phrase appears to have become employed primarily as a title or description for Jesus Christ. The March 4,
1825 *Evangelical Restorationist* stated that "it was sinners only that 'the
Light and the Life of the world,' came to reconcile, or 'call to repentance.'"[16] A work entitled "The Evangelist's Manual," a guide for Trinitarian Universalists published in Charleston in 1827, contains the statement "Jesus Christ declares that he is the light and life of the world."[17]
The phrase appears to have taken on a biblical guise over time and during the early nineteenth century was being used alongside established
titles for Jesus such as "bread of life" and "light of the world," even
though the phrase itself was not directly drawn from the Bible. Through
the use of recognizable religious language borrowed from an authoritative text, the Book of Mormon fashions a recognizable religious identity
for itself by presenting its readers with a Jesus who is both biblical and
ultra-biblical, one who claims biblical provenance yet frequently operates
outside of it. Yet due to the conscious attempts of Joseph Smith or the
context of the allusion itself, not simply the rhetoric of John's words but
the meaning as well as transferred into Smith's text.

2. BORN OF GOD

A second Johannine phrase, "Born of God," appears frequently throughout the writings of one of the Book of Mormon's more poignant figures,
Alma the Younger. In a series of experiences very similar to that of the
biblical Paul, Alma actively rebelled against the church of God until a
divine encounter led him to a life-long devotion to Jesus Christ. As Alma
describes the results of this encounter, he writes: "I have repented of my
sins and have been redeemed of the Lord. Behold, I am born of the Spirit"
(Mos. 27:24). In the following verses, he expounds further upon what
"born of the Spirit" may mean: "And the Lord said unto me: Marvel not
that all mankind, yea, men and women—all nations, kindreds, tongues,
and people—must be born again, yea, born of God, changed from their
carnal and fallen state to a state of righteousness, being redeemed of God,
becoming his sons and daughters" (Mosiah 27:25). Alma then begins a
discussion of what exactly it means to be "born again" or "born of God."
This is the first usage of "born of God" in the Book of Mormon. On the
whole the Book of Mormon will employ the phrase nine times, all but
two by Alma the Younger.[18] The idea that believers in Jesus Christ can
become his spiritual offspring is an idea that had been in development
within the Book of Mormon, at least as early as King Benjamin's speech in
Mosiah 2–5. The question raised by Alma's words directly relates to the

topic of anthropology, namely Alma's view of the human condition in its fallen state.

Due to the significance Alma will attach to the phrase "born of God," it may be useful to examine John's anthropology more closely at this point. The phrase itself is an allusion to John 1:13: "But as many as received him, to them gave he power to become the sons of God, even to them that believe on his name: Which were born, not of blood, nor of the will of the flesh, nor of the will of man, but of God" (John 1:12–13). A useful definition of the scope and limits of John's "anthropology" is provided by Jeffrey Trumbower: "There is always an implicit and sometimes explicit theological anthropology in every Christian speculation on the nature of salvation and how it is achieved. Are all human beings the same, in need of and capable of the same type of salvation? How is salvation itself defined? What is the human beings' status in relationship to God before and after an encounter with Jesus . . . ?"[19]

In John 1:9, readers are told that Jesus brings life through his "light" and his light "lighteth every man that cometh into the world." Thus all men and women begin on an equal footing—they have all received the light. There is no sense from the Prologue that a distinction exists between "believers" and "non-believers" or "elect" and "fallen" prior to birth. It is with verse 12 that a division begins to take place. John tells us that ὅσοι δὲ ἔλαβον αὐτόν, ἔδωκεν αὐτοῖς ἐξουσίαν τέκνα θεοῦ γενέσθαι. Three key points emerge from this sentence. First, the implication of ὅσοι is that not all who receive the "light" actually receive Jesus, and that at some point a choice or decision was made about whether or not to accept him.[20] References in prior verses to ambiguous entities such as "the darkness," "the world," and "his own people" suggest that those who received him were those who separated themselves from these larger bodies of people, who went "against the grain" so to speak. Second, to those who ἔλαβον αὐτόν, he gave to them ἐξουσία. It is difficult to know exactly what this ἐξουσία was. The term itself literally means "'ability to perform an action' to the extent that there are no hindrances in the way, as distinct from δύναμις in the sense of intrinsic ability."[21] In the New Testament, the term can refer to power exercised both by God (Rev. 6:8) and by Satan (Acts 26:18; Col. 1:13), but when the word is used "for the authority imparted to the community the outstanding characteristic is that the Church owes its existence and nature to Christ. It needs 'enablement' even to enter the kingdom of God."[22]

Both these definitions are key to understanding Johannine anthropology. In the Prologue, humanity receives ἐξουσία because Jesus ἔδωκεν it to them—they did not earn it themselves.[23] They were not born with it. They received it solely through the person of the λόγος. This idea corresponds well with the Christological concept presented in John 14 that "I am the way, the truth, and the life: no man cometh unto the Father, but by me" (John 14:6). In order to become "sons of God," one must go through Christ. There are nuances in the pre-New Testament usage, differences between ἐξουσία and δύναμις that illuminate this as well. δύναμις carries with it the sense of "intrinsic ability," and if John had used this term instead of ἐξουσία the implication may have been that man could somehow make himself a "son of God" separate from Jesus.[24] However, ἐξουσία suggests that one is bestowed with an ability or power, but that it was not inherent within them; rather, it is granted by an outside party. One must have "enablement" mediated to them by Jesus even to enter the gate of God's kingdom.

The third crucial point pertaining to Johannine anthropology that emerges from verse 12 comes from the clause τέκνα θεοῦ γενέσθαι. First, what does it mean to be a τέκνον θεοῦ? In the Fourth Gospel, "there is a consistent linguistic distinction between being a son of God and a child of God. Only Christ is now υἱός. In distinction from Him believers are exclusively τέκνα . . . the reference is to communion with God rather than deification, to community religion rather than mystical individualism."[25] So while becoming τέκνα θεοῦ may not bring one up to the level of Christ (and certainly not to the level of the Father), it does denote "a totally new mode of existence, one that belongs to the 'eschatological' renewal of all things by God, which as 'eternal life' has already been initiated by the work of Christ."[26] Additionally, this is not a state of being that man enjoyed prior to "receiving" Christ, since they must γενέσθαι sons of God. The implication again is that this status was not one that was inherent within man or that they had earned based upon a covenant relationship with God—being a "creature" of God does not somehow carry with it the ability to be a "child" of God. It is a completely new form of existence, a transformation in the truest sense, one that comes only through the bestowal of Christ and only τοῖς πιστεύουσιν εἰς τὸ ὄνομα αὐτοῦ, bringing the reader full circle and elaborating upon what exactly "receiving" him entails. Rudolf Bultmann aptly notes the strict limitations as well as the terms of the change imposed upon those who believe: "It is equally clear that the transference into this new mode of existence is given only to the man who believes in the revelation with which he is confronted in Jesus; further that the new existence is characterized by the illumination which comes from understanding oneself in relation to God."[27]

Verse 13 reinforces the inability of man to attain this transformation through his own means. John cites three nouns which cannot accomplish what God can, namely the transformation into τέκνα θεοῦ: ἐξ αἱμάτων, ἐκ θελήματος σαρκὸς, and ἐκ θελήματος ἀνδρὸς. On one hand, John could just be making a general statement here, specifically citing three items but having in mind the idea that nothing mortal can duplicate what God can create. On the other hand, he could have specific intent behind choosing these three nouns as indicators of human impotency. First, the curious plural αἱμάτων may be a reference to human procreation, as "In ancient thought blood was sometimes considered the means of procreation" and thus "Probably the blood of father and mother is meant," with the plural father and mother explaining the use of αἱμάτων.[28] On a smaller scale, αἱμάτων could just be a reference to mortality, as it is blood that courses through the veins of humanity. Second, the θελήματος σαρκὸς could at first appear to be a negative statement, somehow implying carnality or sexual desire.[29] But the reference to procreation through the earlier use of αἱμάτων, as well as the positive use of σάρξ in the next verse suggests a different meaning, one that invokes "the sphere of the natural, the powerless, the superficial, opposed to 'spirit,' which is the sphere of the heavenly and the real."[30] Finally, θελήματος ἀνδρὸς. Ἀνήρ was a term for an adult male, and while sexual conception could be implied again, it may be easier to interpret θελήματος ἀνδρὸς as a generic reference to man, or perhaps humanity in general.[31] What John has done with this tricolon is implicitly construct a series of binary relationships. Τέκνα θεοῦ cannot be "generated" by mortals (αἱμάτων), the natural sphere (θελήματος σαρκὸς), or man (θελήματος ἀνδρὸς), but by a figure who is immortal, spiritual, and God. True spiritual "birth" can only be accomplished by Jesus Christ, and further reinforcing that humanity's anthropology is something that must be overcome or transformed, but certainly does not enable or empower. Humanity has no power in any respect to accomplish the creation of τέκνα θεοῦ.

With this understanding of Johannine anthropology, how should readers of the Book of Mormon interpret Alma's words? Alma's "birth" imagery begins in Mosiah 27:24 with "Behold, I am born of the Spirit." This "birth" comes in response to having "repented of my sins" and having "been redeemed of the Lord." The combination of "repent" and "redeem" is significant, for although Alma can choose to repent of his sins, he cannot bring about his own redemption—only God can perform that act. This reliance upon God is shown by the two verbal tenses involved: "repent" is an active deed performed by Alma, but "been redeemed" is passive, signifying that Alma was not the agent of activity in that process. His redemption is the result of God's will, not Alma's own doing, and in this respect follows very closely the logic of John's Prologue, that while humanity can choose to receive Jesus, only Jesus can validate that choice. With reference to the Prologue of John, C. K. Barrett noted, "No human agency is or can be responsible for such a birth as this."[32] Alma's experience reflects a similar sentiment.

In the following verse, Mosiah 27:25, Alma teaches that we "must be born again, yea, born of God," and in this manner we become "his sons and daughters." As Brant Gardner observes, "modern Saints typically equate 'being born of the spirit' with baptism and the gift of the Holy Ghost, but neither of these events is part of Alma's experience. . . . Rather, his particular 'birth' is redemption from sin. Alma is born of the Spirit because the atonement of Jesus Christ was applied to his soul (not be-

cause of the gift of the Holy Ghost as in modern terminology). It constituted a new birth in that his soul became freed from the bonds of sin—
innocent like a newborn child."[33] Alma's "birth," then, is literally one
that comes "from above,"[34] not by human means but by the agency of
God. It involves a transformation that moves upon the very core of humankind, changing them from a "carnal and fallen state" to one of "righteousness," a change that can only be enacted, one imagines, by the intervention of divine aid. Herman Ridderbos could just as easily have been
thinking of Alma's conversion when he writes of the Johannine "born of
God:" "This gift does not lie within the range of possibilities granted a
person in his or her natural birth. A person is entirely dependent for it on
the Spirit of God, and all the more because the world made by God and
the flesh in which he has given human beings their particular mode of
existence have become the element in which, by human sin and self-will,
people have alienated themselves from God and hence do not know and
accept the light that comes to them in the Word."[35] Alma's concept of
spiritual "re-birth" demonstrates remarkable correlation with the doctrine found in John 1 as well as, interestingly enough, John 3, another
passage where being "born again" often correlates with baptism.[36]

Regarding being "born of God," the Prologue of John helps readers of
the Book of Mormon understand just how inadequate mortals are in
bringing about this "birth," and that it requires the absolute intervention
of God. Alma mirrors this understanding through his recognition that he
needed both "repentance" but also "redemption" in order to truly be re-
born, a concept that can be seen in Alma 36, the point at which Alma's
"born of God" imagery becomes most fully developed. Here Alma re-
counts in harrowing detail his journey from the brink of Hell to finding
the acceptance of God's grace. In all, the phrase appears four times in
Alma 36:

> Now behold, I say unto you: If I had not been *born of God,* I should not
> have known these things. But God hath by the mouth of his holy angel
> made these things known unto me, not of any worthiness of myself.
> (Alma 36:5)

> But behold, my limbs did receive their strength again, and I stood upon
> my feet and did manifest unto the people that I had been *born of God.*
> (Alma 36:23)

> Yea, and from that time even until now I have labored without ceasing
> that I might bring souls unto repentance, that I might bring them to
> taste of the exceeding joy of which I did taste, that they might also be
> *born of God* and be filled with the Holy Ghost. (Alma 36:24)

> for because of the word which he hath imparted unto me, behold,
> many hath been *born of God* and hath tasted as I have tasted and hath
> seen eye to eye as I have seen. Therefore they do know of these things

of which I have spoken as I do know; and the knowledge which I have is of God. (Alma 36:26)

In Alma 36:5, Alma tells his son that "If I had not been born of God, I should not have known these things." Thus the event of being "born of God" is significant enough for Alma that its absence would completely negate whatever experience he has had. There is the hint of divine intervention as well, as Alma claims that his "birth" came from God, by "the mouth of his holy angel." He did nothing to bring about this spiritual birth. It was not something that he earned or worked to achieve—it was purely and completely the intervention of God in his life: "not of any worthiness of myself." This idea correlates well with John 1:13, where the act of being "born of God" comes "not of blood, nor of the will of the flesh, nor of the will of man."

Alma then relays in painstaking detail his experience. He was "struck with such great fear and amazement" (Alma 36:11) and was "racked with eternal torment, for my soul was harrowed up to the greatest degree and racked with all my sins" (Alma 36:12). His pain was such that he even felt that "I could be banished and become extinct, both soul and body" (Alma 36:15). After three days of torment, Alma finds a relief as great as his misery when he remembers the prophecy concerning the coming of Jesus Christ. At this point Alma finds himself "re-born:"

> Now as my mind catched hold upon this thought, I cried within my heart: O Jesus, thou Son of God, have mercy on me, who art in the gall of bitterness and art encircled about by the everlasting chains of death. And now behold, when I thought this, I could remember my pains no more. Yea, I was harrowed up by the memory of my sins no more. And O what joy and what marvelous light I did behold! Yea, my soul was filled with joy as exceeding as was my pains. Yea, I say unto you, my son, that there can be nothing so exquisite and so bitter as was my pains. Yea, and again I say unto you, my son, that on the other hand there can be nothing so exquisite and sweet as was my joy." (Alma 36:18–21)

The final section of chapter 36 finds Alma giving a description of two key parts of his experience. First, he describes the physical effects of his "birth:" "But behold, my limbs did receive their strength again, and I stood upon my feet and did manifest unto the people that I had been born of God" (Alma 36:23). Alma has been spiritually re-born, but the description of that spiritual re-birth mirrors the language of physical birth. Alma describes his body "receiving strength" and being able to once again stand "upon my feet." His re-birth is so complete that it impacts his senses as well. He writes that those who have been born of God "hath tasted as I have tasted and hath seen eye to eye as I have seen" (Alma 36:26). This experience is so significant and overpowering that it transcends merely a physical or spiritual delineation—it affects both completely.

Secondly, Alma relays the effects of his re-birth. As a result of his being "born of God" he desires only to bring the same experience to others: "Yea, and from that time even until now I have labored without ceasing that I might bring souls unto repentance, that I might bring them to taste of the exceeding joy of which I did taste, that they might also be born of God and be filled with the Holy Ghost" (Alma 36:24). Here Alma demonstrates what it means (rather than how it feels) to be "born of God:" Once one has tasted re-birth one is consumed with the desire to spread that same feeling and knowledge to others. But Alma continues to recognize that while he may be the messenger, true spiritual re-birth must come from above and observes that it must be accompanied by being "filled with the Holy Ghost."

While the language of Alma 36, with its repetition of the key phrase "born of God," may be primarily intended to direct attention back to the Gospel of John and thus link the two texts rhetorically, the Book of Mormon manages to incorporate into its own text the meaning behind John's text. Significantly, the Book of Mormon's usage of "born of God" maintains the same distinction present in John 1:13, namely that this re-birth must come through divine mediation or intervention—one must be born "from above." Alma does not bring about the new spiritual state himself, but was in fact engaged in conduct detrimental to the Nephite church at the time of his vision. Baptism is not mentioned a single time as having any part in his re-birth, instead Alma emphasizes his interaction with the divine, whether seeing a "holy angel" (Alma 36:5–6) or a vision of "God sitting upon his throne, surrounded with numberless concourses of angels" (Alma 36:22).[37]

3. ONLY BEGOTTEN SON

The third and final Book of Mormon phrase that will be examined as a biblical allusion is the title "Only Begotten Son." In the Bible, the title "only-begotten" appears nine times. Some of the references are to the only children of parents, such as the son of the widow of Nain (Luke 7:12), the daughter of Jairus (Luke 8:42), or Isaac (Heb. 11:17). Only the Johannine writings use the title for Jesus, where it is found a total of five times. Two of them, John 1:14 and 1:18, are from the Johannine Prologue:

> And the Word was made flesh, and dwelt among us, (and we beheld his glory, the glory as of the only begotten of the Father,) full of grace and truth. (John 1:14)

> No man hath seen God at any time; the only begotten Son, which is in the bosom of the Father, he hath declared him. (John 1:18)

Two others, John 3:16 and 3:18, are from the body of the Gospel of John:

> For God so loved the world, that he gave his only begotten Son, that whosoever believeth in him should not perish, but have everlasting life. (John 3:16)

> He that believeth on him is not condemned: but he that believeth not is condemned already, because he hath not believed in the name of the only begotten Son of God. (John 3:18)

The final occurrence is 1 John 4:9:

> In this was manifested the love of God toward us, because that God sent his only begotten Son into the world, that we might live through him. (1 John 4:9)

Thus the phrase, as it is applied to Jesus, has a Johannine provenance.

For John, the title was likely employed in order to signify Jesus' unique role as the agent of the Father who mediates between heaven and Earth: "Because Jesus is the only Son of God, His sending into the world is the supreme proof of God's love for the world. On the other side, it is only as the only begotten Son of God that Jesus can mediate life and salvation from perdition."[38] But the title also suggests a relationship that goes beyond agency: "As the only-begotten Son Jesus is in the closest intimacy with God . . . there is no other with whom God can have similar fellowship. He shares everything with this Son. For this reason Jesus can give what no man can give, namely, the fullest possible eye-witness account of God. He knows God, not just from hearsay, but from incomparably close intercourse with him."[39] John 1:14 and 18 focus upon the relationship of the λόγος to the Father—he is "in the bosom of the Father," but he is also "full of grace and truth." In John 3:16 and 18 the love of the Father is so great that he will sacrifice even his "only begotten Son" so that belief in him may bring "everlasting life" and the promise that humanity will be "not condemned." Finally, 1 John 4:9 states "In this was manifested the love of God toward us, because that God sent his only begotten Son into the world, that we might live through him." All the Johannine usages of the title stress the importance of this relationship between Father and Son and between Son and humanity. Thus, the title "Only Begotten Son" is appropriately descriptive of Jesus due to 1) his role as agent for the Father in bringing salvation to humanity and 2) his unique, intimate relationship with the Father being "the only one of its kind or class."[40] Jesus qualifies as one who has a "unique" relationship with the Father in that "He is the object of the Father's 'special love'; Jesus is the 'Father's equal'; the Son is the enfleshment of the divine, and He is an 'eternal, not an adopted, Son.'"[41] While there still exists some serious questions as to the theological implications of the title,[42] it was an important one for early Christians and for modern Mormons.

In the Book of Mormon, the title only begotten occurs nine times, and each use mirrors the meaning behind the Johannine usage. All nine references are to Jesus and all maintain the Johannine sense of the title, meaning that it is only used in specific circumstances that elaborate upon Jesus' function as Savior and Redeemer:

> But behold, they shall have wars and rumors of wars. And when the day cometh that *the Only Begotten of the Father*—yea, even the Father of heaven and of earth—shall manifest himself unto them in the flesh, behold, they will reject him because of their iniquities and the hardness of their hearts and the stiffness of their necks. Behold, they will crucify him. And after that he is laid in a sepulchre for the space of three days, he shall rise from the dead with healing in his wings, and all they that shall believe on his name shall be saved in the kingdom of God. (2 Nephi 25:12–13)

> Behold, they believed in Christ and worshpiped the Father in his name; and also we worship the Father in his name. And for this intent we keep the law of Moses, it pointing our souls to him. And for this cause it is sanctified unto us for righteousness, even as it was accounted unto Abraham in the wilderness to be obedient unto the commands of God in offering up his son Isaac, which was a similitude of God and his *Only Begotten Son*. (Jacob 4:5)[43]

> Wherefore, beloved, be reconciled unto him through the atonement of Christ his *Only Begotten Son*, that ye may obtain a resurrection according to the power of the resurrection which is in Christ and be presented as the first fruits of Christ unto God, having faith and having obtained a good hope of glory in him before he manifesteth himself in the flesh. (Jacob 4:11)

> I say unto you that I know of myself that whatsoever I shall say unto you concerning that which is to come is true. And I say unto you that I know that Jesus Christ shall come, yea, the Son, the *Only Begotten of the Father*, full of grace and mercy and truth. And behold, it is he that cometh to take away the sins of the world, yea, the sins of every man which steadfastly believeth on his name. (Alma 5:48)

> And not many days hence the Son of God shall come in his glory, and his glory shall be the glory of the *Only Begotten of the Father*, full of grace, equity, and truth, full of patience, mercy, and long-suffering, quick to hear the cries of his people and to answer their prayers. (Alma 9:26)

> But God did call on men in the name of his Son, this being the plan of redemption which was laid, saying: If ye will repent and harden not your hearts, then will I have mercy upon you through mine *Only Begotten Son*. Therefore whosoever repenteth and hardeneth not his heart, he shall have claim on mercy through mine *Only Begotten Son* unto a remission of their sins; and these shall enter into my rest. (Alma 12:33–34)

or in fine, in the first place they were on the same standing with their brethren—thus this holy calling being prepared from the foundation of the world for such as would not harden their hearts, being in and through the atonement of the *Only Begotten Son* which was prepared— (Alma 13:5)

thus they become high priests forever after the order of the Son, the *Only Begotten of the Father*, which is without beginning of days or end of years, which is full of grace, equity, and truth. And thus it is. Amen. (Alma 13:9)

There is a consistency in how the title "Only Begotten Son" is used throughout the Book of Mormon, centered upon the absolute necessity of the atonement of Jesus Christ as a means of achieving salvation or redemption. It is a title that is used carefully rather than casually. 2 Nephi 25:12 summarizes the passion of Jesus. Jacob 4:5 discusses "Only Begotten Son" in the context of Jesus' sacrifice bearing a typology in common with Isaac's sacrifice. Jacob 4:11 is more explicit, explaining the significance of the atonement as the means of reconciliation, obtaining a resurrection, and being presented as the "first fruits of Christ unto God." Of the remaining uses of the title, it is noteworthy that all six of them occur in two key sermons given by Alma the Younger that further expand the Book of Mormon concept of salvation through Jesus Christ, and all six uses of the title are present in verses specifically intended to invoke the message of salvation in and through the redeeming sacrifice of Jesus. As opposed to some of Smith's subsequent writings, such as the Book of Moses, the Book of Mormon maintains the context of this title in its application to Jesus.

4. ONLY BEGOTTEN SON

The revelations of Joseph Smith continue to use the title to emphasize both Jesus' role as agent of the Father and his unique, intimate relationship with the Father. An early usage of the title that reflects this salvific context comes in D&C 20, one of Joseph Smith's significant creedal documents. In this text, Joseph Smith explicates the relationship between the Father and the Son in one passage: "wherefore the Almighty God gave his *only begotten Son*, as is written in those scriptures which hath been given of him" (D&C 20:21). This verse comes in the midst of a long theological statement. Following a brief account of the creation and fall of humanity (D&C 20:17–20), D&C 20:21 states that the reason why Jesus was sent to Earth was to overcome the effects of the fall. Joseph Smith will go on to state that Jesus, following the crucifixion, went "to reign with almighty power according to the will of the Father" (D&C 20:24) and that the Father, Son, and Holy Ghost are "one God, infinite and eternal, without end" (D&C 20:28).

Two further usages of "Only Begotten Son" appear in a revelation given just months later and both usages occur, as with D&C 20, in a salvific context, in this case in the midst of a long statement regarding the origins and nature of the fall of Adam. The Lord proclaims that "Wherefore I the Lord God caused that he should be cast out from the Garden of Eden from my presence because of his transgression Wherein he became spiritually dead which is the first death even that same death which is the last death which is spiritual which shall be pronounced upon the wicked when I shall say depart ye Cursed" (D&C 29:41). The very next verse, D&C 29:42, explained that Adam and his seed "should not Die as to the temporal death" as long as they had faith "on the name of mine only begotten Son."

The same assertion is true for D&C 29:46, which expounds upon the redemption of little children through "mine only begotten" and thus preserves the idea of Jesus as "agent." Although the revelation began with the voice of Jesus Christ, the voice switches to the Father who begins referencing Jesus in the third person. There are two ways to interpret this shift of speakers, both of which demonstrate the relationship of Father and Son. First, the Father may have intervened in the course of this revelation to speak personally about the sacrifice made by the Son that brings redemption from the fall. Lending more credence to the sacrifice of Jesus, the voice of the Father solidifies the importance of Jesus' role. Second, this may be an example of what has become known in Mormonism as "divine investiture of authority," or the idea that when a verse of scripture reads as if the Father is speaking and Jesus is referred to in the third person, it is really Jesus speaking on behalf of the Father.[44] Thus in D&C 29:42 and 46, Jesus is speaking as if he was the Father, even though he is not the Father.

D&C 49:5 presents a situation almost identical to section D&C 29:42 and 46.[45] "Only Begotten Son" is used once again in the context of "the redemption of the world," and again the Father is speaking instead of the Son.[46] This passage is particularly significant because the revelation was given to the North Union Shaker Community in Ohio. Addressing their particular beliefs that God is a being dual in nature, taking the form of Jesus and Ann Lee, D&C 49 emphasizes the relationship with the Father and Son to challenge their beliefs about Deity and convince them of the Mormon belief in God. Additionally, since the Shakers did not believe in a carnal resurrection, the emphasis on Jesus' redemptive sacrifice to redeem all humankind from death was a striking and purposeful emphasis in the revelation.[47]

A prominent example of Smith's usage of the title "Only Begotten Son" can be found in D&C 76, a record of a mystical experience in which Smith and his associate Sidney Rigdon claimed to have seen, among others things, a multi-tiered heaven.[48] The description of this vision included several usages of the title "Only Begotten Son" as well as the statement that the Son was in the "bosom of the Father."[49] Notably, this is the first occurrence in the revelations of the phrase "bosom of the Father," an allusion to John 1:18 that combines both Jesus' salvific role and his close relationship with the Father. The phrase held a significant function in John's Prologue, as it envisages "not the geographic situation of the Son rather the intimate relation between the Father and Son . . . by its use in the contexts of motherhood, sexual union, and marital fellowship."[50] In the course of the dictation of the vision, the phrase "bosom of the Father" appears twice, in both cases emphasizing the true nature of the relationship between Father and Son.[51]

While these verses stress the close relationship between Father and Son, the idea of salvation or redemption mediated through Jesus, while not explicitly discussed in D&C 76, is hardly forgotten. Significantly, what Joseph Smith and Sidney Rigdon describe viewing consisted of "the things which were from the beginning." This may represent a key shift in Joseph Smith's thought. Prior verses where "Only Begotten Son" was used describe the redemption of humanity, but in the context of this Earthly world, focusing in particular upon the implications of the fall of Adam. In D&C 76, Joseph Smith goes back in the past far enough to witness events that unfolded prior to the creation of the Earth, claiming that events "from the begining" were "ordained of the Father *through* his only begoten son." Joseph Smith depicts a Jesus Christ who is crucial to salvation, both through what he does here *and* what he did prior to his incarnation.

As with D&C 76:13, the close relationship between the Father and Son is emphasized again in D&C 76:23, where Jesus stands "on the right hand of God," and the voice of the Father is heard giving a witness.[52] But the shift away from redemption being the focus of events on this world back to events unfolding prior to creation continues in this verse as well. Joseph Smith continues his elaboration on the mission and purpose of the Son: "by him and through him and of him the worlds are made and were created and the inhabitants thereof are begotten sons and daughters unto God" (D&C 76:24). At this point, Smith's view of salvation expands both spatially and temporally. No longer will he speak of one "world," but now "the worlds" owe their creation to the actions of the Son. The time period for creation also expands, as these worlds "are and were" created, suggesting that the work of the Son began long ago and continues to progress as worlds continue to be created. It is as if Joseph Smith has taken the Johannine idea of "agent" and, as he often does, pushed it to the extent of its biblical limits, finding a *sensus plenior* behind John's often ambiguous language. While he writes that "the world was made by him" (John 1:10), suggesting the existence of only one "world," John also mentions that "all things were made by him" (John 1:3). For Smith, "world" and "All things" have literally (and literarily) become "all worlds."

Additionally, D&C 76:23–24 adds a further nuance to the close relationship between Father and Son. These "worlds" are populated not by
men and women "created" by God, but by "begotten sons and daughters
unto God." The spirits that inhabit bodies of flesh are literally the spirit
children of God. And who does this Father entrust the salvation and care
of his "sons and daughters" to? In 1843, Joseph Smith penned a poetic
version of D&C 76. The following is his rendition of D&C 76:24: "Whose
inhabitants, too, from the first to the last, Are sav'd by the very same
Saviour of ours; And, of course, are begotten God's daughters and sons,
By the very same truths, and the very same pow'rs."[53] The Son is not
merely the agent of the Father to this world, but to all worlds, and his
incarnation and resurrection are not merely for the benefit of "created"
beings, but of begotten sons and daughters of God.

In the following verse, D&C 76:25, Christ's unique filial relationship
continues to be a point of emphasis.[54] Here the "only begotten son" was
the one "whom the father loved" and the one who was "in the bosom
with the father," alluding to John 3:16 and 1:18, respectively. But again,
the idea of "redemption" has been expanded upon. This verse refers to
Satan and his being cast out from the presence of God. The only misdeed
of Satan that receives mention is that he "rebelled against the only begotten son." Unstated in the revelation is the nature of this rebellion, but
Smith hints at it in a revelation received as part of the translation of the
Bible: "That Satan whom thou hast commanded in the name of mine only
begotten is the same which was from the beginning and he came before
me saying Behold I send me I will be thy Son and I will redeem all
mankind that one soul shall not be lost and surely I will do it Wherefore
give me thine honour."[55] Thus this rebellion took the form of "destroying
the agency of man" by presenting an alternate path to salvation directly
in conflict with that of Jesus Christ. Once again, the issue of salvation is at
stake. D&C 76:25 could have stated that "Satan rebelled against Jesus,"
but by framing the rebellion as Satan against "the only begotten son"
Smith employs a meaningful Johannine title to emphasize the depths of
the treachery.[56]

It is apparent that in the early revelations (D&C 20, 29, and 49) the use
of "Only Begotten Son" managed to maintain the Johannine context. Humanity was scarred by the fall beyond all remedy short of the intervention of the Son, who could offer redemption by virtue of his close association with the Father. Yet in D&C 76 Joseph Smith goes beyond this world,
maintaining the fundamental nature of the Son's relationship to the
Father and his crucial role in salvation but expanding its application to
include "worlds" and "begotten sons and daughters of God." In D&C 76,
every stage of salvation—creation of worlds, creation of spirits, pre-mortal decisions, and eternal glory, either its fulness (celestial) or complete
lack thereof (sons of perdition), fully relies upon the actions of the "Only
Begotten Son." This title meant something important to Joseph Smith,

just as it did for John. It describes both the connection of Jesus to the Father and of Jesus to humanity. John teaches us that "the only way to intimacy with the Father is through the Logos," and "the Logos is the one who introduces us to the Father."[57] Smith intuitively takes this fundamental truth from John and magnifies it, as if searching for the "how" and "why," unsatisfied with what the Bible sets forth.

Yet at the same time there is something slightly unnerving about the evolution of Joseph Smith's thought. Terryl Givens has noted the confusion surrounding Mormon concepts of Jesus, writing that "The question of how Christ could be fully divine pre-mortally, and at the same time literally begotten in the spirit by the Father, has never been fully resolved in Mormon doctrine," leading to the formation of a Christology that is "just as imbued with seeming contradiction as the creedal Christ who is 'begotten not made.'"[58] Perhaps this confusion can be seen in how Smith employs the language of the "Only Begotten Son." Following the multiple (and very creative) usages of the title "Only Begotten Son" in D&C 76, the title only occurs two more times, D&C 93:13 and D&C 124:123, both of which appear somewhat cursory. Subsequent revelations after D&C 76 will emphasize how humankind can overcome the gulf between God and sin themselves, primarily through priesthood authority and power. The question this sentiment raises is "As long as this priesthood authority is possessed, what need has humanity for Jesus?" If the usages of "Only Begotten Son" can be used as a reliable indicator, it would appear that as Joseph's anthropology gets higher his Christology gets lower.[59] Prior to D&C 76, Jesus was the "Only Begotten Son" of the Father. Once Smith dictates D&C 76 he now describes innumerable "worlds" where "the inhabitants thereof are begotten sons and daughters unto God" (D&C 76:24). How is Jesus unique, if all are literally "begotten" of God? Is it coincidental that the title "Only Begotten Son" ceases to have any real place or function in the revelations after D&C 76? Can the use or disuse of a title reflect a theological shift? In this case, the answer appears to be yes.

5. & 6. AND THE LIGHT SHINETH IN DARKNESS; AND THE DARKNESS COMPREHENDED IT NOT . . . HE CAME UNTO HIS OWN, AND HIS OWN RECEIVED HIM NOT

In addition to the many occasions of the uniquely Johannine title "Only Begotten Son," Joseph Smith's revelations also utilize two significant statements of the Johannine Prologue in a similar allusive manner. The phrases in question are John 1:5, "And the light shineth in darkness; and the darkness comprehended it not," and John 1:11, "He came unto his own, and his own received him not." The earliest appearance of these phrase is found in D&C 6, a revelation received by Joseph Smith at Harmony Pennsylvania on or around April 7th, 1829.[60] An acquaintance of the Smith family, Oliver Cowdery, had recently arrived in Harmony to act as Joseph's scribe, and this revelation served as validation for Oliver's decision. The revelation begins in a very formal way, as will D&C 11, 12, and 14, where the same Johannine passages are found. But the tone quickly becomes more personal as the Lord reveals to Oliver that he knows Oliver previously sought verification of Joseph's divine calling and even reminds him of an incident known only to Oliver, namely that "you cried unto me in your heart, that you might know concerning the truth of these things" (D&C 6:22). Thus the catalyst for the revelation seems to be the hope for something empirical on the part of Oliver, something to assuage him, which mention of that incident does. As the Lord reminds him, "What greater witness can you have than from God" (D&C 6:23).

The Johannine contribution to D&C 6 is found in verse 21: "Behold I am Jesus Christ, the Son of God. *I am the same that came unto my own and my own received me not. I am the light which shineth in darkness, and the darkness comprehendeth it not.*"[61]

At first glance, this verse provides three possible uses of the Johannine ἐγώ εἰμί formula, although it is most likely that the "I am" is functioning out of grammatical necessity and not attempting to assert a theological meaning as it often does in the Fourth Gospel. More interesting is "I am Jesus Christ, the Son of God." The closest Johannine parallel to this phrase is John 20:31, where John writes "But these are written, that ye might believe that Jesus is the Christ, the Son of God; and that believing ye might have life through his name." But nowhere in the New Testament do we see Jesus identify himself in this exact manner.[62] However, this phrase does occur in the Book of Mormon: "And they shall believe in me, that I am Jesus Christ the Son of God, and shall pray unto the Father in my name" (3 Nephi 20:31; see also 3 Nephi 9:15), as well as multiple times throughout the Doctrine and Covenants (D&C 10:57; 11:28; 35:2; 36:8; 52:44).

This verse presents readers with a further synthesis of Mormon scripture and the Bible that works on at least two levels. On one hand, the speaker of these verses identifies himself as "I" and then quotes passages from the Gospel of John, linking D&C 6 with the Bible. On the other hand, the verse also includes a self-proclaimed title for Jesus found only in the Book of Mormon, which links that text with D&C 6 and the Gospel of John. Through the rhetoric of allusivity, Joseph Smith has carefully woven together the Bible, the Book of Mormon, and his revelations in a way that readers can't reject one without rejecting all three. The presence of language from both the Gospel of John *and* the Book of Mormon give a weight or authority to the newly received revelations.

Of greater significance for this study is the effect of alluding to these particular verses. Obviously there are rhetorical reasons. Adopting a Johannine voice in D&C 6 served as a legitimate for God to identify himself to Oliver Cowdery in a manner that would resonate and be recognizable to a nineteenth-century audience. Joseph Smith may have needed a voice or persona for his Jesus, and the Fourth Gospel, with its combination of unique language and high Christology, provided an advantageous voice for a resurrected deity. But there may be a deeper reason as well, one that goes beyond echo to allusion. First, John 1:11 illustrates the rejection of Jesus by those who ought to have received him, but who apparently didn't get/understand him. This context applies to Joseph Smith as well. According to Smith, when he had asked Jesus what church he ought to join, Jesus had told him "that I must join none of them, for they were all wrong. . . ."[63] The implication of this statement is that even those who faithfully professed a belief in "Jesus" lacked a sufficient knowledge of who he really was. The result was that Jesus had returned again to "restore" that truth to humanity through Joseph Smith; he had again come "unto mine own." Oliver Cowdery, however, did not have that same theophany. By relaying to Oliver that "I am the same that came unto my own, and my own received me not" Jesus implicitly instructs him about the apostasy. The allusion to John 1:11 relayed that the same context that accompanied the original context of John 1:11 applies in 1829 as well: In the meridian of times, Jesus came to "his own" people, the Jews that should have received him as their Messiah. But they rejected him. Now, in a similar fashion, Jesus has been rejected by the Christian world, those who were literally "his own" by taking upon them his name.

With this understanding in mind, the allusion to John 1:5, "I am the light which shineth in darkness, and the darkness comprehendeth it not," becomes clearer. Both statements serve as references to an apostasy and a subsequent restoration of the gospel. In John 1:5, the verb translated as "comprehended" is κατέλαβεν, which can mean "to gain control of someone and overtake" or "to process information, understand, grasp."[64] John's usage of κατέλαβεν remains a topic of discussion among Johannine scholars. As Craig Keener summarizes, various interpretations include the ideas that the "darkness could not 'apprehend' the light intellectually, that darkness did not accept the light, or that darkness could not 'conquer' the light." Keener concludes that John "has introduced a wordplay here: darkness could not 'apprehend' or 'overtake' the light, whether by comprehending it (grasping with the mind) or by overcoming it (grasping with the hand)."[65] This interpretation of John 1:5 can also be applied to the allusion from John 1:5 in D&C 6:21. With this interpretation, Jesus is telling Oliver Cowdery first that the "darkness" did not understand who Jesus was from an intellectual standpoint, a statement that harmonizes quite well with the instruction given Joseph Smith during his "first vision."[66] This understanding of κατέλαβεν highlights one of the primary purposes of Joseph Smith's restoration, namely the belief that Jesus Christ had come to "his own" in the form of those who received the texts penned by Joseph Smith.

Additional insight can be gained from Keener's other possibility for interpreting κατέλαβεν, namely "overcoming" from a physical, rather than an intellectual, standpoint. Early in the Book of Mormon, the prophet Nephi had a vision of the time period after the decline of the early Christian church, in which he sees the rise to power of a force he terms "the great and abominable church" whose intent was "that they might pervert the right ways of the Lord, that they might blind the eyes and harden the hearts of the children of men" (1 Nephi 13:27). At the head of this "church" stands Satan, who "hath great power over them" (1 Nephi 13:29). Fortunately, Nephi is promised that the "church of the Lamb" will overcome the "great and abominable Church": "And when the day cometh that the wrath of God is poured out upon the mother of harlots—which is the great and abominable church of all the earth, whose founder is the devil—then at that day the work of the Father shall commence in preparing the way for the fulfilling of his covenants which he hath made to his people which are of the house of Israel" (1 Nephi 14:17). Nephi's vision reveals that, from its earliest days, Mormonism viewed the relationship between Jesus and Satan as an apocalyptic clash between the forces of "light" and "dark." Jesus' words to Oliver become words of reassurance—though there may have been nearly two millennia of darkness, it will never overcome the light, and the time for the victory of the "light" has arrived.

This second interpretation is supported by the language of the verse. The Gospel of John uses the verbs "shineth" and "comprehended" in John 1:5. In King James grammar, the verb "shineth" is a *present* active indicative, while "comprehended" is a *perfect* active indicative, a tense that suggests a completed action. The grammatical implication is that the light is currently shinning, but the actions of the "darkness" either in "understanding" or "seizing" the light have been completed. It stands to reason that John saw the battle between light and darkness as won once and for all. This same meaning exists in the Greek text, where φαίνει is a present active indicative verb and κατέλαβεν is an aorist active indicative. However, in Joseph Smith's revelation, the verb tense has been changed. "Shineth" remains a present active indicative, but instead of the Johannine "comprehended," the verb has been changed to "comprehendeth," also a present active indicative. This subtle shift in tense suggests that whatever κατέλαβεν signified in the Fourth Gospel, whether the intellectual misunderstanding of Jesus or the attempt to seize him by the darkness (or both), actually remains a pressing, on-going issue in 1829, one to which Smith's restoration will provide a final solution.[67]

The allusions to John 1:5 and John 1:11 receive a second mention in D&C 10, a revelation received by Joseph Smith as a result of the loss of 116 manuscript pages of the Book of Mormon. In language familiar from D&C 6, Joseph Smith is addressed by his Johannine Jesus: "Behold, I am Jesus Christ, the Son of God: *I came unto my own, and my own received me not. I am the light which shineth in darkness, and the darkness comprehendeth it not"* (D&C 10:57–58). D&C 10 was received during the embryonic phase of Joseph's prophetic career, yet the revelation is remarkable in demonstrating how confident Smith is in integrating biblical allusions into his own texts.[68] The last 16 verses of D&C 10 present readers with a pastiche, a rather heavy one, of phrases from both the Gospel of John and the Gospel of Matthew. The allusions to the Prologue of John in D&C 10 are identical to those in D&C 6, and the same analysis that applied there likely applies here. But there are other scriptural allusions in the surrounding verses that may further enhance our understanding of how scripture is being utilized in these early revelations.

Primarily, several passages from the Gospel of Matthew seem intended to establish the concept of a latter-day "church." In D&C 10:53, Jesus states that "And for this cause have I said, if this generation harden not their hearts, I will establish my church among them." Two verses later, in 10:55, Jesus promises that "therefore, whosoever belongeth to my church need not fear, for such shall inherit the kingdom of heaven," an allusion to Matthew 5:5 or 5:13. Jesus goes on to promise that "for behold, I will gather them as a hen gathereth her chickens under her wings, if they will not harden their hearts" (D&C 10:65), an allusion to Matthew 23:37. Finally, in language alluding to Jesus' promise to Peter at Caesarea Philippi, Jesus states "And now, behold whosoever is of my church, and endureth of my church to the end, him will I establish upon my Rock, and the gates of hell shall not prevail against them" (D&C 10:69; cf. Matthew 16: 15–19). In both D&C 9 and 10, language from the Gospel of John gave Jesus a voice. Now, in need of language to describe his "restored" church, Smith applies language from the Gospel of Matthew.

In addition to the allusions from John 1, D&C 10 also borrows from John 10, a dialogue between Jesus and the Pharisees in which Jesus explains that "other sheep I have, which are not of this fold: them also I must bring, and they shall hear my voice; and there shall be one fold, and one shepherd" (John 10:16). This verse can be an enigmatic one for Johannine scholars, who raise questions regarding the identity of the "other sheep."[69] Is it a reference to Diaspora Jews? Second generation Christians? Gentiles? Jesus words are opaque and unclear. In D&C 10:59, not only does Jesus allude to John 10:16 but he also provides a resolution to the identity of the "other sheep:"

> I am he who said other sheep have I which are not of this fold, unto my disciples, and many there were that understood me not. And I will show unto this people, that I had other sheep, and that they were a branch of the house of Jacob; and I will bring to light their marvelous works, which they did in my name; yea, and I will also bring to light my gospel, which was ministered unto them, and behold they shall not deny that which you have received, but they shall build it up, and shall

bring to light the true points of my doctrine: Yea, and the only doctrine which is in me; (D&C 10:59–62)

These verses clearly allude to the coming forth of the Book of Mormon, suggesting that the identity of the "other sheep" is, in fact, the Nephites dwelling upon the American continent, again verbally linking the Gospel of John, the Doctrine and Covenants, and the Book of Mormon together in a three-way dialogue.[70]

In addition to this midrash on John 10:16, one theme that emerges from these verses is the image of "light," used three times in D&C 10:59–62. As we have seen, light plays a significant role in the Gospel of John, often "connecting light with God, life, and knowledge."[71] It is this sense of "light" as "knowledge" that seems to have relevance in D&C 10. One of the purposes of the restoration will be to "bring to light" the role of the Nephites through the production and distribution of the Book of Mormon. Just as the language of John hinted at apostasy and restoration in D&C 6, it plays a similar role here. Jesus' comments that he must "bring to light" his "gospel" and "the true points of my doctrine" suggest that they were previously in "darkness." The addition of "and many there were that understood me not" to the quotation from John 10:16 that "other sheep I have, which are not of this fold" reinforces this point, that loss of knowledge and confusion over the teachings of Jesus necessitated a latter-day restoration of the primitive church. The result of the multiple allusions strewn throughout D&C 10:59–62 is a four-way dialogue with 1) John 10:16; 2) John 1:5; 3) D&C 6:21, and 4) the Book of Mormon. All these texts must be brought into the discussion in order to understand the full weight of Jesus' words.

These allusions are further deepened when we evaluate D&C 10:68–69. Consider the following verses:

> And I say also unto thee, That thou art Peter, and upon this rock I will build my church; and the gates of hell shall not prevail against it. (Matthew 16:18)

> Verily verily I say unto you that this is my doctrine. And whoso buildeth upon this buildeth upon my rock; and the gates of hell shall not prevail against them. And whoso shall declare more or less than this and establisheth it for my doctrine, the same cometh of evil and is not built upon my rock, but he buildeth upon a sandy foundation; and the gates of hell standeth open to receive such when the floods come and the winds beat upon them. (3 Nephi 11:39–40)

> Behold this is my doctrine: whosoever repenteth, and cometh unto me, the same is my church: whosoever declareth more or less than this, the same is not of me, but is against me: therefore, he is not of my church. And now, behold whosoever is of my church, and endureth of my church to the end, him will I establish upon my Rock, and the gates of hell shall not prevail against them. (D&C 10:67–69)

These three passages share a variety of points of contact: 1) The phrase "whoso/whosoever shall declare/declareth more or less than this" is found in both 3 Nephi 11:39–40 and D&C 10:67–69, but not in the Bible; 2) The phrase "this is my doctrine" is found in 3 Nephi 11:30, 32, 35, and 39 as well as D&C 10:67, but also not in the Bible; 3) The passages from 3 Nephi and D&C 10 demonstrate a clear reliance upon Matthew 16:18, with references to the "rock" and the "gates of hell." Finally, 4) all three passages are spoken by Jesus, while the Jesus who speaks in both 3 Nephi and D&C 10 has adopted a Johannine voice. The depth of the allusions is again remarkable. On one hand, Joseph Smith has a grasp of biblical verse to the point where he can alternately incorporate passages from the Gospel of John and the Gospel of Matthew into his own scripture. On the other, there are phrases in this revelation that also appear in the Book of Mormon. From the beginnings of his ministry, Joseph Smith has subtly constructed a dialogue between John, Matthew, 3 Nephi, and D&C 10, a dialogue spanning 2,000 years, four different authors, and two continents.

The presence of 3 Nephi in Smith's revelation adds another layer to the discussion of the phrase "the light shining in darkness" and returns us to our discussion of the Johannine Prologue. In the Gospel of John the phrase "the light shining in darkness" was used to visualize or describe the *kenosis* of the λόγος as it descended to the world. In 3 Nephi, the "light shining in darkness" signified an actual event, as the Nephites had been in darkness and now see Jesus descending in light. Finally, in D&C 10 the phrase "light shining in darkness" is used to signify the restoration of the gospel from the darkness of apostasy. Thus one phrase, used three different ways in three different texts, all converge in D&C 10.

Furthermore, the overall point of D&C 10 was to show how the omniscience of God insured that the plans of Satan would be foiled by preserving the small plates, which themselves become a "light" shining in the "darkness" of Satan's plans. This may symbolize how Joseph Smith's Jesus views "restoration," namely as the introduction of "light" into a state of "darkness," whether physical, literal, or allegorical. Temporally, all three texts (John 1, 3 Nephi, and D&C 10) described how those who should be following Jesus were in a state of apostasy, and all three times this necessitated bringing "light" into "darkness." This understanding gives further depth to the use of John 1:5 both here and in D&C 6:21, where we are told that the "darkness" was unable to "comprehend" (κατέλαβεν) the "light." Understood in a context where "comprehend" means "to seize" or "to overcome," Jesus declares that Satan will never overtake/conquer him, whether in the Old World of the Jews, the New World of the Nephites, or in 1829. God will always have his omniscience and foresight, as he did in having Mormon include the small plates. Thus the use of John 1:5 in both D&C 6 and 10 works well because it reinforces that Jesus has always defeated Satan, both in the first century AD and here in 1829. With this in mind, D&C 10:57 becomes more of a statement of identity, while D&C 10:58 serves as more of a statement of purpose.

In addition to D&C 6 and 10, similar quotations from the Johannine Prologue will appear in several subsequent revelations:

> for behold it is I that speaketh: behold *I am the light which shineth in darkness,* and by my power I give these words unto thee. . . . Behold *I am Jesus Christ, the Son of God: I am the life and the light of the world: I am the same which came unto my own, and my own received me not:* but verily, verily I say unto you, that *as many as receiveth me, them will I give power to become the sons of God, even to them that believe on my name:* Amen. (D&C 11:11, 28–30)

> Behold I am the *light and life of the world,* that speaketh these words: therefore, give heed with your might, and then you are called: Amen. (D&C 12:9)

> Behold I am Jesus Christ the Son of the living God, which created the heavens and the earth; *a light which cannot be hid in darkness.* (D&C 14:9)

> My Son Orson hearken ye and Behold what I the Lord God say unto you even Jesus Christ your Redeemer the *light and the life of the world a light which shineth in darkness and the darkness Comprehendeth it not* Who so loved the world that he gave his own life *that as many as would believe might become the Sons and daughters of God* Wherefore ye *are my Son.* (D&C 34:2–3)

> I am Jesus Christ the son of God who was crusified for the sins of the World *even as will believe on my name that they may become the sons of God* even one in me as I am in the Father as the Father is one in me that we may be one. (D&C 35:2)

> Saying hearken ye and listen to the voice of him who is from all eternity to all eternity the great I am even Jesus Christ th[e] *light and the life of the world* a *light which shineth in darkness and the darkness comprehendeth it not the same which came in the maridian of time unto my own and my own Received me not but to as many as received me gave I power to become my Sons and even so will I give unto as many as Receive me power to become my Sons.* (D&C 39:2–3)

> Saying hearken O ye people of my Church to whom the Kingdom has been given hearken ye and give ere to him who laid the foundation of the Earth who made the Heavens and all the hosts thereof and *by whom all things were made which live and move and have a being.* . . . wherefore Father spare these my Brethren *that Believe on my name* that they may come unto me And have everlasting life. . . . For verily I say unto you that I am Alpha and Omega the Beginning and the end *the light and the life of the world a light that shineth in darkness and the darkness comprehendeth it not I came unto my own and my own Received me not but unto as many as received me gave I power to do many Miricles and to become the Sons of God and even unto them that believed on my name gave I power to obtain eternal life.* (D&C 45:1, 5, 7–8)

It is difficult to determine whether the presence of Johannine language in passages such as the ones above is due to any reason other than biblical allusion. As discussed above, perhaps Joseph Smith wanted a distinct voice in which Jesus would speak in the modern days, and John's language, with its unique language and imagery, provided that voice. Perhaps Joseph Smith, like the epic poets of ancient Greece,[72] relied upon certain stock phrases or "formula quotations" around which to construct his revelations, especially to assist in the reciting of the revelation to a scribe.[73] In addition to the passages from John, readers of Smith's early revelations encounter phrases such as "now behold a marvelous work is about to come among the children of men" (D&C 4:1; see also 6:1; 11:1; 12:1; 14:1), or "behold I am God, and give heed unto my word, which is quick and powerful, sharper than a two-edged sword, to the dividing asunder of both joints and marrow:—Therefore give heed unto my words" (D&C 6:2; see also 11:2; 12:2; 14:2; and, strangely, 33:1). Other "formula quotations" may include "the field is white already to harvest" (D&C 4:4; see also 6:3; 11:3; 12:3; 14:3; and 33:3, 7) and "therefore, if you will ask of me you shall receive; if you will knock it shall be opened unto you" (D&C 6:5; see also 11:5; 12:5; and 14:5). These formula quotations tend to come from the same revelations and usually appear in a consistent sequence throughout. However, as the topics and audience of Joseph Smith's revelations broaden and expand over time, the stock phrases no longer play a role in the construction of the revelations.

This chapter has examined how closely the Bible and Mormon scripture work together from a literary and contextual standpoint through the use of allusion. These allusions went beyond simply signifying the language of the Bible, as did Johannine echo. The significant shift in moving from *echo* to *allusion* is the transference of both *language* and *meaning* to the alluding text. Through examining the three Book of Mormon phrases discussed above, Joseph Smith emerges as an author possessing an ability not simply to restate biblical language in a different setting, but to reproduce accurate settings for the very biblical language he is utilizing. As a result of this process, Smith links his text with the Bible but also opens up a series of dialogues with the Bible in which both texts become interlocutors in a theological discussion about possible understandings of Johannine Christology and anthropology.[74] A similar use of allusion is present in the Doctrine and Covenants. The context of John 1:5, 11–12 itself, not simply a recognition of its biblical provenance, is needed to understand the new contexts created by the weaving of these allusions into the early revelations. As an author, Joseph Smith demonstrates a comfort with biblical language to the point that he can not only re-produce lengthy phrases, sometimes word-for-word, but can also exploit the specific context of those passages to reflect the eschatological or apocalyptic meaning behind his own revelations. To be adept at the first demonstrates an impressive skill in and of itself; proficiency in both suggests an author who goes beyond simple biblical familiarity or knowledge to one who understands the text to such a degree that he can verbally re-create both text and context.

NOTES

1. Annette Merz, "The Fictitious Self-Exposition of Paul: How Might Intertextual Theory Suggest a Reformulation of the Hermeneutics of Pseudepigraphy?," in *The Intertextuality of the Epistles: Explorations of Theory and Practice*, eds. Thomas L. Brodie, Dennis R. MacDonald, and Stanley E. Porter (Sheffield: Sheffield Phoenix Press, 2006), 117.

2. The dividing line between "allusion" and "exegesis" has been the topic of much debate. Karl William Weyde challenges authors such as Sommer and Fishbane on their definitions, arguing that studies examining the relationship between biblical texts must contain more clearly-defined terminology. On the one hand, Weyde writes that "allusion should be distinguished from exegesis; the former does not include the notion of interpretation but evokes only the memory of an older text," although he recognizes that "this definition makes it difficult to draw a clear distinction between allusion and echo." On the other hand, exegesis "intends to apply the meaning of an earlier text to a later setting, in some cases also to modify its meaning" ("Inner-Biblical Interpretation: Methodological Reflections on the Relationship between Texts in the Hebrew Bible," 300). I recognize Weyde's caution, but in this study his definition of allusion would fit my definition of echo, and his definition of exegesis would correlate with my use of allusion (as a category).

3. Sommer, *Prophet Reads Scripture*, 12. In Ben-Porat's own words, "The modification is the result of the interaction between the two texts and reveals the formation of at least one intertextual pattern. Even when marker and marked are identical the local interpretation of the marked . . . must be different from that of the marker . . . because of the different context" ("The Poetics of Literary Allusion," 110).

4. Edenburg, "Intertextuality, Literary Competence," 144.

5. See, for example, D&C 11:28; 34:2; 39:2; 45:7.

6. Craig R. Koester calls this "light/dark" imagery of the Fourth Gospel "probably its most striking motif" (Craig R. Koester, *Symbolism in the Fourth Gospel: Meaning, Mystery, Community* [Minneapolis: Fortress Press, 2003], 141).

7. Leon Morris, *The Gospel According to John* (Grand Rapids: William B. Eerdmans Publishing Company, 1995), 82.

8. Koester notes three ways in which the "light" becomes crucial to the "life" of man: 1) "Light manifests the power and presence of God. It emanates from the λόγος, a term that could designate the creative and sustaining power of God, and the presence of God himself;" 2) "Light manifests the 'life' given to people through God's Word;" 3) "Light means knowing God through faith in Christ . . . to believe in Jesus is to believe in God; to see Jesus is to see God; to know Jesus is to know God. And those who come to know God in Jesus receive the light of eternal life" (Koester, *Symbolism in the Fourth Gospel*, 143).

9. J. Ramsey Michaels, *The Gospel of John* (Grand Rapids: William B. Eerdmans Publishing Company, 2010), 55.

10. Jo-Ann A. Brant, *John* (Grand Rapids: Baker Academic Press, 2011), 23. Viewing the Prologue and the Gospel as a unified document represents a shift from older scholars such as Bultmann who tended to see the Prologue as a pre-Christian hymn tacked-on to the Gospel. However, as Brant notes, the absence of manuscripts lacking the Prologue, and the presence of the Prologue in discussions of the Gospel of John by second-century commentators suggests a unified, original state. Brant also writes that "the way that it [the Prologue] orients the reader to the entire body of the Gospel provides compelling internal evidence" (*John*, 23). The classic statement in support of

unity is J. A. T. Robinson: ". . . the themes of the gospel are played over beforehand, as in the overture to an opera" ("The Relation of the Prologue to the Gospel of St. John," *NTS* 9 [1963]: 122).

11. Koester, *Symbolism in the Fourth Gospel*, 141–74.

12. In addition to this title, there is an abundance of additional Johannine material in Ether 4:12. First, the idea that Jesus is the sole source of light and truth, and that belief upon him is imperative if one is to achieve salvation is hinted at in the second sentence "for good cometh of none save it be of me." Second, there is the curious example of the ἐγώ εἰμί formula with "he that will not believe my words will not believe me—that I am." While instances of the ἐγώ εἰμί formula with a predicate nominative are present in the Book of Mormon, the "absolute" usage—the ἐγώ εἰμί without a predicate nominative—is rare in the Book of Mormon, found in only two other places (3 Nephi 12:1–2). Third, the line "the Father who sent me" with its emphasis upon the Son as "agent" of the Father is one of the prominent themes of Johannine Christology. Finally, the idea that Jesus Christ can be both sent by the Father and also the Father himself, which this verses claims, captures another theme of Johannine Christology, namely that "I and my Father are one" (10:30). This sort of synthesis or blurring of the lines between Father and Son is a thread that runs throughout the Fourth Gospel but also manifests itself in a slightly different fashion throughout the Book of Mormon. With the addition of the final line, "I am the light, and the life, and the truth of the world," there remains little question that the speaker of this verse is the Johannine Jesus.

13. "Light" and "Life" were often connected in Jewish literature and thus one could argue that such a phrase may have had relevance for a group of scattered Jews. See Peder Borgen, "Logos was the True Light: Contributions to the Interpretation of the Gospel of John," *NovT* 14 (1972): 115–30, and Dodd, *Interpretation*, 201–5.

14. Obadiah Sedgwick, *The Bowels of Tender Mercy Sealed in the Everlasting Covenant* (London: 1661), 54

15. Joseph Smith translated a large portion of the Book of Mormon while living with Isaac Hale's family in Harmony, Pennsylvania, a state with a rich Quaker heritage. It is feasible that Joseph Smith was familiar with this specific phrase due to his time in Pennsylvania and inserted it into the Book of Mormon when the translation called for a similar title for Jesus.

16. *Evangelical Restorationist*, Vol. 1 No. 22. March 4, 1825.

17. *The evangelists manual: or a guide to trinitarian Universalists* (Charleston: A. F. Cunningham, 1829), 80.

18. Mosiah 27:25, 28; Alma 5:14; 22:15; 36:5, 23, 24, 26; 38:6.

19. Jeffrey Trumbower, *Born From Above: The Anthropology of the Gospel of John* (Tubingen: J. C. B. Mohr, 1992), 1.

20. The question this statement raises is *when* did this decision take place? The majority opinion up through the 1950s was that this verse referred to the time prior to the incarnate ministry of Jesus, a "pre-incarnation failure to respond to their Creator" (Thomas Brodie, *The Gospel According to John: A Literary and Theological Commentary* [Oxford: Oxford University Press, 1997], 140). For the argument in favor of this opinion, see Rudolf Schnackenburg, *The Gospel According to St. John* (New York: Crossroad, 1969/80, 1979/81, 1982), 1:256–58. However, as Brown notes "most of the phrases found in 10–12 appear in the Gospel as a description of the ministry of Jesus," suggesting that while the beginning of the Prologue may be alluding to the Old Testament creation account, the ministry of Jesus becomes the crucial point in time where the "receiving" and "rejecting" took place (Brown, *The Gospel according to John*, 1:29). Brodie sums up the enigma of this verse well: "What emerges, therefore, is that the text as a whole is ambiguous" (Brodie, *The Gospel According to John*, 140).

21. Gerhard Kittel and Gerhard Friedrich, *Theological Dictionary of the New Testament* (Grand Rapids: William B. Eerdmans Publishing Company, 1972), 2:562.

22. Kittel, *Theological Dictionary*, 2:569.

23. The use of the aorist active indicative (common throughout the New Testament) likely suggests that this bestowal has already happened, and is thus not a future, eschatological event. This would accord well with the realized eschatology so prominent in the Fourth Gospel. However, there is the possibility of the "proleptic aorist" at work here, suggesting that while the transition into becoming τέκνα is a certainty, it awaits future fulfillment.

24. Barrett notes that δύναμις does not actually appear anywhere in the Gospel of John, which could suggest that John consciously rejected any terminology that might imply man's innate or inborn ability. Or perhaps John may have felt the distinction was too vague to warrant any differentiation at all. See Barrett, *The Gospel According to Saint John*, 164.

25. Kittel, *Theological Dictionary*, 5:653.

26. Herman Ridderbos, *The Gospel of John: A Theological Commentary* (Grand Rapids: William B. Eerdmans Publishing Company, 1997), 46.

27. Bultmann, *The Gospel of John*, 59.

28. Barrett, *The Gospel According to St. John*, 164. "More likely, the plural points simply to the participation of two parents in the act of procreation, not to the physiological details of either conception or birth" (Michaels, *The Gospel of John*, 72).

29. ". . . 'desire' or 'will' (*thelema*) refers simply to choice or initiative, not to sexual or any other kind of desire, legitimate or illegitimate" (Michaels, *The Gospel of John*, 72).

30. Brown, *The Gospel According to John*, 1:12. See also Barrett, *The Gospel According to St. John*, 164.

31. Brown writes: "Man was looked on as the principal agent in generation; some considered the woman's role no more than that of a vessel for the embryo" (*The Gospel According to John*, 1:12). See also Michaels, *The Gospel of John*, 73. Köstenberger adds: "The reference to 'a husband's will' implies the OT concept of male headship, in the present context perhaps with reference to the initiative usually taken by the husband in sexual intercourse resulting in procreation. Alternatively, the reference could more generally be to parental determination or will" (*John*, 40).

32. Barrett, *The Gospel According to St. John*, 164.

33. Brant Gardner, *Analytical and Contextual Commentary on the Book of Mormon* (Salt Lake City: Greg Kofford Books, 2007–2011), 3:457. Part of this confusion could be that writers at the time of Joseph Smith presented both a pro- and anti-baptism interpretation to "born of God." According to John Wesley, being "born of God" "implies not barely the being baptized, or any outward change whatever; but a vast inward change, a change wrought in the soul, by the operation of the Holy Ghost; a change in the whole manner of our existence; for, from the moment we are born of God, we live in quite another manner than we did before; we are, as it were, in another world" (John Emory, ed., *The Works of Reverend John Wesley* [New York: J. Collard, 1831], 1:162). Earlier, Jonathan Edwards had written that "being born of God signifies something else than a being brought into the state of professing Christians" (Edward Hickman, ed., *The Works of Jonathan Edwards* [London: Paternoster Row, 1839], 550). There was by no means a consent though. In an 1836 work, Christopher Bethel, Bishop of Bangor, wrote that whenever "born of God" occurs "without mention of baptism, baptism is implied and virtually contained" (Christopher Bethel, *A General View of the Doctrine of Regeneration in Baptism* [London: J. G. & F. Rivington, 1836], 62). Restorationist Walter Scott concurred, writing that "Faith is regenerative, baptism, like birth, is transitional. By the former we are begotten of God; by the latter we are born of God" (Walter Scott, *The Messiahship, or, Great Demonstration, Written for the Union of Christians, on Christian Principles, as Plead for in the Current Reformation* [Cincinnati: H. S. Bosworth, 1859], 59).

34. See discussion in fn. 36.

35. Ridderbos, *The Gospel of John*, 48.

36. Jesus' words to Nicodemus that begin the discussion are: ἐὰν μή τις γεννηθῇ ἄνωθεν, οὐ δύναται ἰδεῖν τὴν βασιλείαν τοῦ θεοῦ (John 3:3). At this point, exegetes of the Fourth Gospel are faced with a dilemma: How ought ἄνωθεν to be understood? This adverb, which occurs five times in John, can mean either "from above" or "anew/

again" (Horst Balz and Gerhard Schneider, *Exegetical Dictionary of the New Testament* [Grand Rapids: William B. Eerdmans Publishing Company, 1982], 1:112). The question then becomes significant from a theological standpoint: Is Jesus insisting that man must be born *a second time*, or that he must be born *with divine assistance*? The other usages of ἄνωθεν in the Fourth Gospel (John 3:7, 31; 19:11, 23) suggest that the latter is the most likely and "must be regarded as the primary meaning" (Barrett, *The Gospel According to St. John*, 206). Raymond Brown concurs, stating "Jesus' primary meaning in vs. 3 was 'from above'" (Brown, *The Gospel According to John*, 1:130). However, this does not rule out that Jesus intended the secondary meaning of "again" to be understood as well, although such a play on words on the part of Jesus would require a Semitic phrase with an amount of play equal to ἄνωθεν. Regardless, Jesus' statement has crucial anthropological implications: "Thus right at the beginning it is stated uncompromisingly that man, as he is, is excluded from salvation, from the sphere of God; for man as he is, there is no possibility of it" (Bultmann, *The Gospel of John*, 135). Jesus then instructs Nicodemus that ἐὰν μή τις γεννηθῇ ἐξ ὕδατος καὶ πνεύματος, οὐ δύναται εἰσελθεῖν εἰς τὴν βασιλείαν τοῦ θεοῦ. Again, there is some confusion about how to interpret this verse. The confusion revolves around ἐξ ὕδατος καὶ πνεύματος. Should this phrase be interpreted as an expansion of the earlier birth "from above/again" from verse 3, or should it be interpreted as a recapitulation of both Jesus' statement in verse three *and* Nicodemus's follow-up question in verse 4? So, on one hand, Jesus' words could be interpreted as referring to a baptismal ordinance, followed by a spiritual confirmation. For a Christian audience ingrained with 2,000 years of theology and practice, this would be the logical interpretation in today's society, and Barrett does state that "it is probable . . . that it included a reference to Christian baptism" (Barrett, *The Gospel According to St. John*, 209). But the second possibility, namely that Jesus is referring to two different births, is suggested both by the context of verse 4 and also by verse 6. Nicodemus had asked about "entering his mother's womb a second time," and Jesus responds that both ὕδωρ and πνεῦμα are necessary. Ὕδωρ, in this case, would refer either to semen or to amniotic fluid, a possibility entertained by some scholars. Cf. Ben Witherington III, *John's Wisdom* (Louisville: Westminster John Knox Press, 1995), 97. From a Mormon perspective see Joseph Fielding McConkie and Robert L. Millet, *Doctrinal Commentary on the Book of Mormon* (Salt Lake City: Deseret Book, 1988), 2:307.

37. This is not to say that Joseph Smith couldn't have gained this understanding of "born of God" from his own religious environment. Biblical commentator Adam Clarke wrote of being "born of God" that "this new birth must come through the will of God—through his own unlimited power, and boundless mercy, prescribing salvation by Christ Jesus alone. It has been already observed that the Jews required circumcision, baptism, and sacrifice, in order to make a proselyte. They allow that the Israelites had in Egypt cast off circumcision, and were consequently, out of the covenant: but at length they were circumcised, and they mingled the blood of circumcision with the blood of the paschal lamb, and from this union of *bloods*, they were again made the children of God. . . . This was the only way by which the Jews could be made the sons of God; but the evangelist shows them that under the Gospel dispensation, no person could become a child of God but by being spiritually regenerated" (Adam Clarke, *The New Testament of Our Lord and Savior Jesus Christ, Containing the Text Taken from the Most Correct Copies of the Authorised Translation, Including the Marginal Readings and Parallel Texts, with a Commentary and Critical Notes* [New York: J. Emory and B. Waugh, 1831], 1:486). John Wesley wrote that "Every one that is born of God, though he be as yet only a 'babe in Christ,' has the love of God in his heart; the love of his neighbor; together with lowliness, meekness, and resignation" (John Emory, ed., *The Works of the Reverend John Wesley* [New York: J. Emory and B. Waugh, 1831], 2: 488). A nineteenth-century description of what it meant to be "born of God" that bears some remarkable similarities to Alma's own experience can be found in Ambrose Searle's *The Church of God: or, Essays on Various Names and Titles Given to the Church, in the Holy Scriptures: To*

which are Added, Some Papers on Other Subjects (London: H. D. Symonds, and M. Jones, Paternoster-Row, 1806), 98–109.

38. Kittel, *Theological Dictionary*, 4:740

39. Kittel, *Theological Dictionary*, 4:740.

40. Walter Bauer, *A Greek-English Lexicon of the New Testament and Other Early Christian Literature*, revised and edited by Frederick W. Danker, 3rd edition (Chicago/London: University of Chicago Press, 2000), 658. Hereafter *BDAG*.

41. Dan Lioy, *The Search for Ultimate Reality: Intertextuality between the Genesis and Johannine Prologues* (New York: Peter Lang Publishing, 2005), 82.

42. The problem largely stems from the interpretation of μονογενὴς as "only-begotten," which has been used to support the idea of "eternal generation" of the Son from the Father. While this interpretation is a possibility, most scholars stop short of stating that this interpretation is the preferred one, and the debate surrounds the question of whether John uses the title μονογενὴς to indicate Jesus' unique status or to indicate the manner of his creation. In other words, should the point of emphasis be "only" or "begotten?" Schnackenburg writes that "According to the Greek, the notion of origin cannot be excluded from μονογενὴς, but in view of the Hebrew sub-stratum, it cannot be certainly affirmed" (*The Gospel According to St. John*, 1:271). Brown goes further and states that "Although *genos* is distantly related to *gennan*, 'to beget,' there is little Greek justification for the translation of *monogenes* as 'only begotten'" (Brown, *Gospel of John*, 1:13). Barrett disagrees, stating that "though μονογενὴς means in itself 'only of its kind,' when used in relation to *father* it can hardly mean anything other than only (-begotten) son" (Barrett, *Gospel according to St. John*, 166). Bultmann gives three possible interpretations in his commentary, that μονογενὴς can mean "unique in its γένος," "uniform in its manner," or "only begotten" (Bultmann, *The Gospel of John*, 71 fn. 2). Also notable is the observation of Dwight Moody Smith, who surveys uses of μονογενὴς in the Septuagint and notes that in that context the term is restricted to "unique" or "only" (Dwight Moody Smith, "God's Only Son: The Translation of John 3:16 in the Revised Standard Version" *JBL* 72 [1953]: 219). D. A. Fennema has examined the title specifically in the context of John 1:18 and has concluded "We discover that every undisputed NT occurrence of μονογενὴς denotes a unique filial relationship, whether or not it modifies υἱός or θυγάτηρ. Accordingly, when John applies this term to the Son of God it is correctly translated as 'only son'" (D. A. Fennema, "John 1:18: 'God the only son,'" *NTS* 31 [1985]: 126).

43. The use of "Only Begotten Son" in Jacob 4:4–5 is a curious one and worth further examination for an additional reason. The only other place in the New Testament where "Only Begotten Son" is used outside of Johannine literature is Hebrews 11:17: "By faith Abraham, when he was tried, offered up Isaac: and he that had received the promises offered up his only begotten son." Thus both Hebrews 11:17 and Jacob 4:4–5 both use "Only Begotten Son" within the context of Abraham's sacrifice of Isaac. But the title "Only Begotten Son" has been switched from referring to Isaac in Hebrews 11:17 to referring to Jesus in Jacob 4:4–5. This, along with the fact that Jacob tends to echo Paul more than John, may suggest that the provenance of this verse is Hebrews rather than John, even though the way the title is being used is more in harmony with John. This suggests a great versatility on how the Bible is used within the Book of Mormon, preserving the context of Hebrews for the larger setting of Jacob 4:5 while altering the title to allude to John. Of course, it could merely be that the author of the Book of Mormon saw, as did Paul, that the sacrifice of Isaac by Abraham functioned as a type of the sacrifice of Jesus.

44. Mormons would look at a passage such as Revelation 22:7–13 as biblical justification for this idea. The doctrine has its roots in the understandable confusion in Mormon scripture between the Father and the Son, particularly in the Book of Mormon and the Book of Moses. Mormon scholar Thomas G. Alexander writes "A clarification of this point was necessary because of the apparent confusion in various scriptures relating to the unity of the Father and the Son, the discussion of Jesus Christ as Father, and the ambiguity over the roles of the Father and Son in the creation. The

church undertook to do this in 1916, through a statement prepared by the First Presidency and Council of the Twelve and published to the church membership. The effect of the statement was to make clear the separation of the two beings and to indicate the roles of God and Christ" (Thomas G. Alexander, *Mormonism in Transition: A History of The Latter-day Saints, 1890–1930* [Chicago: University of Illinois Press, 1986], 280).

45. "Thus saith the Lord for I am God and and have sent mine *only begotten Son* into the world for the redemption of the world and have decreed that he that receiveth him shall be saved and he that receiveth him not shall be damned" (D&C 49:5).

46. Harper writes "Often in the Doctrine and Covenants we hear Christ speaking of himself as the Son of God. D&C 49 ends that way, but most of the revelation is in the Heavenly Father's voice. This is one of only two places in the Doctrine and Covenants where we hear the Father speak of Christ as his Only Begotten Son" (Harper, *Making Sense of the Doctrine and Covenants*, 170).

47. MacKay, et al., *The Joseph Smith Papers: Documents, vol. 1*, 297–303; See Lawrence R. Flake, "A Shaker View of a Mormon Mission," *BYU Studies*, 20, no. 1, (Fall 1979).

48. Godfrey, et al., *The Joseph Smith Papers: Documents, vol. 2*, 179–91.

49. "Even the things which were from the begining before the world was which was ordained of the Father through *his only begotten Son* who was in the *bosom of the father* even from the beginning" (D&C 76:13).

50. Peter M. Phillips, *The Prologue of the Fourth Gospel* (London/New York: T&T Clark, 2006), 218.

51. One interesting grammatical note is the use of the verb "was" in D&C 76:13, rather than the "is" of John 1:18. John's language suggests that Jesus remains, even after his incarnation and resurrection, in the "bosom of the Father," perhaps a way of stating that the intimate relationship between the two continues to exist no matter what form the Son is in. Joseph Smith, by using the past tense, seems to imply that the "bosom of the Father" referred only to a pre-mortal Jesus, and that a resurrected and post-mortal Jesus no longer requires this imagery, suggesting that, at least on some level, Joseph may have interpreted the phrase in terms of geography rather than intimacy. This same shift in verb tense is also present in D&C 76:25 and 39, the other two places where the phrase "bosom of the Father" appears.

52. "For we saw him, even on the right hand of God and we heard the voice bearing record that he is the *only begotten of the Father*" (D&C 76:23).

53. Joseph Smith, "The Answer," *Times and Seasons* 4 (February 1, 1843): 83. For the argument that W. W. Phelps, not Smith, was the author of the poem, see Michael Hicks, "Joseph Smith, W. W. Phelps, and the Poetic Paraphrase of 'The Vision,'" *Journal of Mormon History*, 20.2 (1994): 63–84.

54. "And this we saw also and bear record that an angel of God who was in authority in the presence of God who rebelled against the *only begotten son* whom the Father loved who was *in the bosom with the Father* and was thrust down from the presence of God and the son" (D&C 76:25).

55. And I, the Lord God, spake unto Moses, saying: That Satan, whom thou hast commanded in the name of mine Only Begotten, is the same which was from the beginning, and he came before me, saying—Behold, here am I, send me, I will be thy son, and I will redeem all mankind, that one soul shall not be lost, and surely I will do it; wherefore give me thine honor. But, behold, my Beloved Son, which was my Beloved and Chosen from the beginning, said unto me—Father, thy will be done, and the glory be thine forever. Wherefore, because that Satan rebelled against me, and sought to destroy the agency of man, which I, the Lord God, had given him, and also, that I should give unto him mine own power; by the power of mine Only Begotten, I caused that he should be cast down; And he became Satan, yea, even the devil, the father of all lies, to deceive and to blind men, and to lead them captive at his will, even as many as would not hearken unto my voice (Moses 4:1–4).

56. The same is true for D&C 76:35, "Having denied the holy ghost after having received it and having denied the *only begoten son of the Fathe[r]* crucifying him unto themselves and putting him to an open shame."

57. Phillips, *The Prologue of the Fourth Gospel*, 204.

58. Terryl L. Givens, *Wrestling the Angel* (Oxford: Oxford University Press, 2014), 120–21.

59. This lowering of Christology reaches its culmination in D&C 93, where Joseph appears to teach something of a "moral example" theory of atonement. This shift demonstrates the difficulty in maintaining both a high Christology and a high anthropology. If humanity has divine origins and a divine destiny, what is the function of a Savior?

60. For dating and context of D&C 6, see MacKay, et al., *The Joseph Smith Papers: Documents, vol. 1*, 34–35.

61. On something of a technical level, it is interesting to note that the original revelations had "my" in place of "mine," and then at some point, probably after 1920, the language is changed to its modern "mine." For more, see Herbet Schendl, "Morphological Variation and Change in Early Modern English: *my/mine, thy/thine*," in *Language History and Linguistic Modelling: A Festschrift for Jacek Fisiak on His 60th Birthday*, eds. Raymond Hickey and Stanisław Puppel (Berlin: Walter de Gruyter, 1997), 179–91.

62. To be clear, the point is that nowhere in the New Testament does Jesus himself ever say "I am Jesus Christ, the Son of God." Other writers do, however, present third-person renditions. Mark 1:1 reads "The beginning of the gospel of Jesus Christ, the Son of God." Acts 8:37 has Philip state "And Philip said, If thou believest with all thine heart, thou mayest. And he answered and said, I believe that Jesus Christ is the Son of God." Finally, Paul writes to the Corinthians "For the Son of God, Jesus Christ, who was preached among you by us, even by me and Silvanus and Timotheus, was not yea and nay, but in him was yea" (2 Cor. 1:19). The phrase "Jesus Christ, Son of God" becomes much more prominent in the Book of Mormon, occurring (although also not in the first person) in 2 Nephi 25:19; Mosiah 3:8; 4:2; Alma 6:8; 36:17; Helaman 3:28; 14:12; 3 Nephi 5:13, 26; 30:1; Mormon 7:5; 9:22; Ether 4:7;

63. Davidson, et. al, *The Joseph Smith Papers: Histories, vol. 1*, 214.

64. *BDAG*, 520.

65. Keener, *The Gospel of John*, 1:387. See also Brown, *The Gospel According to John*, 1:8.

66. After being instructed to join "none" of the churches, Jesus explains why: "all their Creeds were an abomination in his sight, that those professors were all corrupt, that 'they draw near to me with their lips but their hearts are far from me, They teach for doctrines the commandments of men, having a form of Godliness but they deny the power thereof'" (Karen Lynn Davison, et al., *The Joseph Smith Papers: Histories, vol. 1*, 214).

67. It is also possible that this change in the spelling of the verb could have been completely unintentional by Joseph Smith and thus not signify anything important. The problem is that while many of Joseph Smith's early revelations were preserved in their original, unedited form in the Kirtland Revelation Books, the earliest extent copy of D&C 6 available comes from the 1833 Book of Commandments and thus may have been edited if, in fact, the original rendering of 6:21 was "comprehended" instead of "comprehendeth." See MacKay, et al., *The Joseph Smith Papers: Documents, vol. 1*, 34–37.

68. D&C 10 is one of the more difficult revelations to contextualize and provide a date. See MacKay, et al., *The Joseph Smith Papers: Documents, vol. 1*, 37–39.

69. See Brown, *The Gospel According to John*, 1:396–98 and Keener, *The Gospel of John*, 1:818–20.

70. This view will be confirmed by the Book of Mormon itself, where Jesus proclaims "And verily I say unto you, that ye are they of whom I said: Other sheep I have which are not of this fold; them also I must bring, and they shall hear my voice; and there shall be one fold, and one shepherd. And they understood me not, for they supposed it had been the Gentiles; for they understood not that the Gentiles should be converted through their preaching" (3 Nephi 15:21–22).

71. Koester, *Symbolism in the Fourth Gospel*, 142.

72. In ancient epics such as Homer's *Iliad* and *Odyssey*, often the reader will encounter segments of text of various length that repeat certain lines or even lengthy passages. One useful definition of "epic formula" quotation is "A ready-made semantic unit for insertion in the verse as necessary" (Chris Carey, ed., *Aeschines* [Austin: University of Texas Press, 2000], 67 fn. 140). Sometimes these formula quotations are short, such as the ornamental epithet "swift-footed" to describe Achilles, used even when Achilles is standing still. Other formula quotations can go on for much longer. The most common explanation for the presence of these "formula quotations" is that it allowed the bard a measure of versatility in real-time composition of oral poetry—instead of needing to memorize lengthy epics, the poet would combine a series of formula quotations with an established narrative. Often this was done to maintain the appropriate measure, but it surely simplified the narrative construction process. For further reading see Alfred Lord, *The Singer of Tales* (Cambridge: Cambridge University Press, 2000), and Milman Parry, *The Making of Homeric Verse: The Collected Papers of Milman Parry* (Oxford: Oxford University Press, 1991).

73. One of the purposes of formula quotations in epic poetry was to assist in recitation: "The practical utility of formulas as mnemonic devices was to facilitate immediate recitation under the pressure of telepathic tension between singer and audience" (Edmund de Chasca, "Toward a Redefinition of Epic Formula in the Light of the *Cantar de Mio Cid*," *Hispanic Review* 38.3 [1970]: 252).

74. "An *intertextual* relationship which can enhance the meaning of a text is present when the reading of a passage evokes one or more other texts, thus generating a dialogue between texts which introduces interpretive aspects that go beyond the possible *intratextual* links" (Merz, "The Fictitious Self-Exposition of Paul," 117).

THREE

Mormon Scripture and the Expansion of John

In addition to *echo* and *allusion*, Mormon scripture also presents several examples of what could be termed *expansion*. As with echo and allusion, expansion is also part of the "rhetoric of allusivity" due to its borrowing and re-fashioning of biblical texts. However, what separates expansion from echo and allusion is that expansion builds upon the meaning of the biblical text, constructing scripture that goes *beyond* the meaning of the biblical source. Paul R. Noble, in his study of inner-biblical allusion in the Hebrew Bible, writes: "Thus an author who weaves into his text numerous allusions to another writing will not usually do so just to give the perceptive reader the pleasure of recognizing the resemblances, but rather to add thereby *significant new dimensions* to the text's meaning."[1] With expansion, the author uses familiar biblical verse to make "a new point not necessarily related to the topic of the older text."[2] So while the language is familiar, the meaning is innovative and new.[3] This type of expansion can be viewed as the discovery of a *sensus plenior* within the text. Michael Fishbane, who terms the expansion of an ancient text by a more recent text "aggadic exegesis," states that this can be accomplished through either "creative recombination of earlier words or topoi," or through "complex transformations of them."[4] The key, according to Fishbane, is to find "dense occurrence in one text of terms, often thoroughly reorganized and transposed, found elsewhere in a natural, uncomplicated form."[5]

An example of expansion within the Book of Mormon is Nephi's use of Isaiah, in particular Nephi's construction of his own prophecy found in 2 Nephi 25. Speaking of Nephi's injunction to "liken scripture" unto ourselves, Joseph Spencer and Jenny Webb observed:

That Nephi feels comfortable weaving his own prophecies into the text of Isaiah is itself a telling thing. That he not only adds his own statements to the Isaianic text but also adjusts the "quoted" scripture freely is still more telling. It appears that Nephi's work of likening implies at least two things about the nature of scripture and its application: (1) The work of likening allows what might otherwise become the "dead letter" of a scriptural text to come back to life. Likening thus appears to be a kind of scriptural resurrection, a way of giving new life to scripture. (2) The work of likening a text may only be able to breathe life into a text through a prophetic editing process in which the text may be adjusted, recontextualized, and intentionally appropriated.[6]

This idea that a text might become "resurrected" by a future author is particularly important when discussing the Book of Mormon and the Doctrine and Covenants, both of which utilize a heavy pastiche of biblical verse. But what makes this discussion particularly germane is that Nephi can "adjust, recontextualize, and appropriate" biblical language to create a new text. Significantly, it is Nephi's assumption of a prophetic role that allows for this textual re-creation to occur:

First, it should be noted that likening a text is, for Nephi, a question of weaving into the scriptural text *not* the banalities of everyday life (an application of the scriptures to everyday life), but rather truths one has learned regarding the meaning and importance of the Abrahamic covenant through some kind of revelatory or prophetic experience. It might thus be said that it is only a *prophet*—though that word must be taken in its broadest definition as referring to anyone who has "the spirit of prophecy" (see 2 Nephi 25:4)—who can authoritatively give new life to a scriptural text.[7]

Understood this way, *expansion* represents an organic, creative approach to scripture, one that increases demands upon the reader who must recognize not only the origin of the quoted text but who also must evaluate *how* the text has been "adjusted, recontextualized, and appropriated." In order to better understand the function of *expansion*, we will examine three distinct Johannine phrases that appear in the Book of Mormon and five that appear in the Doctrine and Covenants.

1. FULL OF GRACE AND TRUTH

In Alma 5, Alma the Younger, the Nephite high priest and former chief judge, delivers a discourse to the inhabitants of the Nephite city of Zarahemla intended to illustrate the importance of truly believing in deliverance from bondage, the power of Jesus, and the establishment of the church of God. At the apex of this speech Alma bears witness to his belief in the delivering power of Jesus Christ: "I say unto you that I know of myself that whatsoever I shall say unto you concerning that which is to come is true. And I say unto you that I know that Jesus Christ shall come, yea, the Son, the Only Begotten of the Father, full of grace and mercy and truth. And behold, it is he that cometh to take away the sins of the world, yea, the sins of every man which steadfastly believeth on his name" (Alma 5:48). This statement by Alma the Younger confirms that this deliverance can only come about through the efforts of Jesus Christ. The reasons why Jesus Christ is capable of saving those (and only those) who "believe on his name" are twofold: because of his special, uniquely divine status as "the Only Begotten of the Father" and his state of being "full of grace, mercy, and truth."[8]

Readers familiar with John will notice that while "full of grace and truth" is an allusion to John 1:12 (the only place in the Bible where the phrase occurs), "mercy" has been inserted between "grace" and "truth." At first glance, it is difficult to understand why Joseph Smith would make this addition, rather than simply maintain the wording of the Johannine subtext, but there are a few possibilities.[9] First, Smith simply may have felt that "grace and truth" were inadequate in expressing the full range of Jesus' capability and so he added "mercy." A second, more likely possibility, directly relates to allusivity. Some Johannine scholars[10] have argued that the phrase "full of grace and truth" in John 1:14 was intended as an allusion to Exodus 34:6, where Yahweh uses the phrase "abundant in goodness and truth" to describe himself to Moses upon Mt. Sinai.[11] Along with the qualities of "goodness and truth," Yahweh also calls himself "merciful," meaning that three adjectives from Exodus 34:6 are used to construct the passage in Alma 5:48, building upon the two of John 1:14. This combinative process is certainly quite creative and demonstrates a biblical fluency on the part of the author. In order for this to work, the author would have to be aware of both the language of John 1:14, that Jesus was "full of grace and truth," and that John 1:14 was an allusion to Exodus 34:6, from which he would borrow the word "mercy."

Furthermore, the insertion of "mercy" within "grace and truth" fits well within the context of Alma's argument, which describes Jesus Christ as a being who is "full of grace, mercy, and truth." Yet at the same time the inclusion of "mercy" creates some dissonance—readers familiar with John recognize that the word doesn't belong, subtly intruding upon the text. This intrusion serves to focus the attention of the reader upon the concept of mercy, a prominent theological thread that runs throughout Alma 5. Alma the Younger could directly address the topic of mercy, but by placing it where it doesn't belong, in the middle of a well-known biblical phrase, the reader is urged to confront it. In this way, the presence of "mercy" between "full of grace and truth" acts as a signpost for the reader, a poetic breaking of expectations that draws attention to the text and foreshadows the mercy that Jesus will show toward those in Zarahemla who repented and became truly converted.[12]

In a subsequent discourse, this time to wicked Nephites living in the city of Ammonihah, Alma the Younger again employs a variation of "full of grace and truth:" "And not many days hence the Son of God shall come in his glory, and his glory shall be the glory of the Only Begotten of the Father, full of grace, equity, and truth, full of patience, mercy, and long- suffering, quick to hear the cries of his people and to answer their prayers" (Alma 9:26). Instead of placing "mercy" between "grace" and "truth," as he did at Zarahemla, Alma the Younger now inserts "equity" between "grace" and "truth." [13] The term "equity" occurs ten times in the KJV Old Testament and is limited to the books of Psalms, Proverbs, Ecclesiastes, Isaiah, Micah, and Malachi. Other than Alma 9:26, it occurs seven times in the Book of Mormon, often paired with "justice." Of the five usages referring to Jesus Christ, none occur following his appearance to the Nephites. The word is fully absent from the KJV New Testament. It does occur twice in the Doctrine and Covenants, in both instances paired with "justice." (The inclusion of a second tricolon of adjectives describing Jesus, "full of patience, mercy, and long-suffering," is found only here in all of Mormon scripture.) The closest parallel in the Bible is again Exodus 34:6–7, where both "mercy" and "long-suffering" are mentioned as qualities of God, although "patience" is absent in that case. The combination of "mercy" and "long-suffering" without "patience" occurs as a pair seven times in the Book of Mormon, with five of those found in Alma.

These variations on a familiar Johannine phrase beg the question: Why does Joseph Smith change the wording, and why change it in this specific context? Furthermore, how does it relate to Alma 5:48, where "mercy" was similarly woven between "grace" and "truth" in a speech also given by Alma? Not only must readers deal with the insertion of an unfamiliar adjective sandwiched between "grace and truth," but readers must also sort out why that unfamiliar adjective has changed. "Equity," unlike "mercies," appears to have little in common with "grace" and "truth."

One possible explanation for the additions of "mercy" and "equity" to "full of grace and truth" comes from Rudolf Bultmann, who wrote of John 1:14 that "χάρις and ἀλήθεια describe God's being; not 'in itself,' but as it is open to man (in his receptivity) and in its activity towards man: they refer, that is, to the benefits in which God (or the Revealer) abounds, and which he bestows on the believer." [14] The Nephites in Zarahemla responded well to Alma's call to repentance, and thus God "bestowed" upon them mercy. However, God is also a God of justice, of fairness. When the Nephites in Ammonihah fail to respond properly to Alma's warning, even going so far as to burn the wives and children of those who are sympathetic to Alma's message, God "bestows" upon them his "equity" by allowing the Lamanites to completely destroy them, leaving their formerly powerful stronghold a "desolation." By inserting one adjective, either "mercy" or "equity," in between the well-established "grace and truth" of John's Prologue, the text foreshadows how God is going to react to each of the cities in question.

This explanation does not, however, explain the presence of the second tricolon "full of patience, mercy, and long-suffering." The closest biblical parallel is again Exodus 34:6–7, a passage that also provides a possible source for John 1:14. "Patience" does not occur in the Gospel of John or in the Johannine epistles, although it does occur seven times in the "Johannine" Book of Revelation. "Mercy" likewise is absent from the Gospel of John, but does appear once in 2 John 1:3. Finally, "long-suffering" is absent from any Johannine literature. This presents readers of Alma 9:26 with an expansion of the same question raised by Alma 5:48. Again, the attention of readers is turned toward the connection between John 1:14 and Exodus 34: 6–7. Alma 9:26 clearly demonstrates a reliance upon John 1:14 with its use of "full of grace and truth," but also demonstrates a reliance upon Exodus 34 with the addition of "mercy" and "long-suffering." Read in this way, the Book of Mormon presents readers with a passage (Alma 9:26) alluding to another passage that hasn't been written yet (John 1:14) that is itself alluding to a passage from the Old Testament (Exodus 34:6–7).[15] Here Smith demonstrates a creativity of scriptural adaption surpassing the echoes and allusions we've examined thus far. Smith has not simply taken John 1:14 and placed it within the Book of Mormon, he has taken the Old Testament passage alluded to in John 1:14 and woven both of them together in a new, Book of Mormon context. This exegetical step, assuming it was a conscious move, would require Smith to know the Bible well enough to not only weave allusions from John, but *also the sources for those allusions*, into his work.

2. GRACE FOR GRACE

A second Johannine expansion is found in Helaman 12, a lament inserted by Mormon in the middle of the violent encounters between the Gadianton Robbers and the Nephites in chapter 11 and the prophecies of Samuel the Lamanite in chapters 13–15. Mormon specifically identifies the unfaithfulness of the Nephites, who "do forget the Lord their God and do trample under their feet the Holy One" (Hel. 12:2). Mormon states that he hopes "all men might be saved," but is aware that "in that great and last day there are some which shall be cast out, yea, which shall be cast off from the presence of the Lord" (Hel. 12:25). Throughout this chapter, Mormon grapples with the idea of salvation, who will be saved and who will not, and what issues factor into a determination of salvation. It is in the midst of this discussion that Mormon makes the statement that "And may God grant in his great fullness that men might be brought unto repentance and good works, that they might be restored unto *grace for grace* according to their works" (Helaman 12:24).

This phrase provides readers with one of the most significant usages of the Johannine Prologue, for while it appears only here in the Book of Mormon it will place a crucial role in understanding D&C 93 of the Doctrine and Covenants. "Grace for grace" is unique to John, appearing only in John 1:16, where its meaning remains "a bone of contention" among Johannine scholars.[16] Lexically, the Greek preposition ἀντὶ usually signifies "instead of/in place of" and thus connotes a sense of "replacement."[17] This interpretation raises the question of why Jesus would be replacing one "grace" with another "grace." For this reason, Johannine scholars often attempt to find different meanings for ἀντὶ. Ruth Edwards suggests five possible interpretations: 1) opposite, in front of; 2) instead of, in place of; 3) in return for; 4) corresponding to; 5) upon, in addition to.[18]

Scholars differ as to which one they prefer. Herman Ridderbos states that "More appealing is the view that interprets that 'grace for grace' accumulatively,"[19] thus demonstrating a preference for #5.[20] C. K. Barrett also prefers to interpret χάριν ἀντὶ χάριτος as a statement of accumulation, but also sees relevance in #3: "The meaning of this phrase seems to be that Christian life is based at all points upon grace; as it proceeds one grace is exchanged only for another."[21] Thomas Brodie favors #2: "The idea that the text is concerned with the transition and continuity between the old order and the new is confirmed by what follows" and "suggests that the grace of the incarnation replaces or surpasses the grace (*hesed*) of the OT."[22] Keener, while believing that the "most likely" interpretation is that of Jesus' grace "superseding that of the old covenant," does acknowledge an additional possibility of "Christ's grace matching ours" and that "other texts may suggest that the phrase signifies a compensatory exchange."[23] Also noting the potential of #3 is Peter Phillips, who points out that the idea of "exchange" was a viable interpretation based upon how ἀντὶ was used by Euripides and Dionysius of Antioch.[24] #1 and #4 are not really entertained as possibilities by scholars, as #1 is never found in the New Testament and #4 is not found in Greek usage at all.

Through the application of these different hermeneutical possibilities to Helaman 12:24, the Book of Mormon's usage of "grace to grace" becomes clearer. The verse presents readers with two parallel subordinate clauses: "that men might be brought unto repentance and good works," and "that they might be restored unto grace for grace," both the objects of "And may God grant, in his great fullness." The relevant question is whether these two subordinate clauses should be read as parallel, and thus two different restatements of the same idea, or whether they should be seen as two different statements. The former may suggest that "grace for grace" is identical to a repentant state that yields good works, while the latter may suggest that "grace for grace" is the result of being repentant and performing good works. Thus three things must be considered: "grace for grace" must be "granted" by God, "grace for grace" is a state of being "restored," and "grace for grace" comes about "according to their works." Based particularly upon the term "restored," the former seems more likely. The Book of Mormon tends to use "restore" and "restoration" as either a *geographical* restoration, like of a land to a people, or a more *spiritual* restoration. Consider the following verses:

> And this death of which I have spoken, which is the spiritual death, shall deliver up its dead, which spiritual death is hell. Wherefore death and hell must deliver up its dead, and hell must deliver up its captive spirits and the grave must deliver up its captive bodies. And the bodies and the spirits of men will be restored one to the other; and it is by the power of the resurrection of the Holy One of Israel. (2 Nephi 9:12)

> O my son, this is not the case. But the meaning of the word restoration is to bring back again evil for evil or carnal for carnal or devilish for devilish, good for that which is good, righteous for that which is righteous, just for that which is just, merciful for that which is merciful. Therefore my son, see that ye are merciful unto your brethren. Deal justly, judge righteously, and do good continually. And if ye do all these things, then shall ye receive your reward. Yea, ye shall have mercy restored unto you again; ye shall have justice restored unto you again; ye shall have a righteous judgment restored unto you again; and ye shall have good rewarded unto you again. For that which ye doth send out shall return unto you again and be restored. Therefore the word restoration more fully condemneth the sinner and justifieth him not at all. (Alma 41:13–15)

> Therefore, O my son, whosoever will come may come and partake of the waters of life freely. And whosoever will not come, the same is not compelled to come. But in the last day it shall be restored unto him according to his deeds. If he hath desired to do evil and hath not repented in his days, behold, evil shall be done unto him according to the restoration of God. (Alma 42:27–28)

> He hath given unto you that ye might know good from evil. And he hath given unto you that ye might choose life or death. And ye can do good and be restored unto that which is good, or have that which is good restored unto you; or ye can do evil and have that which is evil restored unto you. (Hel. 14:31)

According to these usages of "restoration," in particular Alma 41:13–15, the idea of restoration is that you become what you perform or do. Thus, if you perform "carnal" deeds you are "restored" to a carnal state. But if you perform "good" deeds and works, ones that exhibit justice and mercy, then God "restores" unto you justice and mercy. The acts themselves have no necessarily ontological value, but they signify what eschatological state we should expect to find ourselves. Thus Alma advises Corianton "Therefore my son, see that ye are merciful unto your brethren. Deal justly, judge righteously, and do good continually. And if ye do all these things, then shall ye receive your reward. Yea, ye shall have mercy restored unto you again; ye shall have justice restored unto you again; ye shall have a righteous judgment restored unto you again; and ye shall have good rewarded unto you again" (Alma 41:14). Alma even uses the same pattern in Alma 41:13 that readers find in Helaman 12:24 with "grace for grace:" "evil for evil or carnal for carnal or devilish for devilish, good for that which is good, righteous for that which is righteous, just for that which is just, merciful for that which is merciful."

With this paradigm in mind, readers could interpret Mormon's use of "grace for grace" in the sense that as individuals repent and turn their minds and hearts toward performing "good works," they enter into a relationship with God where he "exchanges" or bestows upon them his "grace" for the "grace" they have shown to others through their works. It is not our works that save us, rather the grace we receive by virtue of performing those works. We perform good works, and in doing so our being becomes transformed into "good." With this understanding in mind, Mormon is employing "grace for grace" in a manner that corresponds most closely to #3, the idea of "exchange" or "compensation." We receive Jesus' grace when we demonstrate grace. It is the ultimate method of equity: Who you are and how you act determines what you become in the long term. The Book of Mormon's use of "grace for grace" correlates well with its Johannine context, but the Book of Mormon has taken a Johannine phrase and not just employed it for "biblicizing" the text (echo) or one that mirrors the language and the theology (allusion), but used a Johannine phrase as a springboard for a creative construction of a new idea, an *expansion*. In the process, Joseph Smith has taken a simple phrase from John and crafted it into an expression of the concept of restoration. There is no radical re-definition of "grace for grace" (or for that matter "full of grace and truth"), yet Smith has adopted and adapted biblical language into his own, preserving the structure while altering the language. This process results in such innovative phrases as "evil for evil," "carnal for carnal," and "good for that which is good," expressions that clearly have their foundation in John 1:16 but in the Book of Mormon have been transformed into a theology of restoration.

3. BECOME THE SONS OF GOD

The third and final Johannine expansion comes in Moroni 7, where the final Book of Mormon editor and author, Moroni, inserts a "few of the words" of his father Mormon into his own record (Mor. 7:1). Moroni states that these words were delivered by his Father "in the synagogue which they had built for the place of worship" (Mor. 7:1) and would thus theoretically be a sermon delivered by Mormon and then written down by Moroni or another Nephite. While there are hints of Johannine language in this chapter, such as "faith in his name" in Moroni 7:26 and

Moroni 7:38, the biblical context for this chapter is largely Pauline and takes much of its language from 1 Corinthians 13.

The first use of "become the sons of God" comes in the midst of a discussion upon the nature and significance of faith. Mormon emphasizes that faith in Jesus was required of all believers prior to the birth and ministry of Jesus, that even though Jesus had not yet atoned for the sins of humanity God had still manifested the reality of the atonement through "divers ways" (Mor. 7:24). But the question becomes, now that Jesus has actually come to the Earth, died, and been resurrected, is faith still a requirement? Can one have faith in something that has actually happened? Or has faith ceased to matter, since believers have the written witness of those who have seen Jesus? Mormon strongly believes in the continued reality of faith, asking "have miracles ceased because Christ hath ascended into heaven?" In fact, even after the death of Jesus men remain "saved by faith in his name" and it is "by faith" that believers "became the sons of God" (Mor. 7:26).

From a Johannine perspective, this is a curious verse. In the Fourth Gospel, "faith" plays almost no role in the teachings of Jesus. Whereas the word appears 230 times in the New Testament, it is completely absent from the Gospel of John. Instead, the Fourth Gospel prefers the verb πιστεύω, "to believe," which appears 98 times throughout the Gospel.[25] In addition to John 1:12, the term appears in other, often crucial verses:

> But if I do, though ye believe not me, believe the works: that ye may know, and believe, that the Father is in me, and I in him. (John 10:38)

> Believe me that I am in the Father, and the Father in me: or else believe me for the very works' sake. (John 14:11)

> But these are written, that ye might believe that Jesus is the Christ, the Son of God; and that believing ye might have life through his name. (John 20:31)

Significantly, most of the occurrences of πιστεύω are in the present tense, suggesting that John views "belief" not as a static, singular experience but a continual, progressive one. One does not "believe" only at one point or at one time, nor is "believing" something that one possesses.[26] The ability to "believe" (and continue to believe) becomes crucial for the disciple, the only method by which one can truly obtain salvation and understand the true nature of the Son:

> For God so loved the world, that he gave his only begotten Son, that whosoever believeth in him should not perish, but have everlasting life. (John 3:16)

> And said unto the woman, Now we believe, not because of thy saying: for we have heard him ourselves, and know that this is indeed the Christ, the Saviour of the world. (John 4:42)

> Verily, verily, I say unto you, He that heareth my word, and believeth on him that sent me, hath everlasting life, and shall not come into condemnation; but is passed from death unto life. (John 5:24)

> Jesus saith unto her, Said I not unto thee, that, if thou wouldest believe, thou shouldest see the glory of God? (John 11:40)

> While ye have light, believe in the light, that ye may be the children of light. These things spake Jesus, and departed, and did hide himself from them. (John 12:36)

The necessity of "believing" is even explicitly noted as a purpose behind penning the Fourth Gospel: "But these are written, that ye might believe that Jesus is the Christ, the Son of God; and that believing ye might have life through his name" (John 20:31).

This Johannine concern with "belief" has relevance for this discussion of Moroni 7:26. Mormon appears to use faith, even down to the phrase "faith in his name" in place of "believe on his name," in a very similar fashion as John uses "believe." This similarity comes out in the way Mormon develops his argument. Mormon writes that those who have faith "will cleave unto every good thing" (Mor. 7:28), meaning that "those who truly follow the Savior make the commitment to live the gospel."[27] Just as "believing" was a progressive, continual process for John, having "faith" for Mormon is not a one-time occurrence, but something that must be pursued and developed over the course of a lifetime.

Mormon, however, does not stop with faith, but continues to lay out the process by which believers "become the sons of God" through an explication of "hope" and "charity," thus inviting Paul into this discussion. It is remarkable that the author of Moroni 7 is able to take "faith," a word that is completely absent from the Gospel of John and use it at the center of a theological discussion that is so very Johannine, one that directs readers towards "becoming the sons of God." Joseph Smith appears to be aware of this, and it is with a fair amount of irony that he uses the phrase "faith in his name" in Moroni 7:26, a phrase that may be a synthesis of "faith" and "believe on his name" from John 1:12. In this instance, Smith has taken "believe on his name" and quite literally replaced "believe" with "faith," in the process constructing something of a "theological hybrid."

This "theological hybridity" only increases in depth with the second Johannine verse from Moroni 7, Moroni 7:48: "Wherefore, my beloved brethren, pray unto the Father with all the energy of heart that ye may be filled with this love which he hath bestowed upon all who are true followers of his Son Jesus Christ, that ye may *become the sons of God*, that when he shall appear, we shall be like him—for we shall see him as he is—that we may have this hope, that we may be purified even as he is pure. Amen" (Moroni 7:48).[28] There are at least two possibilities for how to interpret the phrase "become the sons of God" in Moroni 7:48: 1) as a catalogue of individual items in a purpose clause, or 2) as deliberate links in a result clause following a purpose clause. If we interpret it as a catalogue of individual items, then the verse would read "Wherefore, my beloved brethren, pray unto the Father with all the energy of heart (in order) that (1) ye may be filled with this love which he hath bestowed upon all who are true followers of his Son Jesus Christ, (in order) that (2) ye may become the sons of God, (in order) that (3) when he shall appear, we shall be like him—for we shall see him as he is—(in order) that (4) we may have this hope, (in order) that (5) we may be purified even as he is pure. Amen." Taken this way, the verse becomes a catalogue or list of five things one ought to pray for. In this context, "become the sons of God" is essentially a rhetorical device—there is no sense of what the term "sons of God" means or how one goes about becoming one, only that one ought to pray about becoming one.

However, if we read this verse as deliberate links in a chain we get this: "Wherefore, my beloved brethren, pray unto the Father with all the energy of heart (in order) that (1) ye may be filled with this love which he hath bestowed upon all who are true followers of his Son Jesus Christ, (so) that (2) ye may become the sons of God, (so) that (3) when he shall appear, we shall be like him—for we shall see him as he is—(so) that (4) we may have this hope, (so) that (5) we may be purified even as he is pure. Amen." The former presented a list of things to pray for, the second a series of clauses where each one is dependent upon the previous, where the achievement of one results in the next link being put in place. Thus being "filled with this love" causes or results in one becoming the "sons of God," which then causes us to appear "like him," which then causes us to "have this hope," which leads finally to us becoming "purified even as he is pure." Interpreted this way, "becoming sons of God" takes on greater significance, as we see that it is a state of being obtained only through the bestowal of the Father through the Son, and that it is a necessary step that leads to us becoming more like him.

This latter interpretation corresponds well with the context of Moroni 7 and John 1. The overall point of Mormon's sermon is that *who* you are, not *what* you do is what truly matters. He stated earlier in the chapter that

> For behold, God hath said: A man being evil cannot do that which is good. For if he offereth a gift or prayeth unto God, except he shall do it with real intent, it profiteth him nothing; for behold, it is not counted unto him for righteousness. For behold, if a man being evil giveth a gift, he doeth it grudgingly; wherefore it is counted unto him the same as if he had retained the gift. Wherefore he is counted evil before God. And likewise also is it counted evil unto a man if he shall pray and not with real intent of heart. Yea, and it profiteth him nothing, for God receiveth none such. (Moroni 7:6–9)[29]

Mormon's intent is to stress "the need to achieve the state where we not only *act* the right way, but we *are* the right way."[30] Thus the emphasis throughout Moroni 7 is on the progression from faith to charity, since "if ye have not charity, ye are nothing" (Mor. 7:46). Mormon then goes on to define charity as "the pure love of Christ," which carries the plenary meaning of both "the love which Christ possesses" and "the love we must have for him." This helps us understand why we must "be filled with this love" if we are truly to "become the sons of God" (Mor. 7:48).

This interpretation harmonizes well with the Gospel of John as well on at least three counts. First, the emphasis on the pivotal nature of love is a recurring theme and even becomes the token or signifier of true discipleship: "A new commandment I give unto you, That ye love one another; as I have loved you, that ye also love one another. By this shall all men know that ye are my disciples, if ye have love one to another" (John 13:34–35). One cannot become a true disciple without love—it is a *sine qua non* for belief. Second, the Johannine Prologue informs us that the state of becoming the "sons of God" is bestowed only through the "power" held by the λόγος. Without Jesus, one cannot reach this state of "son" or "daughter."

This is true for Mormon's sermon as well, as he states that true charity is bestowed by the Father "upon all who are true followers of his Son, Jesus Christ." The only difference is that in John the λόγος bestows the power, while in Moroni 7 charity comes from the Father, but the origins remain divine in both texts.[31] Finally, in John 8 Jesus argues with the Jews concerning paternity. The Jews claim that Abraham is their father, which in turn leads Jesus to remark that "If ye were Abraham's children, ye would do the works of Abraham" (John 8:39). Jesus further points out to the Jews that "If God were your Father, ye would love me "(John 8:42), but their desire to kill him proves that "Ye are of your father the devil, and the lusts of your father ye will do" (John 8:44). Jesus' point in this debate is that "conduct, or more precisely one's response to the word of God, is the criterion for identifying paternity."[32] Mormon argues a similar point: Those who are granted this charity, the "pure love of Christ," who become the "sons of God" shall "be like him."[33] They are his "sons" and he is their "Father" because they possess charity, because by virtue of their charity they perform works and exercise a conduct reflective of their paternity.

Notably, the primary dialogue present in Moroni 7 appears to be between Mormon and Paul. Mormon has gone to great lengths to ensure that Moroni understands the crucial nature of charity. The word used by Paul in 1 Corinthians that was translated as "charity" in the King James Bible is the Greek ἀγάπη, a word which "relates for the most part to the love of God, to the love of the higher lifting up the lower, elevating the lower above others."[34] For Paul, ἀγάπη becomes absolutely crucial for salvation, for it is when believers develop within themselves the capacity for ἀγάπη that they learn "to be toward others the way God in Christ has been toward us."[35] It is within this understanding of the Paul/Mormon dialogue that a second dialogue is initiated, this time between Mormon and John, centered on the phrase "sons of God." One point of emphasis that can be traced throughout the Book of Mormon is the idea of becoming "spiritually begotten." King Benjamin told his people that by virtue of their covenant relationship "ye shall be called the children of Christ, his sons and his daughters; for behold, this day he hath spiritually begotten you" (Mos. 5:7). In a similar fashion Alma inquired of the Nephites in Zarahemla "Have ye spiritually been born of God? Have ye received his image in your own countenances?" (Alma 5:14). Just as a child resembles his Father physically, so must the children of Christ resemble him spiritually. For Mormon, this *imitatio Christi* is most fully accomplished through our acquiring charity, and in the process becoming "the sons of God."

By incorporating the language of John, Mormon has brought John into this discussion of ἀγάπη and observant readers now reflect upon how ἀγάπη is used not only in the Pauline epistles but also in the Fourth Gospel. C. K. Barrett notes the significance of ἀγάπη in John: "ἀγαπᾶν, ἀγάπη, are among the most important words in John. . . . Love seems to be, for John, a reciprocal relation. The Father loves the Son (3:35; 10:17; 15:9f.; 17:23f., 26), and the Son loves the Father (14:31); Jesus loves his own (11:5; 13:1, 33, 34; 14:21; 15:9(f.), 12; 21:7, 20), and his own love, or should love, one another (13:34f.; 15:12f., 17; 17:26). They must also love him (14:15, 21, 23f., 28; 21:15f.)."[36] Thus utilization of both Paul and John becomes crucial for Mormon in relaying to his readers not just that charity is important, but *why* it is so crucial. We become "sons of God" because we learn to love others with the same love that both the Father and the Son demonstrate toward each other and toward us. While the Book of Mormon writers have consistently returned to the idea of spiritual birth, they have not been as consistent in relating how that process is accomplished. This is where Paul and John come into play. 1 Corinthians 13 may be the best contained discussion of charity in the New Testament, providing useful language and framework for Mormon. But there are nuances of charity not found in Paul, such as the reciprocal nature of charity and its relevance in our becoming "sons of God," that are more clearly explicated in the Gospel of John. Understood in both its Pauline and Johannine contexts, Mormon's letter is perhaps the most explicit and thorough discussion of what true spiritual birth entails in the Book of Mormon. But part of its power comes through the ways he brings Paul and John into the discussion. Mormon could simply have told Moroni that charity was necessary, or he could have just quoted Alma or Benjamin. But by merging the voices of Paul and John through the mouth of Mormon, Joseph Smith invites the modern reader to examine this discussion of charity and its significance with John and Paul in mind, as if the full implications of Mormon's letter can't be fully gleaned without their participation.

4. D&C 45:1, 5, 7–8, 28–29

Throughout the Doctrine and Covenants, readers encounter a similar expansion of John's Prologue. One prominent example comes in D&C 45. If D&C 42 represented the "law" of the Lord, then D&C 45 represents the "prophets," continuing Joseph Smith's recapitulation of the Old Testament.[37] Biblical prophecies, many from the Olivet discourse, are effortlessly woven together with contemporary warnings. The revelation relays a strong sense of immediacy. Jesus pleads with the early Mormons to "hearken" and "listen" to him, because there is not much time before the end, and those who fail to heed will find that "death shall overtake you in an hour when ye think not the Summer shall be past and the harvest ended and your souls not saved" (D&C 45:2). Time, in this revelation, is linear, building up to a momentous *kairos*. But time in D&C 45 also functions cyclically. Jesus promises to the Saints that "I will reason as with men in days of old" and "I will speak unto you and prophecy as unto men in days of old" (D&C 45:10, 15). Jesus mentions Zion, the city of Enoch, and how he saved its members, promising to treat the Saints in a similar fashion. Jesus repeats much of his Olivet discourse, promising to reveal eschatological events to the Saints as "plainly" as "I shewed it unto my Deciples as I stood before them in the flesh" (D&C 45:16). It is as if the early Saints are reliving events that have happened in the past, having encountered a deity who takes literally the statement "Jesus Christ the same yesterday, and today, and forever" (Heb. 13:8; cf. D&C 20:12). As Steven Harper has noted, this revelation "cements a connection between the Old Testament, New Testament, and the restoration of the gospel through Joseph Smith."[38] But what is notable is *how* Joseph Smith accomplishes this. He does not just reproduce biblical prophecies verbatim, as if this would prove any sort of divine inspiration; rather he re-molds and re-works them in a way that suggests that he sees himself standing at the end of a long prophetic tradition. Consider the following verses:

> and then shall the Jews look upon me and say what are these wounds in thine hands and in thy feet then shall they know that I am the Lord for I will say unto them these wounds are the wounds With which I was wounded in the house of my friends I am he that was lifted up I am Jesus which was crusified I am the Son of God. (D&C 45:51–52)

These verses are an allusion to Zechariah 13:4–6:

> And it shall come to pass in that day, that the prophets shall be ashamed every one of his vision, when he hath prophesied; neither shall they wear a rough garment to deceive: But he shall say, I am no

prophet, I am an husbandman; for man taught me to keep cattle from my youth. And one shall say unto him, What are these wounds in thine hands? Then he shall answer, Those with which I was wounded in the house of my friends.[39]

It is significant that Joseph Smith doesn't merely quote from Zechariah 13:6 and say "this applies to Jesus." Rather he has Jesus speak in the first person and apply the verses to himself. The result of this action is that even if the original context of Zechariah 13:6 (which likely refers to a false prophet) didn't apply to Jesus, it does now. Smith is literally re-writing scripture in a way that focuses the attention of heaven and earth, past, present, and future, upon himself while bestowing a "divine" stamp-of-approval upon his reading of Zechariah. The importance of Joseph Smith and his work now becomes clear: It will be the restoration of the gospel, the gathering of Israel, the building of Zion, that will usher in the glorious events of the end of times, when Jesus "shall come in my glory" (D&C 45:56). As was the case with several previous revelations, the speaker of this dense and extremely imaginative revelation identifies himself using language from the Gospel of John, including allusions from John 1:3, 4, 5, 11, and 12. Due to the range of Johannine language in this revelation, each one will be examined individually.

The phrase "by whom all things were made which live and move and have a being" is literally created out of two New Testament passages. "By whom all things were made" appears to be an allusion to the first few verses of John 1, in particular John 1:3, which reads "All things were made by him." The second half of the phrase is likely dependent upon Acts 17:28: "For in him we live, and move, and have our being; as certain also of your own poets have said, For we are also his offspring."[40] The emphasis in John appears twofold: The prepositional phrase δι' αὐτοῦ states unequivocally that Jesus is the agent of the Father, and thus God himself, while the terms πάντα and οὐδὲ serve to affirm the superiority of Jesus to any created being.[41] The emphasis in both John 1:3 and Acts 17:28 is upon Jesus Christ as not simply creator, but as giver of life. Inanimate objects, such as rocks or books, are not explicitly mentioned, although perhaps their creation is implied by interpreting "have a being" as "existing" rather than "alive." The phrase sets the reader up to encounter a deity who brings life with him, one breathes life both into history through his appearance to Joseph Smith and into scripture through his recasting of prophecy. A few months later, Joseph Smith would produce a revelation that would again link Jesus and "life:" "and also those to whom these commandments were given might have power to lay the foundation of this Church and to bring it forth out of obscurity and out of darkness the only true and living Church upon the face of the whole Earth with which I the Lord am well pleased speaking unto the Church collectively and not individually" (D&C 1:30).

D&C 45:5 presents yet another variation on the "believe on my name" of John 1:12, with added nuances. First, Jesus directly pleads with the Father to "spare" men and women that "believe on his name." "Spare" them from what? From the eschatological trials on the horizon? From death? From damnation? It's difficult to say. Second, those who do "believe on my name" will be allowed to "come unto me and have everlasting life." There is no mention of any other requirements such as faith, repentance, or baptism, as there was in previous revelations. There is, however, some measure of dissonance between this verse and John 1:12. In John 1:12, salvation came to those who "believe on his name" because he is God, the λόγος incarnate. In D&C 45 it is the idea that Jesus performed the atonement and was crucified that brings salvation to those who "believe on my name": "Father behold the sufferings and death of him who did no sin in whom thou wast well pleased Behold the Blood of thy son which was shed the blood of him whom thou gavest that thyself might be glorified" (D&C 45:4). Smith again expands upon scriptural borderlines, reconstructing them to include more than what was originally stated. The phrase "believe on his name" is clearly Johannine, and the phrase "have everlasting life" is found only three times in the Gospels, two of which are John 3:16 and John 6:40. Additionally, the idea that salvation can come to humanity by virtue of their belief is very much a Johannine idea. But the linking of Jesus' atonement and crucifixion with this salvation seems theologically closer to the Synoptics than to John. The Fourth Gospel never mentions a shedding of blood occurring in Gethsemane, and the Johannine crucifixion scene is much different than the Synoptic account. The Synoptic Gospels, especially Mark, emphasize the pain endured by Jesus, yet the Johannine Jesus is, as always, completely in control and even at ease upon the cross.

A similar dissonance is present in D&C 45:3: "listen to him who is the advocate with the Father who is pleading your case before him." This statement is likely an allusion to 1 John 2:1, the only usage of the title "advocate" for Jesus in the Bible, but a word that occurs five times in Joseph Smith's revelations. In some earlier verses in the Doctrine and Covenants it was easy to pick out and isolate the provenance of certain verses, whether they were from John or Matthew, the Old Testament or the New Testament, the Bible or the Book of Mormon. But here we have in D&C 45:3 a Christological title for Jesus borrowed from 1 John 2, in D&C 45:4 soteriology borrowed from the Synoptics, and in D&C 45:5 soteriology from John 1, all woven together in a blending of different theological concepts that may initially seem counter-intuitive but are presented almost seamlessly by Joseph Smith in a comprehensible fashion. Joseph Smith is moving away from a "reciter" of scripture toward more of a "creator" or "fashioner" of scripture.

This "fashioning" can be seen beginning with D&C 45:7, where the Johannine source becomes more apparent. Readers first encounter the familiar phrases "the light and the life of the world," and "a light that shineth in darkness and the darkness comprehendeth it not." The "light and the life" brings to mind the earlier emphasis upon "life" in D&C 45:1, while quotations from John 1:5 could be interpreted as allusions to the apostasy and restoration of the gospel under Joseph Smith. This appears to be how they were used in the earlier revelations, and their usage here, in a revelation emphasizing the reality and power of prophecy in nineteenth-century America, seems to fit that earlier mold. This same emphasis on apostasy and restoration carries over to D&C 45:8 as well. However, what is new in this verse is the idea that those who "receive" Jesus get "power to do many Miricles" in addition to the Johannine promise of becoming "sons of God." This promise to perform miracles ties in well with the larger theme of the chapter, namely the return to the world or reality of charismatic gifts such as prophecy. But is this promise "to perform many Miricles" an elaboration of "receive me" or "become sons of God?" In other words, do those who receive him get a) power to perform miracles and b) power to become the sons of God, or is part of becoming a "son of God" that you obtain power to do many miracles? Interestingly, this promise to perform miracles, while it appears out of place within this allusion to John 1:12, actually meshes quite well with the Johannine provenance of the verse. Out of the sixteen usages of "miracle" in the four Gospels, thirteen of them come from the Fourth Gospel. Jesus, the Son of God, performs miracles, thus it is only natural that those to whom he gives power to become "sons of God" should possess a similar power.

In the Fourth Gospel the typical word for "miracle" is σημεῖον, which means more literally a "sign." This is a key term for John, and "in distinction from both general use of the Greek word and our word 'sign,' use of this word in John does not refer primarily to a deeper or symbolic dimension of meaning but to a miracle as a sign of authentication or legitimation." [42] The inclusion in D&C 45:8 of the promise to bestow "power to do many Miricles" can be understood as God providing for the Latter-day Saints the means by which they can prove themselves—just as Jesus proved his sonship through his "signs," Mormons will prove their "sonship" through their "signs." For Joseph Smith, the Book of Mormon stood as a prime example of a σημεῖον and the ability to pronounce prophesy in the name of Jesus Christ likely counted as well. If so, then D&C 45, where Joseph Smith does just that, provides the evidence to support the claim of D&C 45:8, rather cleverly establishing Joseph Smith as a "son of God" as well as one "endowed with power from on high."

With D&C 45:28, Smith continues his deconstruction and reconstruction of scripture: "and when the times of the gentiles is come in a light shall break forth among them that sit in darkness and it shall be the fulness of my Gospel but they receive it not for they perceive not the light and they turn their hearts from me because of the precepts of men." Previously Joseph Smith took quotations from John and expanded upon them, adding words or sentences to broaden meaning. In these two verses Smith takes a number of Johannine terms—light, darkness, fulness, receive—and reworks them into a fully legitimate theological statement. In John, the light was the λόγος—it was He who was not "comprehended" by the darkness, and it was his "fulness" that we have all "received." In D&C 45, Joseph redefines the terms while preserving the language. In D&C 45:28, the "fulness of my Gospel" has now become the "light," and rather than the "light" it is now the "fulness of my Gospel," rather than Jesus, that is neither "received" nor "perceived."

This usage of the Johannine Prologue goes far beyond the use of "formula" quotations as a voice for Jesus, even when the verses appropriated from John receive minor tinkering, as they did in D&C 45:8. But D&C 45:28–29 represents the most complete example of Joseph Smith's reconstruction of scripture seen thus far. Up to this point, Joseph Smith has respected the language of the Bible. He quotes it extensively, either in brief clauses or in full passages. Sometimes, he makes small additions or changes. But here he begins to "misread" scripture as a way of legitimizing new ideas, pushing the boundaries of scripture, so to speak. In D&C 45:28–29 Joseph Smith can take the language of John and weave his own theology through it. It is true that Joseph Smith has often used John 1:5 and John 1:11 to give a voice to the apostasy, but in D&C 45 he literally does so, using the language of John 1:5 and John 1:11 to legitimize the "times of the Gentiles." There is a certain audacity in replacing Jesus, the "light" of John 1, with the "restored gospel," of Mormonism, a certain boldness in equating the rejection of Mormonism with the rejection of Jesus, both of which Joseph Smith does in his crafting of these two verses.[43] It is not just prophecy that is reworked in D&C 45, but scripture as well. In D&C 45, Joseph announces that he is both a new prophet *and* a new author, placing a divine claim upon his right to magnify, alter, elaborate, or simply re-define the word of God, both spoken and written.

5. D&C 67:11

In November 1831 a conference was held regarding the publication of the Book of Commandments. A handful of church elders were asked to sign a revealed statement about the nature and truthfulness of the revelations that would be published with the Book of Commandments.[44] Some of the elders were troubled by imperfections they perceived in the revelations, and apparently they hoped for a divine witness to confirm the decision for publication. While those present at the conference may have been hoping for something more grandiose, what they received was this short revelation. The revelation declares that the Lord has indeed heard their prayers and knows their hearts (D&C 67:1), but "there were fears in your hearts and verily this is the reason that ye did not receive" (D&C 67:2).

The Lord then validates the language of the revelations, stating that "for ye know that there is no unrighteousness in it and that which is righteous cometh down from above from the father of lights" (D&C 67:9).[45] The Lord then states that the members must strip themselves from "Jealesies and fears and humble yourselves before me," at which point "the veil shall be wrent and you shall see me and know that I am" (D&C 67:10).[46] At this point, the revelation alludes to John 1:18, the only time this verse is quoted in all of Mormon scripture: "No man hath seen God at any time; the only begotten Son, which is in the bosom of the Father, he hath declared him."

Following the promise that "the veil shall be wrent and you shall see me and know that I am," Smith begins his expansion on John 1:18. He states that this ability to "see me and know that I am" cannot be accomplished "with the carnal neither natural but with the spiritual for no man hath seen God at any time in the flesh but by the Spirit of God neither can any natural man abide the presence of God neither after the carnal mind ye are not able to abide the presence of God now neither the ministering of Angels wherefore continue in patience untill ye are perfected" (D&C 67:10–13). Johannine scholars see the function of John 1:18 as demonstrating that "for no one, not even for Moses, can God be an object of direct observation and that the human person cannot even exist in God's unveiled presence."[47] God himself had stated the same to Moses on Mt. Sinai: ". . . for there shall no man see me, and live" (Ex. 33:20).[48] One of the purposes of John 1:18 was to elevate the status of Jesus, the "only Son who has not only seen the Father but is ever at His side."[49] Thus Jesus' statement that "He who has seen me has seen the Father."

This verse serves at least two important functions for Joseph Smith and the church. First, it re-enforces Smith's supersessionist idea that he and his followers are the legitimate, latter-day heirs of the Jewish covenant. In June 1830, Joseph Smith began a "translation" of the Bible, part of which involved "restoring" a lengthy vision in which Moses "was caught up into an exceeding high Mountain" (Moses 1:1).[50] While on this mountain, Moses sees God "face to face and he talked with him and the glory of God was upon Moses therefore Moses could endure his presence" (Moses 1:2). At the conclusion of the first part of this vision, Moses speaks in language reminiscent of D&C 67:10–11: "And it came to pass, that it was for the space of many hours before Moses did again receive his natural strength like unto man, and he saith unto himself Now for this once I know that man is nothing, which thing I never had supposed, *but now mine eyes, mine own eyes but not mine eyes for mine eyes could not have beheld* for I should have withered and died in his presence but his glory was upon me and I beheld his face for I was transfigered before him" (Moses 1:10–11).[51] This vision establishes that Moses was "transfigured," or temporarily changed, in order to abide in the presence of God and still remain alive.

According to D&C 67, Moses' experience was not meant to be unique. D&C 67 promises that those who "strip yourselves" of faults and act humbly may also "see me," not with the "natural mind" but with the "spiritual mind." Smith's church may employ biblical terms like "priesthood" and "prophet," but it was also to be grounded in the democratic ideals of nineteenth-century America. In a few short months, Smith would receive a revelation granting priesthood authority to all worthy male members, regardless of lineage, and his vision of the afterlife promised all but the worst among humanity a "degree of glory." D&C 67 thus represents the democratization of prophet-hood. Visions of God would no longer be limited only to men like Moses and Isaiah, but to all who "have been ordained unto the ministry" (D&C 67:10), who, "when ye are worthy in mine own due time ye shall see and know that which was confirmed upon you by the hands of my Servant Joseph Amen" (D&C 67:14).[52]

A second function John 1:18 may have served for Joseph Smith was in regards to his own spiritual background. Joseph Smith's life was a living example of the sacred collapsing into the profane. He spoke of having seen[53] or heard[54] or being visited by numerous divine figures and claimed to have seen the Son on several occasions. Especially noteworthy are the five occasions he would claim to see God the Father.[55] One might think that John 1:18 would appear in Smith's writings more frequently, if for no other reason than explaining that it was possible to see the Father, as long as the circumstances warranted it. What Joseph Smith does in D&C 67:11 is push back against the idea that God remains a distant, unseen presence. While it may be generally true that no man can see God, according to D&C 67:11 this visitation can occur if one is acted upon "by the Spirit of God." Thus for Joseph Smith, John 1:18 was not an inaccurate claim, it was simply incomplete. D&C 67, with its caveat that "for no man hath seen God at any time in the flesh but by the Spirit of God" may have allowed Smith to feel more comfortable in relaying his own encounters with God the Father. A short time after the reception of D&C 67, Joseph Smith and Sidney Rigdon produced an "inspired" translation of John 1:18, which would read, in a manner echoing D&C 67:11: "And no man hath seen God at any time, except he hath born record of the Son." In a similar fashion, 1 John 4:12, with its assertion that "No man hath seen God at any time" was followed in Smith's revised version with the proviso "except them who beleive." Statements like these may have served to alleviate questions about what Smith himself may have experienced, to help him understand how he was able to see God when the New Testament seemed to claim the exact opposite. Those skeptical of Smith's visionary claims may see D&C 67:11 as Smith laying the groundwork for his multiple stories about visitations from the Father. By expanding upon John 1:18 through the addition of the caveat "except quickened in the flesh" Smith introduced a way in which it would be possible to see God, anticipating potential critics who would point to John 1:18 as proof of Smith's fraudulence.[56]

6. D&C 76

*D&C 76 serves as a watershed moment for Joseph Smith in his prophetic growth and begins a series of revelations termed by Richard Bushman the "the exaltation revelations."[57] These revelations find Joseph looking beyond the establishment of Zion upon the Earth to what may lay beyond this world.[58] Readers encounter in D&C 76 a vision of the heavens, in D&C 84 an explication of priesthood, in D&C 88 a blueprint of the cosmos, and D&C 93 the potential for humanity to become divine beings. The catalyst for the vision recorded in D&C 76 was, Smith relates, a reading of John 5:29. John 5:29 itself is a succinct, tantalizingly short statement by Jesus regarding the eschatological fate of both the righteous and the wicked: "And (they) shall come forth; they that have done good, unto the resurrection of life; and they that have done evil, unto the resurrection of damnation." Smith expressed some dissatisfaction with such a thoroughly dualistic approach to salvation when other scripture, as well as common sense, told him otherwise. He wrote that "It appeared self evident from what truths were left, that if God rewarded every one according to the deeds done in the body, the term 'heaven,' as intended for the Saints eternal home, must include more kingdoms than one."[59] Smith intuited that behind John 5:29 lay greater and grander truths, and as a result he and Sidney Rigdon "meditated upon these thing," a pondering that was rewarded when "the Lord touched the eyes of our understandings and they were opened and the glory of the lord shone round about" (D&C 76:19).[60]

A key Johannine phrase that appears several times through D&C 76 is "receive a fulness," language that appears in John 1:14 and John 1:16:

> And the Word was made flesh, and dwelt among us, (and we beheld his glory, the glory as of the only begotten of the Father), *full* of grace and truth. (John 1:14)

> And of his *fulness* have all we *received,* and grace for grace. (John 1:16)

The Greek word translated as "fulness" is πλήρωμα, a loaded term that can mean anything from a numerical "full measure"[61] to the Gnostic "totality of aeons,"[62] but is perhaps most easily understood as "totality." In John 1:16, the statement is made that the disciples have received of "his πλήρωμα." It is this word πλήρωμα that links John 1:14 to John 1:16, where Jesus is said to be "full" (πλήρης—the same root as πλήρωμα) of grace and truth."[63] Thus those who "receive" Jesus are promised the opportunity to partake "the full measure of grace and truth present in him, not just the partial, veiled measure in the law."[64] In John 1:16, the verb for "receive" is λαμβάνω, a rather common verb that can mean "to get hold of something by laying hands on," "to acquire," "to accept," or "to comprehend" from an intellectual standpoint.[65]

What John constructs in these verses is a crucial connection or link between the Father, the Son, and humanity, specifically those who "receive" Jesus. Jesus is the only being who can be called the "only begotten son," and as such (or due to) he is "full of grace and truth," qualities associated with God in the Old Testament.[66] This links the Father and the Son. Additionally, those who "receive" Jesus receive of His "fulness," specifically "grace for grace." John identifies the incarnation as the pivotal moment where this relationship is fulfilled. Jesus becomes "the Word made flesh," and now he "dwelt among us." For the first time, the Father, through his Son, has contacted humanity, and offered them the means by which they can return. Raymond Brown writes that "it is quite possible that . . . the Prologue is reflecting the idea that Jesus is now the *shekinah* of God, the locus of contact between the Father and those men among whom it is His delight to be."[67] The Prologue thus establishes the groundwork for the crucial events of John 17, where Jesus, in his intercessory prayer, will ask the Father:

> That they all may be one; as thou, Father, art in me, and I in thee, that they also may be one in us: that the world may believe that thou hast sent me. And the glory which thou gavest me I have given them; that they may be one, even as we are one: I in them, and thou in me, that they may be made perfect in one; and that the world may know that thou hast sent me, and hast loved them, as thou hast loved me. (John 17:21–23)

This unity between Father, Son, and believers is fundamental to John, establishing on Earth a pattern that is fundamental to Heaven.[68] It is not surprising, then, that Joseph Smith would find meaning in the language of John 1 (and John 17) as the scope of his revelations begins to move further and further out into the heavenly realm. Specifically, the concept of a "link" or "connection" with the divine and how it may be rationally explained beyond the "grace" of John will be the critical question that D&C 76, 84, 88, and 93 will attempt to answer.

In D&C 76, readers encounter seven instances where "receive" and "fulness" are used together.

> and we beheld the glory of the son on the right of the Father and *received of his fulness*. (D&C 76:20)

> they are they who are priests and kings who *having received of his fulness* and of his glory. (D&C 76:56)

> and again we saw the terrestrial world and lo these are they who are of the Terestrial whose glory differeth from that of the church of the first

born who have *received the fulnes* of the father even as that of the moon differeth from the sun of the firmament. (D&C 76:71)

these are they who *receive of this glory but not of the fulness*. (D&C 76:76)

these are they who *receive of the presence of the son but not of the fulness of the father*. (D&C 76:77)

these are they who *receive not of his fullness* in the eternal world, but of the holy ghost through the ministration of the Terestrial. (D&C 76:86)

they who dwell in his presence are the church of the first born and they see as they are seen and know as they are known having *received of his fulness* and of his grace. (D&C 76:94)

With the exception of D&C 76:20, all the uses of "received of his fulness" appear in the context of kingdoms of glory, whether celestial, terrestrial, or telestial. In this context, "received of his fulness" seems intended to serve as a signifier or indicator of glory. Those who inhabit the celestial, or highest, kingdom, "having received of his fulniss and of his glory" (D&C 76:56). Those who inhabit the terrestrial "receive of this glory but not of his fulness" (D&C 76:76). The former clause is elaborated upon further in verse 77, where to "receive of this glory" is to "receive the presence of the son," while "not of his fulness" refers specifically to the "fulness of the father." Finally, those who inhabit the telestial "receive not of his fullness in the eternal world" but instead receive "the holy ghost through the ministration of the Terestrial" (D&C 76:86).

Once again Joseph Smith, perhaps reacting against the ambiguity of "grace and truth" imaginatively expands upon his Johannine source. To simply state that believers "receive of his fulness" is inadequate. Smith takes the phrase and re-crafts it until it serves as a measuring stick for eternal worthiness and reward. In D&C 76:56, the antecedent of "his" is the "father" of the previous verse. In John it was the "fulness" of the λόγος that all believers "received," but now for Joseph the truly righteous receive the "fulness" of the Father.

What exactly constitutes this "fulness" of the Father? In his poetic rendition of D&C 76, Smith wrote that those in the celestial kingdom "receive a fulness of glory and light." In a similar fashion, he stated that those in the celestial kingdom "will there enjoy a fulness of that light Glory and intelligence."[69] In later years, Joseph Smith would further narrow down this idea of "fulness" to mean something akin to priesthood ordinances that must be "received" in the Temple. Smith stated that "If a man gets the fulness of God he has to get [it] in the same way that Jesus Christ obtain it and that was by keeping all the ordinances of the house of the Lord."[70] Celestial marriage, in particular, was a crucial step in obtaining this "fulness:" "And as pertaining to the new and everlasting covenant, it was instituted for the fulness of my glory; and he that receiveth a fulness thereof must and shall abide the law, or he shall be damned, saith the Lord God" (D&C 132:6). The titles given to those celestial heirs, "kings" and "priests" (D&C 76:56), are titles that carry overtones of authority,[71] and it seems that at some point Joseph Smith viewed "fulness" as a "fulness of priesthood," meaning that what was bestowed upon the truly righteous, what made the Father the Father, was access to and bestowal of priesthood. This may very well be the meaning of D&C 76:95, that those who are saved in the celestial kingdom are "equal in power and in might and in dominion." Thus the "fulness" that gives one "power, might, and dominion" is priesthood power and authority, accessible only to those at the highest levels of the celestial kingdom.[72] Those in the terrestrial will not receive of the "fulness" of the Father, rather they will enjoy the presence or "glory" of the Son, while those in the telestial will receive only the presence of the "Holy Ghost."

With D&C 76, Smith continues to demonstrate a penchant for mining a deeper richness and fruitfulness out of John's text, not simply appropriating the language of John but expanding on themes that lay beneath the surface of the text. The fascinating work of Blake Ostler has done much to emphasize just how important unity is in understanding crucial theological tenets such as the atonement, particularly in Mormon thought. In his discussion of the Mormon concept of deification, Ostler elaborates on the nature of this "fulness:"

> The concept of "a fulness" is intimately connected with the divine glory that characterizes the divine life. "A fulness" in Joseph Smith's revelations refers to the fulness of life and glory that is given by the Father to the Son and which is received by grace from one glory to another in a process of growth and progression. It is this same fulness of glory and light that quickens those who accept Christ and continue to grow in his grace from one glory to another.[73]

The end result of this growth, according to Ostler, is deification:

> Thus, the Mormon doctrine of deification consists of a fulness of the mind, power, and glory of the Father dwelling in the Son by virtue of sharing the common mind which is the Holy Ghost, and because the Saints dwell in the Son through the Holy Spirit, they share the same fulness of divine mind and become one with the Father. In so doing, they are transformed into the same image and likeness as the Father and the Son.[74]

Ostler's observations on the Mormon concept of deification are noteworthy and very much in line with Johannine thought. The teleological purpose of spiritual growth is unity with the Father through the Son. D&C 76 demonstrates that Joseph was beginning to grapple with greater spiritual concerns, attempting to define, as were many of his contemporaries, the relationship between God and man.

While to some readers Joseph Smith's reconstruction of John 1:14 and John 1:16 in these verses may be as frustratingly ambiguous as John 1:16

itself, with its abstract and opaque idea of "fulness," it does reveal something of Joseph Smith's intellectual character. He had a keen sense for finding the "holes" or "knots" present in the scriptures, those places where a writer makes a statement that pushes the reader, taunting them with ambiguity. Much of the Gospel of John, and in particular the Prologue, is filled with ambiguity, and this ambiguity may explain Smith's fondness for expanding upon its language. A statement like "and of his fulness have we all received" demanded something more than a cursory reading. Rather, it invited a theological exploration, summoning Smith to construct a multi-tiered kingdom where humanity would "receive" different levels of "fulness." After all, "receiving" a "fulness" implies that it is possible to receive something less. It is perhaps the myriad of possible explanations behind scriptures such as John 1:14 and 16 that proved tantalizing for Joseph Smith, and he responded with a cogent construction of heaven. Yet it was not enough merely to imagine a three-tiered heaven; Smith further explored and re-defined the means by which the "fulness" could be received. The end result was something of a divine *cursus honorum* that became a *sine qua non* for heavenly exaltation. With D&C 76, and the Johannine language he expanded upon, Joseph Smith endeavored to transform the abstract into reality, devoting time and money to creating the temples where these ordinances could be performed, heavenly gateways of a sort, providing access that was otherwise unavailable.

7. D&C 88:29–31, 48–50

D&C 88 continues the revelatory outburst that had begun months earlier with D&C 76 and is, in many ways, an extension of D&C 76. Where D&C 76 laid out the hierarchy of the afterlife, D&C 88 presents a blueprint for the organization of the universe. During 1832 Joseph Smith had been occupied with the effort to construct his Zion, the kingdom of God on Earth. In this revelation, received in late December 1832,[75] Smith learned that organization is required on even the highest levels of heaven. Much as D&C 76 did, D&C 88 borrows heavily from the language of the Fourth Gospel. D&C 88, termed "the olive leaf," opens with the voice of the Lord proclaiming "wherefore, I now send upon you another comfortor, even upon you my friends; that it may abide in your hearts, even the holy spirit of promise which other comforter, is the same, that I promised unto my deciples, as is recorded in the testamony of John" (D&C 88:3). This verse refers to and even quotes from John 14:26, where Jesus had said "But the Comforter, which is the Holy Ghost, whom the Father will send in my name, he shall teach you all things, and bring all things to your remembrance, whatsoever I have said unto you."[76]

Likely borrowing from the Johannine image of light in John 1, Joseph Smith begins this revelation by constructing what may be termed a "theology of light." Throughout the Gospel of John, light and darkness were significant motifs, serving to distinguish those who believed from those who did not. Nicodemus comes to Jesus "at night" (John 3:2; Cf. 9:4, 11:10, 19:39), but Jesus as the "light of the world" has the power to remove the "darkness" and make men see who once were "blind." Joseph takes this "light" and constructs an emanating force he calls the "light of Christ." Richard Bushman has called D&C 88 a "cohesive compound of cosmology and eschatology united by the attempt to link the quotidian world of the now to the world beyond,"[77] and Smith seems to have two very distinct worlds in mind as he crafts this revelation. On the one hand, the light of the Sun, Stars, and Moon are all manifestations of the light of Christ. But "light" holds a deeper meaning as well in Smith's cosmology: "and the light which now shineth; which giveth you light, is through him which enlightneth your eyes; which is the same light that quickneth your understandings" (D&C 88:11). Here readers learn that the source of knowledge and understanding is this light, and thus it plays both a physical and a spiritual role, providing light for our eyes to see and for our souls to understand. As if an emanation akin to the Gnostic pleroma, this light "procedeth forth from the presence of God; to fill the emencity of space" (D&C 88:12). One gets the sense that without the presence of this "light," the entire universe would cease to exist.

Having established that this "Light of Christ" permeates and affects the entire universe, Smith moves on to the implications of the idea that Jesus is both the "light" and the "life." For Smith, "light" and "life" are not merely two different adjectives used to describe Christ, but a progression toward exaltation. Because Jesus is the "light" that fills the expanse of the universe, he has the power to grant "life" to all those who believe— he is the "life" because he is the "light:" "the light which is in all things which giveth life to all things, which is the law by which all things are govorned, even the power of God, who sitteth upon his throne; who is in the bosom of eternity, who is in the midst of all things" (D&C 88:13).

This "life" is described in the next verses: "Now verily I say unto you, that through the redemption, which is made for you; is brought to pass the resurection from the dead; (and the spirit, and the body is the soul of man) and the resurection from the dead, is the redemption of the soul; and the redemption of the soul, is through him, who quickneth all things, in whose bosom, it is decreed, that the poor, and the meek of the earth, shall inherit it; therefore it must needs be sanctified, from all unrighteousness, that it may be prepared for the celestial glory" (D&C 88:14–17). True "life" is a "quickened" or "resurrected" body, and, significantly, the "redemption of the soul" cannot fully take place until the body has been restored. Again, one sees Smith's high anthropology behind this concept. Men and women will be the creators and propagators of "worlds without number," and in order to accomplish this they require new and improved "enlightened" bodies. God reveals that the primary purpose for there being a "celestial" kingdom is so that perfected men and women have a kingdom in which to dwell: "for this intent was it made, and created, and for this intent, are they sanctified" (D&C 88:20). Ultimately, the Johannine "light" and "life" come together in Smith's three-tiered heaven, as those enlightened by "celestial" light will dwell in a "celestial" kingdom (D&C 88:20), while those who are "not able to abide the law of a celestial kingdom cannot abide a celestial glory" (D&C 88:22), and must either dwell in the terrestrial or telestial kingdoms (D&C 88:23–24). For Smith, light becomes more than just a description of Jesus' place amongst "blind" unbelievers who dwell in the "dark." Rather, the "light of Christ" becomes the means and power by which the universe maintains order, by which men and women learn and grow, and finally the measure by which they are judged and allotted a heavenly kingdom. It flows out from the presence of God into the most intimate of spaces, bringing life to all who receive it.

Joseph Smith next continues the "receive of his fulness" thread which he had begun in D&C 76, although with minor alterations. In D&C 76, it was only the celestial beings who would "receive the fulness" of the Father. Terrestrial and telestial would receive some measure of glory, but not the "fulness." Note the subtle shift in the wording of D&C 88: "ye who are quickened, by a portion, of the celestial glory, shall then receive of the same, even a fulness, and they, who are quickened, by a portion of the Terestriall glory, shall then, receive of the same even a fulness; and also they who are quickened by a portion, of the Telestial glory, shall then receive of the same, even a fulness" (D&C 88:29–31). According to these verses, now inhabitants of each kingdom "receive a fulness," but in D&C 88 the definition of "fulness" appears to have been changed or altered from what it was previously in D&C 76. It is no longer a specific reference to the "fulness" of the Father, but a "fulness" of glory that corresponds to each kingdom. This does not appear to be a reference to the "fulness of priesthood," which is what D&C 76 indicated. Rather, now each kingdom has a certain class or type of "glory," and those who inhabit a certain kingdom receive the "fulness" of that glory.

This usage of fulness differs not only from D&C 76 but from D&C 93 as well, where the use of this phrase next occurs. There are at least two possible reasons for this: 1) Joseph Smith has not yet defined the specific parameters for terms like "fulness." He is comfortable using them, but the temporal proximity of these revelations has not allowed him enough time to sort how exactly he wants a term to be understood. 2) Joseph Smith not only considers the boundaries of the Bible to be malleable, but his own scriptural texts as well. Just as he can borrow a title such as "another comforter" from John 14 and expand it into a "Holy Spirit of Promise," he also considers his own terminology to be adaptable. "Fulness" can mean one thing in D&C 76, another in D&C 88, and then yet another in D&C 93. It is almost as if there are terms or phrases that he is drawn to, that he enjoys using, so much so that he applies them to various circumstances. This certainly seems the case with words like "intelligence" and "light," and may be the case with "fulness" in D&C 88.

The final usage of the Prologue in D&C 88 is somewhat jarring: "I say unto you, he hath seen him, nevertheless, he who came unto his own, was not comprehended, the light shineth in darkness, and the darkness comprehendeth it not, nevertheless, the day shall come, when you shall, comprehend even God, being quickened in him, and by him" (D&C 88:48–49). Readers haven't seen these verses used by Joseph Smith since the early revelations, where they were used mainly in the context of apostasy and restoration. Those ideas are still present in D&C 88, but in what may be a sign of Joseph Smith's intellectual growth or at the very least confidence in his prophetic abilities, he takes these same verses from John 1 and constructs what can best be defined as a teleological argument for the existence of God. Beginning in D&C 88:41, Smith states, speaking of Jesus Christ and returning again to the emanation ideas advanced earlier in D&C 88, that "he comprehendeth all things, and all things, are before him, and all things, are round about him, and he is, above all things, and in all things, and is through all things, and is round about all things and all things are by him, and of him, even God for ever, and ever."

Having established the absolute thoroughness with which God permeates the universe, Smith then elaborates upon the significance of this idea: "And again verily I say unto you, he hath given a law, unto all things, by which they moove in there times, and there seasons, and there cources are fixed, even the cources of the heavens, and the earth which, comprehend the earth, and all the planets" (D&C 88:42–43). Because Jesus Christ permeates every particle of the universe, or, to borrow a Johannine term, "comprehends" them, he is able to impose a law and a course upon "all things," allowing him to determine how the universe will function. One gets the picture of a watch-maker, leaning over a work-bench and carefully adjusting all the gears of a watch, causing it to keep time in perfect fashion. The purpose of this universal illustration is presented in D&C 88:47: "behold all these are kingdoms, and any man, who hath seen, any, or the least of these, have seen God, moving in his magesty and power." It is not necessary for man to see God, all one has to do is look around him, at this world or to the heavens, to observe the divine craftsmanship that has so carefully constructed "all things."

At this point, D&C 88 appropriates language from John 1:9: "I say unto you, he hath seen him, nevertheless, he who came unto his own, was not comprehended, the light shineth in darkness, and the darkness comprehendeth it not, nevertheless, the day shall come, when you shall, comprehend even God, being quickened in him, and by him" (D&C 88:48–49). On at least two fronts, this continues the apostasy/restoration thread from earlier in the Doctrine and Covenants. First, regarding apostasy, the verse more forcefully condemns those who did not receive Jesus, whether speaking of the Jews in the first century or Christians in the nineteenth century. The "nevertheless" of D&C 88:48 hints at a frustrated deity. All "hath seen him," yet there were/are many who still rejected him, and when he "came unto his own his own was not comprehended." Yet there is still hope, for while those in the past may have been unable to "comprehend" the true nature of Jesus, He promises that "the day shall come when you shall comprehend even God."

Second, these verses appear to be promoting the crucial nature of the restoration in a way that hasn't been made explicit yet in the revelations. The "light that shineth in the darkness" in John was Jesus Christ, the incarnate λόγος. It was "belief on his name" that determined those who would "receive" him. Furthermore, it was the testimony of the "witnesses" to the λόγος that provided the impetus for "receiving" him. From the beginning of the Fourth Gospel up to the end, this theme of "witnesses" was crucial, as "the Word is the ultimate truth for all of human history, but is made known through witnesses."[78] John the Baptist (John 1:7, 15, 32, 34; 3:26; 5:33), the Samaritan woman at the well (John 4:39), Jesus' own works (John 5:36; 10:25), the Old Testament (John 5:39), the multitude (John 12:17), the Holy Spirit (John 14–17), John the Evangelist (John 19:35; 21:24), and God himself (John 5:32, 37; 8:18) all bore witness to the divine nature of Jesus.[79] The importance of these numerous witnesses was due to a theological problem: "If God was invisible till Jesus revealed him (1:18), he and Jesus would now remain invisible apart from the believing community modeling in their lives the character of Jesus."[80] In the absence of Jesus, Christians would need to rely upon the witnesses provided in the New Testament documents.

What Joseph Smith accomplishes with the expansion of the language of John 1:5 and 11 in D&C 88:48–49 is to reduce the importance of these witnesses (and by extension the Bible). They were not necessary, since all one needed to do was look around and, in an Emersonian fashion, recognize the divine. There were, in fact, witnesses on a universal scale that would prove to all that God had never left, but remained in "all things." Joseph Smith seems to have believed that Christianity had made a major mistake in assuming that Jesus' physical departure meant a complete departure, forgetting the words of the intercessory prayer, "I in them, and thou in me" (John 17:23), or the image of Jesus as the "true vine:" "Abide in me, and I in you" (John 15:4). Christianity had missed the greatest witness, the universe, the light around them, even their own selves. What Joseph Smith aspired to do is "restore" this vision of Johannine unity. But it would not come *sola scriptura* or *sola fide*. While "the day shall come when you shall comprehend even God," divine intervention would be required: "being quickened in him, and by him" (D&C 88:49).

Finally, we must consider the theme of unity with the divine that Joseph had begun to develop in D&C 76. In that section, it was the "fulness" of the Father that the celestial "receive." In D&C 84, Joseph delved into the idea of priesthood hinted at in Hebrews 7. The result was a genealogy of authority originating with God and passed down through the patriarchs of the Old Testament. This priesthood

> continueth in the church of God in all generations and is without begin-ing of days or end of years and the Lord confirmed a priesthood also upon Aaron and his seed throughout all the generations of the Jews. which priesthood also continueth and abideth for ever with the Priest-hood which is after the holiest order of God, and this greater Priest-hood adminestereth the gospel and holdeth the key of the misteries of the kingdom, even the key of the knowledge of God therefore in the ordinences thereof the power of Godliness is manifest (84:17–20).

Joseph then further refines the Johannine language of "receiving" from D&C 76 to further unite those who have this priesthood with Jesus him-self and the Father:

> and also all they who receive this Priesthood receiveth me saith the Lord for he that receiveth my servants receveth me, and he that receiv-eth me recieveth my father, and he that receiveth my father, receiveth my fathers kingdom, therefore all that my father hath shall be given unto him. (D&C 84:35–38)

In D&C 88, Smith would find a third element connecting humanity to the divine. In a statement that brings all the elements of D&C 88 together Jesus promises, in language clearly borrowed from the Fourth Gospel, that "then shall ye know, that ye have seen me, that I am, and that I am the true light, that is in you, and that you are in me, otherwise ye could not abound" (D&C 88:50). Readers encounter repeated efforts by Joseph Smith to bind together the human and the divine, to bridge the chasm between heaven and earth, to find at the end of humanity's long journey a unity with God. What Joseph Smith's Zion could offer was the realiza-tion of this unity, whether through the construction of temples, where man would be brought into the presence of God, or through preparing the Earth for the millennium, where God would be manifest physically upon the Earth.

In evaluating the different places where Joseph Smith expands upon the language of the Johannine Prologue in the Book of Mormon and the Doctrine and Covenants, a significant feature of Joseph Smith's role as author is revealed. This ability and desire toward the expansion of a biblical text demonstrates both how *familiar* and how *confidant* Smith was with the biblical text. He possesses the capacity not only to repeat or mimic the biblical text, but also the awareness to slightly alter the biblical text in a way that the biblical source is still apparent but the newly-presented text asserts its own unique identity and meaning, one that goes beyond the subtext. This comfort becomes increasingly apparent as Smith produces the "exaltation revelations." Smith is not creating scriptural texts *ex nihilo*; rather in creating scripture he borrows from the scripture that he knows, namely the Bible. Yet what Smith does goes beyond a simple pilfering of holy verse. In her study of Paul's use of Jeremiah, biblical scholar Gail O'Day wrote: "it is the essence of biblical texts to be reinterpreted,"[81] and one can see "reinterpretation" in Smith's expansion of his source, as if he and John were partners in creation, each bringing something to the final product. Theirs is a collaborative effort—John provides the language and the context, Joseph Smith both the re-contextualization of John's language and the confidence or audacity to provide the hermeneutic lens through which John's words ought to be understood. A result of this collaboration comes in the increased expectations they place upon the reader, who is expected to grasp 1) John's language; 2) John's context; and 3) how Joseph Smith has "expanded" upon John, whether by inserting a single word such as "equity" or by re-defining what a phrase such as "grace for grace" can mean. The finished product is a remarkable synthesis of scripture both past and present.

NOTES

1. Paul R. Noble, "Esau, Tamer, and Joseph: Criteria for Identifying Inner-Biblical Allusions," *VT* 52.2 (Apr. 2002): 252. Italics added.

2. Sommer, *Prophet Reads Scripture*, 30.

3. One of the possible implications of expansion is "bi-directional reading," meaning that in addition to allusion, where "an intertextual reference can enhance the meaning of the text that *makes the allusion*," expansion "can extend the potential meaning of the text that is *quoted*" (Merz, "The Fictitious Self-Exposition of Paul," 117). Theoretically, the presence of a passage from the Gospel of John (John 1:13) in the Book of Alma (Alma 36:5) has an impact upon both texts, as Alma 36:5, due to the presence of a Johannine phrase, becomes a possible lens through which to interpret John 1:13. See also Ben-Porat, who writes "It is very probable that the creation of intertextual patterns affects and enriches the evoked text . . . as well. Even if the evoked text preceded the alluding text by several hundred years, a simultaneous activation is possible for the reader of both. Consequently, familiarity with the later text . . . can change or modify the interpretation of the evoked text" ("The Poetics of Literary Allusion," 114 fn. 9).

4. Fishbane, *Biblical Interpretation in Ancient Israel*, 283.

5. Fishbane, *Biblical Interpretation in Ancient Israel*, 291.

6. *Reading Nephi Reading Isaiah*, eds. Joseph M. Spencer and Jenny Webb (Salem: Salt Press, 2011), 10.

7. Spencer and Webb, *Reading Nephi*, 11.

8. The phrases "the only begotten of the Father" and "believe on his name" appear prominently though the literature of the nineteenth century. However, while "full of grace and truth" is also quite common, the insertion of "and mercy" is without precedent in the period. No other writers use that combination of attributes.

9. Joseph Smith's addition (or subtraction) of words within biblical allusions should not be seen as the result of forgetfulness or disrespect for the biblical text: "Indeed, the greater the respect for the text, the more need for deliberate changes to make it appear to say what one wants it to say" (Ferguson, "Factors Leading to the Selection," in *The Canon Debate*, 299).

10. Craig Keener writes: "Although the phrase recurs frequently in the Hebrew Bible and appears elsewhere in Jewish texts, the accumulation of allusions to Exod. 33–34 in John 1:14–18 leaves little doubt that John's phrase is a conscious allusion to

the occurrence in that context" (Keener, *The Gospel of John*, 1:471). See Keener, *The Gospel of John*, 1:495 fn. 395 for a summary of scholarship on this issue.

11. Part of the issue as to whether this allusion is legitimate comes from the problem of language. In the Hebrew, the phrase translated in the KJV as "goodness and truth" is חסד ואמת. In the Greek Septuagint, this becomes ἔλεος καὶ ἀληθινὸς, not the χάριτος καὶ ἀληθεία of John 1:14. However, by the first century AD, it is likely that χάρις has replaced ἔλεος as the preferred rendering of חסד, meaning that first-century readers of the Fourth Gospel would likely recognize 1:14 as an allusion to Exodus 34:6. See C. H. Dodd, *The Interpretation of the Fourth Gospel* (Cambridge: Cambridge University Press, 1958), 175–76.

12. This becomes more apparent when "full of grace, mercy, and truth" is recognized as an example of an *inclusio*, namely the bracketing of something by two similar ideas. Thus the strictly Book of Mormon "mercy" is enveloped or bracketed by the biblical "grace" and "truth." The effect on the reader is to mentally link the Book of Mormon with the Bible, Alma's words with John's, in a way that makes it difficult to distinguish between the two—the phrase is biblical, yet it isn't biblical. Joseph Smith has created something entirely new out of pieces that are two thousand years old. Therein, some might say, lies his genius, namely to create something new and innovative out of archaic building blocks, the deconstruction and reconstruction of scripture in a manner that doesn't merely regurgitate the Bible, but expands upon it.

13. To my knowledge, the phrase "full of grace, equity, and truth" does not appear in literature outside of the Book of Mormon between 1820–1830.

14. Bultmann, *The Gospel of John*, 73.

15. This verse raises a significant question in regards to source. On the one hand, for those who believe the Book of Mormon to be a legitimate record of an ancient American society who had access to the documents constituting the Hebrew Bible, the connection between the connection between Alma 9:26 and Exodus 34:6–7 is to be expected, but how to account for the presence of John 1:14 in a text that supposedly pre-dates the birth of Jesus? On the other hand, for those skeptical of the origins of the Book of Mormon who see the work as the product of Joseph Smith's mind, the connection with John 1:14 is easily explained, but how to account for the connection between Exodus 34:6–7 and Alma 9:26? Joseph Smith would have to know the Fourth Gospel well enough to not only weave quotations from John, but also the sources for those quotations, into his work.

16. J. S. King, "The Prologue to the Fourth Gospel: Some Unresolved Problems," *The Expository Times* (1986): 373.

17. *BDAG*, 87–88.

18. Ruth Edwards, "χάριν ἀντὶ χάριτος (John 1:16): Grace and Law in the Johannine Prologue," *JSNT* 32 (1989): 3–15. Edwards herself prefers #2, writing that χάριν ἀντὶ χάριτος "referred to the replacement of the Mosaic Law by the Gospel." Edwards's survey is an expansion of Brown's three categories of "replacement," "accumulation," and "correspondence." See Brown, *The Gospel of John*, 1:15–16.

19. Ridderbos, *The Gospel of John*, 56.

20. Ridderbos is joined in this belief by Rudolf Bultmann, Edwyn Hoskyns, Joachim Jeremias, J. B. Lightfoot, Barnabas Lindars, and Leon Morris, among others.

21. Barrett, *The Gospel According to St. John*, 168.

22. Thomas Brodie, *The Gospel According to John*, 144. Brown favors an interpretation of "replacement" as well, seeing a similarity between the χάρις of John and the חסד of the Old Testament (Brown, *The Gospel of John*, 1:16).

23. Keener, *The Gospel of John*, 1:420–21.

24. Phillips, *The Prologue of the Fourth Gospel*, 212–13.

25. Balz and Schneider, *Exegetical Dictionary of the New Testament*, 3:95.

26. Robert Kysar writes "The Fourth Evangelist never uses the noun 'faith' or 'belief,' but always and only the verb 'to believe.' . . . What does this mean? . . . Faith is not a state of being but a dynamic becoming. If faith is always a verb, that surely implies that faith is not something one does once and for all time. Rather, faith as a verb means

that believing is a decision made once only to have to be made over and over again, or a gift accepted not once but again and again. Faith is a continuing dynamic, not a state of being" (Robert Kysar, *John: The Maverick Gospel* [London: Westminster John Knox Press, 1993], 94).

27. Gardner, *Second Witness*, 6:376.

28. Out of all the Book of Mormon verses discussed in this work, Moroni 7:26 and 48 represents perhaps the most difficult verses for which to claim a Johannine provenance. The primary reason is that so much of Moroni 7 reflects the language and theology of Paul, with heavy emphasis upon "salvation by faith" and "charity." Paul also uses the phrase "sons of God" in his epistles (Rom. 8: 14–21, for example), but the phrase "become the sons of God" does not appear in Paul, while it does appear prominently in John 1:12. Significantly, Paul does not use "sons of God" in his discussion of charity in 1 Corinthians 13, which is clearly an influence upon Moroni 7. Furthermore, Paul's use of "sons of God" tends to be more centered around corporate election that will be most fully realized in an eschatological sense, while John's use of "sons of God" is more about personal transformation through belief "on his name" toward a state of "abiding" in him. Thus Moroni 7 presents readers with a text heavily influenced by Paul, one that includes the phrase "sons of God," a title with both a Pauline and Johannine provenance. One might expect, in a text so similar to Paul, for "sons of God" to be used in a Pauline sense, but its usage correlates more closely to John.

29. Again, astute readers will note the heavy reliance upon Paul in this chapter, as the phrase "For behold, it is not counted unto him for righteousness" is clearly derived from Romans 4:3 and 5, which were themselves building upon Genesis 15:6. However, the Book of Mormon demonstrates its typical creativity by not simply quoting a passage from the Bible, but expounding on it, pushing its boundaries, as it does in Mormon 7:6–9.

30. Gardner, *Second Witness*, 6:369.

31. This is not to say that there exists a definite correlation between the "power" mentioned in John 1:12 and the "charity" discussed in Moroni 7:48, only that both texts explicitly state that the means of becoming "sons of God" requires divine bestowal.

32. R. Alan Culpepper, "The Pivot of John's Prologue," *NTS* 27 (1980–1981): 28.

33. This clause is clearly an allusion to 1 John 3:2: "Beloved, now are we the sons of God, and it doth not yet appear what we shall be: but we know that, when he shall appear, we shall be like him; for we shall see him as he is."

34. Kittel, *Theological Dictionary*, 1:37.

35. Gordon Fee, *The First Epistle to the Corinthians* (Grand Rapids: William B. Eerdmans Publishing Company, 1987), 631.

36. Barrett, *The Gospel According to St. John*, 215.

37. For the background and context of D&C 45, see MacKay, et al., *The Joseph Smith Papers: Documents, vol. 1*, 274–75.

38. Harper, *Making Sense of the Doctrine and Covenants*, 158.

39. Joseph Smith was not alone in interpreting these verses as a reference to Jesus. Adam Clarke wrote that while "I do not think that these words are spoken at all concerning Jesus Christ," nevertheless "I have heard them quoted in this way; but I cannot hear such an application of them without horror. In quoting from the Old Testament in reference to the New, we cannot be too cautious. We may wound the truth instead of honouring it" (Adam Clarke, *The Holy Bible, Containing the Old and New Testaments* [New York: T. Mason & G. Lane, 1837], 4:795).

40. The quotation of Acts 17:28 in D&C 45:1 is notable on two points: First, D&C 45:1 is the only place in Mormon scripture where Acts 17:28 is quoted. Seeing as how Paul is alluding to humanity being the "offspring" of God, an idea which Joseph Smith will interpret literally, it is curious that he never returns to this verse. Second, Acts 17:28 is composed of two quotations which Paul links together in his discussion with the Athenians. The phrase "in him we live, and move, and have our being" is likely a quotation from a work attributed to Epimenides the Cretan: "For in thee we live, and

move, and have our being." The line "For we are also his offspring" is a quotation from Aratus of Soli: "In every way we have all to do with Zeus, for we are truly his offspring" (see F. F. Bruce, *The Book of the Acts* [Grand Rapids: William B. Eerdmans Publishing Company, 1988], 339). The question this raises for readers of Joseph Smith is how to interpret his appropriation of a biblical verse that is itself an appropriation of earlier sources. Should an intertextual dialogue discussing D&C 45:1 now include Joseph Smith, Paul, Epimenides, and Aratus? Speaking of Paul's use of these earlier poets, F. F. Bruce makes a statement pertinent to Joseph Smith's own use of scripture: "In both these poems Zeus is considered not as the ruler of the traditional pantheon of Greek mythology but as the supreme being of Greek, and especially Stoic, philosophy. But did Paul intend to identify the Zeus of Greek philosophy *simpliciter* with the God of biblical revelation, whom in his letters he repeatedly calls 'the God and Father of our Lord Jesus Christ'? Quite certainly not. Is he then simply detaching from their original contexts sentiments which, so far as their actual phraseology goes, lend themselves to incorporation into his Judaeo-Christian context? Again, no. Even in their contexts, the words quoted (especially those of Aratus) could be taken as pointing to some recognition of the true nature of God" (Bruce, *The Book of the Acts*, 339).

41. See Keener, *The Gospel of John*, 1:380, and Ridderbos, *The Gospel of John*, 36.

42. Ridderbos, *The Gospel of John*, 113.

43. The current situation of Joseph Smith and the Mormons may explain why this revelation so closely links the restored gospel of Joseph Smith and Jesus, with its suggestion that if you reject the former you are rejecting the latter. Joseph Smith's history notes that at the time of the reception of D&C 45, "many false reports, lies, and fo[o]lish stories were published in the newspapers, and circulated in every direction, to prevent people from investigating the work, or embracing the faith." Thus D&C 45, with its outpouring of prophecy and appropriation of the Bible, may have served to directly address the criticism lobbed at Joseph Smith and his prophetic claims.

44. Godfrey, et al., *The Joseph Smith Papers: Documents, vol. 2*, 110–13.

45. This title "father of lights" stands out in a revelation filled with Johannine language and imagery. However, the provenance for the title, and this verse as a whole, is likely James 1:17: "Every good gift and every perfect gift is from above, and cometh down from the Father of lights, with whom is no variableness, neither shadow of turning." This is the only appearance of the title in Mormon scripture and provides an example of how useful an intertextual study of Mormon scripture and the Bible would be outside of merely a Johannine Prologue study.

46. The phrase "know that I am" may allude to John 8:28, which itself likely alludes to the phrase "know that I am the Lord," found nearly 100 times in the Old Testament, again demonstrating Joseph Smith's proclivity for appropriating both the Old and New Testament. This phrase will make a crucial reappearance in D&C 93:1.

47. Ridderbos, *The Gospel of John*, 59.

48. Many scholars see John 1:18 as echoing the theophany of Moses in Exodus 33. See Keener, *The Gospel of John*, 1:442 fn. 562.

49. Brown, *The Gospel According to John*, 1:36.

50. All references to the Joseph Smith Translation (including the Book of Moses) are taken from Scott H. Faulring, Kent P. Jackson, and Robert J. Matthews, eds. *Joseph Smith's New Translation of the Bible: Original Manuscripts* (Provo: Religious Studies Center, 2004).

51. The similarities between this statement and D&C 67 were made more explicit when Moses 1:11 was edited to read: "But now mine own eyes have beheld God; but not my natural, but my spiritual eyes, for my natural eyes could not have beheld; for I should have withered and died in his presence; but his glory was upon me; and I beheld his face, for I was transfigured before him."

52. This is possibly an early reference to what would become known in Mormonism as the "Second Comforter." Joseph Smith taught that Mormons can progress to a certain point at which their "calling and election is made sure," borrowing from the language of 2 Peter 1. This means that their salvation in the highest kingdom, the

celestial kingdom, is assured. Part and parcel with this process is the accompaniment of the "Second Comforter," borrowing from the language of John 14, although meaning in a Mormon context that one enjoys the close association of Jesus Christ himself. Is this revelation, with its promise to rend the veil and "see me and know that I am" a precursor to this idea? Part of the problem is a possible confusion over "God." In John 1:18, the Father is clearly meant when John states that "no one has seen God at any time." But what does it mean in D&C 67? Is Jesus referring to himself as "God," speaking in the third person, or does the context of John 1:18 apply here as well and D&C 67:11 refers to the Father? The fact that D&C 67:10 speaks of the promise to "see me and know that I am" suggests that D&C 67:11 refers to Jesus, not the Father. This does not necessarily invalidate the above argument, however, as Mormons believe that the "God" of the Old Testament, Jehovah, is actually the pre-mortal Jesus Christ, and therefore Moses' vision of "God" would have been of Jesus Christ.

53. Historian Alexander Baugh has identified D&C 76 "visionary experiences" of Joseph Smith. See Alexander L. Baugh, "Parting the Veil: Joseph Smith's Seventy-Six Documented Visionary Experiences," in *Opening the Heavens: Accounts of Divine Manifestations 1820–1844*, ed. John W. Welch (Provo: Brigham Young University Press, 2005), 265–326.

54. Joseph Smith wrote in 1842: "And again, what do we hear? Glad tidings from Cumorah! Moroni, an angel from heaven, declaring the fulfilment of the prophets—the book to be revealed. A voice of the Lord in the wilderness of Fayette, Seneca county, declaring the three witnesses to bear record of the book! The voice of Michael on the banks of the Susquehanna, detecting the devil when he appeared as an angel of light! The voice of Peter, James, and John in the wilderness between Harmony, Susquehanna county, and Colesville, Broome county, on the Susquehanna river, declaring themselves as possessing the keys of the kingdom, and of the dispensation of the fulness of times! And again, the voice of God in the chamber of old Father Whitmer, in Fayette, Seneca county, and at sundry times, and in divers places through all the travels and tribulations of this Church of Jesus Christ of Latter-day Saints! And the voice of Michael, the archangel; the voice of Gabriel, and of Raphael, and of divers angels, from Michael or Adam down to the present time, all declaring their dispensation, their rights, their keys, their honors, their majesty and glory, and the power of their priesthood; giving line upon line, precept upon precept; here a little, and there a little; giving us consolation by holding forth that which is to come, confirming our hope!" (D&C 128:20–21).

55. These five occasions were the June 4, 1831 conference in Kirtland, D&C 76, a March 18, 1833 appearance to the School of the Prophets, a vision of the celestial kingdom on January 21, 1836, and the 1838 account of his "first vision." See Baugh, "Parting the Veil: Joseph Smith's Seventy-Six Document Visionary Experiences," 265–306.

56. The tension between John 1:18 and Smith's vision continues to be noted by those seeking to debunk Mormonism. One such book writes of John 1:18 that "Since Joseph Smith claimed to have seen God the Father, this verse proved to be a problem for him. However, rather than back off from his claim of having seen God, he sought to change Scripture" (John R. Farkas and David A. Reed, *Mormons Answered Verse-by-Verse* [Grand Rapids: Baker Books, 1992], 71). In their treatment of Mormonism, Richard Ostling and Joan K. Ostling wrote that "Mormons believe that spirit is matter, and that those biblical passages implying that God is immaterial must be a mistranslation. Smith freely rewrote biblical passages that conflicted with his own concepts" (*Mormon America: The Power and the Promise* [New York: HarperCollins, 1999], 299).

57. Bushman, *Rough Stone Rolling*, 195. Bushman adds: "During the previous years, the revelations had dealt primarily with establishing the Church and building the City of Zion. They established policy, made assignments, or dealt with current Church problems. The emphasis was on this world. Gathering to Zion received more attention than preparing for the afterlife. The revelations promised an inheritance on earth with little mention of a reward in heaven." However, with the reception of "The Vision,"

this earthly emphasis changed: "It was the first of four revelations over the next fifteen months introducing the theme of exaltation. . . . With 'The Vision,' exaltation took its place alongside the Zion project as a second pillar of Mormon belief."

58. For the background and context of D&C 76, see Godfrey, et al., *The Joseph Smith Papers: Documents, vol. 2*, 179–83.

59. Karen Lynn Davidson, et al., *The Joseph Smith Papers: Histories, vol. 2* (Salt Lake City: The Church Historian's Press, 2012), 222.

60. While Joseph was not the first to attempt pulling back the curtain to offer an illustration of heaven (Emanuel Swedenborg, Alexander Campbell, and Walter Scott all attempted something similar), the impact of Joseph's Vision upon the early Saints was substantial. Mark Staker notes that "The Vision's long-term effect was to set a distinctive mark on Mormon theology; but its short-term effect was to change the Church's relationship with the other Christian denominations in the Western Reserve. Although most revelations were given strictly through Joseph Smith, this vision had two witnesses, two testimonies, two resounding affirmations that the Vision was divinely inspired. When it was recorded, both Joseph and Sidney's names appeared at the end, to affirm that it was a joint witness as found on contemporary legal documents. Joseph Smith recorded the Vision as the first revelation in a new ledger, probably purchased for the purpose, writing parts of it in his own hand" (Staker, *Hearken O Ye People*, 325).

61. Kittel, *Theological Dictionary*, 6:302.

62. Kittel, *Theological Dictionary*, 6:300.

63. Cf. Ridderbos, *The Gospel of John*, 56: "Vs. 16 is intended as a confirmation of vs. 14, and its causal 'for' (ὅτι) is not isolated by the insertion of vs. 15."

64. Keener, *The Gospel of John*, 1:420.

65. Kittel, *Theological Dictionary*, 4:583–85.

66. "'Grace' and 'truth' are used together frequently in the Old Testament of God's relationship to humankind and speak first of all ('grace') of God's favor, benevolence, and mercy" (Ridderbos, *The Gospel of John*, 54).

67. Brown, *The Gospel According to John*, 1:33–34.

68. Ernst Käsemann sees John 17 as the template for understanding the entirety of John's gospel. Of interest to this discussion is the following observation: "But the unity of the community may not be detached from the unity of the Father and Son which is its foundation. For John, unity is a mark and a quality of the heavenly realm in the same way in which truth, light and life are a quality and mark of the heavenly reality" (*The Testament of Jesus According to John 17* (Philadelphia: Fortress Press, 1968), 68.

69. Cook and Ehat, *The Words of Joseph Smith* (Orem: Grandin Books Co., 1991), 109.

70. Cook and Ehat, *The Words of Joseph Smith*, 213.

71. Orson Hyde elaborated further on this point: "Such as have not received the fulness of the priesthood, (for the fulness of the priesthood includes the authority of both king and priest) and have not been anointed and ordained in the temple of the Most High, may obtain salvation in the celestial kingdom, but not a celestial crown. Many are called to enjoy a celestial glory, yet few are chosen to wear a celestial crown, or rather, to be rulers in the celestial kingdom" ("A Diagram of the Kingdom of God." *Millennial Star* 9 [15 January 1847]: 23–24).

72. Joseph Smith defined "fulness of the Priesthood" as "Now for Elijah; the spirit, power and calling of Elijah is that ye have power to hold the keys of the revelations, ordinances, oracles, powers and endowments of the fulness of the Melchizedek Priesthood and of the Kingdom of God on the Earth and to receive, obtain and perform all the ordinances belonging to the kingdom of God . . . [to] have power to seal on earth and in heaven" (Cook and Ehat, *The Words of Joseph Smith*, 306).

73. Blake T. Ostler, *Exploring Mormon Thought: Of God and Gods* (Salt Lake City: Greg Kofford Books, 2008), 366–67.

74. Ostler, *Of God and Gods*, 367.

75. For the background and context of D&C 88, see Godfrey, et al., *The Joseph Smith Papers: Documents, vol. 2*, 334–36.

76. Although outside the scope of this work, this comparison is useful for understanding how Joseph Smith deconstructs and reconstructs scripture. In the Fourth Gospel, Jesus clearly identifies this "comforter" as the Holy Spirit, whose task for the early Christian church was to "bring to your remembrance" the words of Jesus, seeming to function solely as an additional witness that would point Christians toward the truth once Jesus had been resurrected and departed from the world. Yet Joseph Smith takes this reference to another "comforter" and molds it into a figure pivotal for obtaining exaltation. This "Holy Spirit of promise," as he terms it, is a "promise which I gave unto you of eternal life, even the glory of the Celestial Kingdom; Which glory is that of the Church of the first born, even of God the holiest of all, through Jesus Christ his Son" (D&C 88:4–5). On another occasion, Smith stated that "Come to God! Weary him until he blesses you. We are entitled to the same blessings; Jesus, revelations, just men, and angels. Not laying again the doctrine of Christ, go on unto perfection. Obtain that Holy Spirit of Promise, then you can be sealed to eternal life." Smith would later elaborate on the specific function of the Holy Spirit of Promise, stating that it was one of the duties of the Holy Spirit to act as a "ratifier" or "sealer" of eternal covenants, and thus a pivotal figure in Smith's scheme of progression toward exaltation (D&C 132:7).

77. Bushman, *Rough Stone Rolling*, 206.

78. Keener, *The Gospel of John*, 1:391.

79. Barrett, *The Gospel According to St. John*, 159.

80. Keener, *The Gospel of John*, 1:393.

81. Gail R. O'Day, "Jeremiah 9:22–23 and 1 Corinthians 1:26–31: A Study in Intertextuality," *Journal of Biblical Literature*, 109.2 (1990): 260.

FOUR

Mormon Scripture and the Inversion of John

The final category of allusivity as it pertains to Mormon scripture is what has been termed *inversion*. In his study of how the language of the Old Testament figured into the composition of the Book of Revelation, G. K. Beale wrote that "There are some allusions which on the surface are distinctly contradictory to the Old Testament contextual meaning."[1] Beale cites as one example Revelation 3:9, a verse which collectively alludes to statements such as the following in Isaiah: "Thus saith the LORD, The labour of Egypt, and merchandise of Ethiopia and of the Sabeans, men of stature, shall come over unto thee, and they shall be thine: they shall come after thee; in chains they shall come over, and they shall fall down unto thee . . ." (Isa. 45:14).

The passage from Revelation that quotes Isaiah keeps much of the language and meaning, "Behold, I will make them of the synagogue of Satan, which say they are Jews, and are not, but do lie; behold, I will make them to come and worship before thy feet, and to know that I have loved thee," but the context has changed from the nations that will bow down to the Jews (Isaiah) to the Jews who will bow down to the Christians (Revelation). The allusion to the passage in Isaiah by Revelation "shows a consistent ironic understanding of some of the major themes in Isaiah 40–66," but "while such a view arises out of a contextual awareness of the Old Testament, the New Testament use is so diametrically opposite that it is best to categorize it as an inverted or ironic use."[2] Thus inversion is accomplished when a second author adapts the language of a previous author but completely re-contextualizes it to the extent that an opposite meaning is intended by the author. Again, inversion is a function of allusivity, requiring even further that the reader understand the biblical allusion in order to understand how the text has become inverted.

D&C 93 presents one of Joseph Smith's deepest engagements with any text of the Bible and results in what is arguably his greatest theological construction. It also exemplifies within Mormon scripture a use of the Johannine Prologue that qualifies as an "inversion." Here are the first eighteen verses of D&C 93, an example of how Joseph Smith's revelations wove together biblical verses linked with Smith's own biblical language.

> Verely thus saith the Lord, it shall come to pass, that evry soul who forsaketh their sins and cometh unto me and calleth on my name and obeyeth my voice and keepeth all my commandments shall see my face and *know that I am* (John 8:28) *and that I am the true light that lighteth evry man who cometh into the world* (John 1:9); *and that I am in the father and the father in me and the father and I are one* (John 10:30; 14:11) the father because he gave me of his *fulness* and the son becaus I was in the world and *made flesh my tabernacle and dwelt among the sons of men* (John 1:14) I was in the world and received of my father, and the works of him were plainly manifest and John saw and bear record of the *fulness* of (my) glory and the *fulness* of Johns reccord is hereafter to be reveiled and he bear reccord saying I saw his glory that he *was in the begining* (John 1:1) before the world was therefore *in the beginning the word was* (John 1:1) for *he was the word* (John 1:1) even the messenger of salvation *the light* and the reedeemer of the world the *spirit of truth* (John 14:17; 16:13) who came into the world *becaus the world was made by him* (John 1:3) *and in him was the (Life of men) and the light of men* (John 1:4) the worlds were made by him men were made by him *all things were made by him* (John 1:3) and through him and of him and I, John bear reccord that I *beheld his glory as the glory of the only begotten of the father full of grace and truth* even the *spirit of truth* which came and dwelt *in flesh and dwelt among us* (John 1:14) and I John saw that he *received not of the fulness* at the first but received *grace for grace* (John 1:16) and he *received not of the fulness* but continued from *grace to grace* until he *received a fulness* and thus he was called the son of God because he *received not of the fulness* at the first and I John bear reccord and lo the heavens were opened *and the holy ghost decended upon him in the form of a dove and set upon him* (John 1:32) and there came a voice out of heaven saying this is my beloved son, and I John bear reccord *that he received a fulness* of the glory of the father and he receivd all power both in heaven and on earth and the glory of the father was with him for he dwelt in him and it shall come to pass that if you are faithful you shall *receive the fulness* of the reccord of John. (D&C 93:1–18)

Of the sheer scope encompassed by D&C 93, Truman Madsen wrote that this revelation "defines beginningless beginnings, the interrelationships of truth, of light, of intelligence, of agency, of element, of embodiment, of joy. Every sentence, every word, is freighted with meaning. In one fell swoop it cuts many Gordian knots."[3] In addition to providing possible solutions to age-old philosophical issues such as *creatio ex nihilo* and the nature of humanity, Joseph Smith also creates a "vocabulary of exaltation," employing terms such as "intelligence," "light," and "truth," in ways that were unfamiliar or unexplored. Through arguments both ontological and teleological, Smith will essentially arrive at the conclusion that "exaltation" equals the accumulation of "intelligence." But this "intelligence," while it may have included "knowledge" in the sense of facts or data, went beyond the natural and empirical. This "intelligence" was a "capacity for comprehension and insight, accounting for past, present, and future, grasping the moral and spiritual meaning of things, and radiating power. . . . That capacity for seeing and comprehending supernaturally—with the spiritual mind, as he called it—was to him the zenith of human experience."[4] Intelligence is, to put it quite simply (and in Johannine language), "light and truth" (D&C 93:36).

D&C 93 relies upon the Prologue of John in ways heretofore unseen in Smith's corpus, and it is through a (deliberate?) misreading of the Johannine Prologue that Smith found the pieces necessary to construct a theological position that further distorted the borderlines between Christology and anthropology, between heaven and earth, between the sacred and the profane. Stephen Prothero has written that "More than any other great American thinker, with the possible exception of Emerson, Smith blurred the distinction between divinity and humanity."[5] Nowhere is that more clear than D&C 93, a document that stands as Smith's first and perhaps greatest statement on the divine potential of humankind, providing a scriptural justification for the Mormon idea that humanity not only shares its origins with God, but that they can become Gods themselves.[6]

The occasion for receiving the revelation is unclear.[7] Many of Joseph Smith's revelations were sparked by questions he had concerning biblical passages he was revising for his new "translation" of the Bible, but he had already completed work on the New Testament in February of 1833, three months prior to the reception of D&C 93. It is clear, however, that the Gospel of John played a key role. In addition to the language of John, the D&C alludes to something termed "the fulness of Johns reccord," which "is hereafter to be reveiled" (D&C 93:6). Joseph Smith's earlier work, the Book of Mormon, had argued that many biblical texts had been altered over the centuries, stripped of the truth by "that great and abominable church," which had "taken away from the gospel of the Lamb many parts which are plain and most precious; and also many covenants of the Lord have they taken away" (1 Nephi 13:26). It is possible that this "record of John" may have fallen under the knife of the "great and abominable church" as well. To date, this additional "record of John" has not been revealed to the members of the LDS church.

The revelation begins with a promise from the Lord: "Verely thus saith the Lord, it shall come to pass, that evry soul who forsaketh their sins and cometh unto me and calleth on my name and obeyeth my voice and keepeth all my commandments shall see my face and know that I am" (D&C 93:1). This verse lays out five qualifications, in a logical progression, that of necessity occur prior to having an encounter with Jesus Christ. In a way, this is a thesis statement for the revelation. One of the purposes of D&C 93 is to establish the capacity for humanity to become like God. D&C 93:1 informs readers that becoming like God is a process; one does not just choose to become like God and then sit back and let it happen. Rather Jesus requires full commitment from his disciples. The language in this verse is key. Jesus uses five actions verbs—"forsaketh," "cometh," "calleth," "obeyeth," and "keepeth." It is the responsibility of believers to seek out Jesus and align themselves fully with him. Jesus will not force them, but neither will he allow them to wait passively for their turn. Full commitment on every level is expected if one truly hopes to "see my face."

There are at least two points of intersection between this verse and the Gospel of John. The first is the phrase "and know that I am," in which the reader encounters the use of the ἐγώ εἰμί title in the Doctrine and Covenants. As noted above, this absolute usage of the ἐγώ εἰμί was rare in the Fourth Gospel but is more prevalent in Mormon scripture. The title signified the revelation of the true identity of Jesus Christ, by imparting "a theological meaning which involves the idea of a heavenly, unique figure among human beings, to whom the quality of the divine is to be attached."[8] One of the extraordinary aspects about D&C 93 is how easily and completely it collapses the boundaries between sacred and profane. From the very first verse readers are alerted to this quality, as they are told that by progressing through a series of steps, they "shall see my face and know that I am." In the Old Testament these types of theophanies were rare. Moses saw Jehovah on Mount Sinai (Exodus 34:5) and Isaiah had a vision of God sitting upon his throne (Isaiah 6), but these encounters were few and far between. Even the Ark of the Covenant, which symbolized the presence of God on Earth, could only be visited once a year at Yom Kippur, and then only by the High Priest. But D&C 93 offers something different. Now "every soul" is presented with the opportunity for a divine visitation. Furthermore, while the New Testament promised an eschatological encounter with Jesus Christ at some future point in time (1 John 3:2), Joseph's revelations, in particular D&C 88, hint at this encounter taking place in this life, further collapsing the boundaries of the sacred.[9]

This democratization of the sacred provides the second point of intersection with the Gospel of John, in particular the Prologue. One of the purposes of the Prologue was to demonstrate that the status quo *vis a vis* the relationship between Jehovah and his people had changed. Craig S. Keener explains, "As in Exodus, in John's prologue the Word comes to God's people; but here the one who tabernacles among his people and whose glory is revealed is the Word. Here (as in 2 Cor. 3) not Moses but the eyewitnesses of Jesus behold and testify to God's glory; and here the character of covenant love and faithfulness which is the substance of that glory is expressed in Jesus' enfleshment as a mortal human being, which enfleshment climaxes (in the course of the Gospel) in the cross."[10] Thus the Prologue becomes the perfect illustration of the supersessionism of Christianity over Judaism: Whereas only Jews were the "children of God," now the title of "son" was offered to all those who "receive" him. Instead of following the 613 stipulations of the Law of Moses, now Jesus asks that his disciples "believe on his name." The Law may have been "given by Moses," but "grace and truth came by Jesus Christ." Moses could not witness the full glory of God, because God decreed that "Thou canst not see my face: for there shall no man see me, and live" (Ex. 33:20). But with Jesus, the Father becomes available: "he that hath seen me hath seen the Father" (John 14:9). With this in mind, the Prologue becomes the ideal literary platform upon which to construct a doctrine of deification because, just as the Johannine Prologue signified the supersessionism of Christianity over Judaism,[11] Joseph Smith's reworked Prologue will signify the supersessionism of Mormonism over Christianity. He does not merely adopt the language of the Prologue, but the spirit and intent of the Prologue as well.

An additional reason why the Johannine Prologue served as a useful text for Joseph Smith was due to its depiction of the descent of the divine λόγος into a mortal body. The Prologue speaks of how the λόγος was "in the beginning" with God, and that the λόγος itself was divine. At some point, the λόγος descended to the Earth and "was made flesh," before eventually returning to the Father. One of the major themes of D&C 93 is that humankind enjoyed similar origins. D&C 93 aspires to take this same "journey of the Soul" and, again to democratize it. Now everyone, not just Jesus, has embarked on a similar "journey." All began with God, beings constructed out of eternal elements (D&C 93:33). All will descend to earth and "tabernacle" themselves, with the opportunity to follow in the footsteps of Jesus and progress "grace to grace." All who "keepeth his commandments" (D&C 93:27) and learn to "act" (D&C 93:30) for themselves through exercising their "agency" and receiving "the light" (D&C 93:31) will "receive of his fulness" (D&C 93:20) and become "glorified in truth" (D&C 93:28). Just as the λόγος was "in the beginning" with the Father, so "ye were also in the begining with the father" (D&C 93:23). Just as the λόγος descended to Earth and "dwelt among us" in an incarnate state, so also "man is the tabernacle of God" (D&C 93:35).[12] If Joseph Smith sought to introduce and develop the idea that man has divine origins and a divine destiny, the Prologue of John served as the perfect model upon which to construct that theology.

D&C 93:2 continues to explore Johannine language, in this case beginning to hone in specifically on the language of the Johannine Prologue: "and that I am the true light that lighteth evry man who cometh into the world." This statement is an allusion to John 1:9, although the speaker has shifted from third person to first person. The passage continues the promise made in D&C 93:1 that those who fulfill certain requirements "shall see my face and know that I am." Two important ideas emerge from this verse. First, readers learn that Jesus is "the true light." While there may exist other philosophies or avenues that purport to possess the ability to lead one toward immortality or salvation, those types of "light" are empty, for only Jesus is the "true light," the only being who possesses the ability to offer divine aid.[13] As Bultmann notes, Jesus "is the *proper, authentic* light, who alone can fulfil the claim to give existence the proper understanding of itself."[14] Thus the exclusivity of John's Gospel makes a re-appearance, although this time it is beautifully cast in the language of Smith's revelations, as if to say that only by offering belief in the God described by Joseph Smith can one obtain divine status.[15] But while the term "true light" implies exclusivity, the promise that "every man" will receive some of this light is inclusive, suggesting that those who fall short of the true understanding of the light do so due to their own inadequacies, not because Jesus was unavailable to them.

A second important point is the development of "light," an image that appears repeatedly throughout D&C 93. The verb translated as "lighteth" in John 1:9, φωτίζει, can mean either "to cause to be illumined" or "to make known in reference to the inner life or transcendent matters and thus enlighten."[16] Johannine scholars differ on how to interpret the term "light." According to C. K. Barrett, "light" is best understood in John 1:9 (and throughout the Gospel) in the first sense: ". . . the function of light is judgement; when it shines, some come to it, others do not. It is not true that all men have a natural affinity with the light . . . the light shines upon every man for judgement, to reveal what he is."[17] Raymond Brown takes the opposite approach, stating that "Verse 7 . . . seems to imply a light that one believes in."[18] Herman Ridderbos takes a position in between the two, writing that John 1:9 "does not say that every individual is in fact enlightened by the light but that by its coming into the world the light is for every human being that by which alone he or she can live."[19]

Joseph Smith himself seems to have viewed "light" in a variety of ways: 1) Smith likely saw "light" as the means by which things were, literally, made visible. In an earlier revelation, Joseph Smith had said: "this is the light of Christ as also he is in the sun, and the light of the son, and the power thereof by which it was made, as also he is in the moon, and is, the light of the moon, and the power thereof, by which it was made, as also the light of the stars, and the power thereof; by which they were made; and the earth also, and the power thereof, even the earth upon which you stand" (D&C 88:7–10). 2) Smith also, like Barrett, saw the "light" as an instrument of judgment, where insufficient light brings down condemnation: "behold here is the agency of man and here is the condemnation of man because that which was from the begining is plainly manifest unto them and they receive not the light" (D&C 93:31). 3) However, Joseph Smith also viewed "light" as the ability to perceive the spiritual and the sacred, a sort of "spiritual I.Q." D&C 88 states of the light that "the light which now shineth; which giveth you light, is through him which enlightneth your eyes; which is the same light that quickneth your understandings, which light, procedeth forth from the presence of God; to fill the emencity of space; the light which is in all things which giveth life to all things, which is the law by which all things are govorned, even the power of God, who sitteth upon his throne; who is in the bosom of eternity, who is in the midst of all things" (D&C 88:11–13). In D&C 93, the full implications of the "light" are made apparent. Jesus states that "he that keepeth his commandments receiveth truth and light untill he is glorified in truth and knoweth all things" (D&C 93:28). Future happiness depends heavily upon the accumulation of "light." Both these points serve to establish, from the beginning of the revelation, the crucial idea that there exists a definite link between Jesus and humanity, one made manifest through "light."

D&C 93:3 emphasizes the close relationship shared by Jesus and the Father: "and that I am in the father and the father in me and the father and I are one." This is the third appearance of this phrase thus far in the revelations. In addition to D&C 93:3, the phrase is found in D&C 35:2 and D&C 50:43:

> I am Jesus Christ the son of God who was crusified for the sins of the World even as will believe on my name that they may become the sons of God *even one in me as I am in the Father as the Father is one in me that we may be one.* (D&C 35:2)

> *and the father and I are one I am in the father and the father in me and* I in as much as ye have received me ye are in me and I in you. (D&C 50:43)[20]

All three seem to be allusions to John 17:21–23:

> That they all may be one; *as thou, Father, art in me, and I in thee,* that they also may be one in us: that the world may believe that thou hast sent me. And the glory which thou gavest me I have given them; that they may be one, even as we are one: I in them, and thou in me, that they may be made perfect in one; and that the world may know that thou hast sent me, and hast loved them, as thou hast loved me. (John 17:21–23)

The allusion to John 17 is significant for understanding both the theology behind D&C 93 and how the Johannine Prologue interacts with Joseph Smith's revelations. In John 17, one of the key terms is "unity." Jesus prays that the disciples may "be one" just as Jesus and the Father "are one." Jesus, who has received the glory of the Father, bestows that glory upon the disciples, with the end result that "I in them, and thou in me, that they may be made perfect in one" (John 17:23). It is almost as if Jesus functions as a mediator or "middle-man," linking the Father and the disciples through himself, and just as he is the "agent" acting on behalf of the Father, the disciples become "fellow agents."[21] Thus John 17 serves to establish a connection or link between three groups: the Father, the Son, and the disciples. While the exact nature of this connection or link remains disputed, the purpose of the union is to serve as a witness of the mission of the Son and of the love of the Father for the world.[22]

As with D&C 76, 84, and 88, in D&C 93, this concept of "unity" linking the Father, Son, and the disciples becomes pivotal, and in this section Smith gives his most fully developed idea of what that link entails.[23] Joseph Smith is going to suggest that there is both an *ontological* link and a *teleological* link between the Father, the Son, and humanity.[24] First, Joseph teaches that humanity is constructed of something he calls "spirit" (D&C 93:32). This "spirit" is a tangible material, since "There is no such thing as immaterial matter. All spirit is matter, but it is more fine or pure, and can only be discerned by purer eyes" (D&C 131:7). Thus men and women of the Earth share the material or elements out of which God the Father and the Son are constructed, to some degree. The only difference is the level of refinement of the matter and the degree of intelligence.[25]

Next, there exists a teleological trajectory similarly found in the Father, the Son, and humanity. D&C 93 establishes that Jesus "received not of the fulness at the first but received grace for grace" (D&C 93:12). Jesus then tells Joseph that "if you keep my commandments you shall receive of his fulness and be glorified in me as I am glorified in the father, therefore I say unto you you shall receive grace for grace" (D&C 93:20). Both Jesus and humanity did not "receive of his fulness" at first, and both must "receive grace for grace."[26] Jesus becomes the example for all others to follow—if we wish to be like him, we must follow in his footsteps. In his discussion of D&C 93, Samuel M. Brown has noted that "While Americans have famously recast Christ in their own image for centuries . . . Mormons radically recast themselves in the image of Christ."[27] Nowhere is this more apparent than the trajectory established by Smith as he pondered Jesus Christ's divine evolution. By 1844, Smith made a statement that synthesized the language of John 17 and D&C 93 even further: "What did Jesus do? Why I do the things I saw my Father do when worlds came rolling into existence. I saw my Father work out his kingdom with fear and trembling, and I must do the same; and when I get my kingdom I shall present it to my Father, so that he obtains kingdom upon kingdom, and it will exalt his glory, so that Jesus treads in his tracks to inherit what God did before."[28] Jesus followed the path laid out by the Father, and it is then up to us, as his disciples, to do the same: "Here then is eternal life, to know the only wise and true God. You have got to learn how to be Gods yourselves; to be kings and priests to God, the same as all Gods have done; by going from a small degree to another, from grace to grace, from exaltation to exaltation, until you are able to sit in glory as doth those who sit enthroned in everlasting power."[29] Blake T. Ostler notes the significance of John 17 for the Mormon concept of deification: "In the Gospel of John, the indwelling love of the Father and the Son is shared by the disciples and is the basis of salvation for the disciples through a process of deification. We share the same unity in the divine relationship that is shared by the Father and the Son."[30] Although D&C 93:3 did not borrow language from the Prologue of John, its use of John 17 established a point crucial for the forthcoming verses that will utilize John 1, namely that humanity and divinity share common, significant links, and through these links we have the potential to be "one" in the Father and the Son.

By alluding to John 17, D&C 93:3 focused the reader's attention upon the unity of the Father and the Son.[31] But D&C 93:4 takes that expectation and expounds upon it by introducing the Book of Mormon concept of how Jesus is both the Father and the Son: "the father because he gave me of his fulness and the son becaus I was in the world and made flesh my tabernacle and dwelt among the sons of men." In Mosiah 15, Abinadi taught that Jesus was the "Father" because "he was conceived by the power of God" and the "Son" "because of the flesh" (Mos. 15:3). The result of this was a unity where "the will of the Son" was "swallowed up in the will of the Father" (Mos.15:7). D&C 93:4 offers a further explanation for how Jesus can both be "Father" and "Son" and in the process seamlessly links John 17 and Mosiah 15, the Bible with the Book of Mormon. Additionally, D&C 93:4 contains allusions to the Johannine Prologue and thus foreshadows the proto-Prologue that will follow in the subsequent verses.

First, Joseph Smith says that Jesus is the Father "because he gave me of his fulness." The term "fulness" appears once in the Fourth Gospel, in John 1:16: "And of his fulness have all we received, and grace for grace." The term in the Greek is πλήρωμα, which, as we have seen, is a rather loaded term means something akin to "totality" but is perhaps best understood in John 1:16 as alluding back to John 1:14, namely that that all those who receive the λόγος receive of the "grace and truth" with which he himself is "full." But Joseph Smith adds a twist to this idea—the Son can be called the "Father" because the true "Father" bestowed upon the Son his "fulness." One of the primary purposes of the opening verses of D&C 93 has been to establish something of a chain linking the Father, the Son, and humanity. D&C 93:4 continues this theme. John 1:16, which teaches that humanity can receive of the "fulness" of the Son, provides half of the "link," D&C 93:4, which teaches that the Son received "fulness" from the Father, the other half. Thus the Father bestows upon the Son, the Son bestows upon humanity. D&C 93:4 further strengthens or reenforces this chain of unity, but the reader only grasps the full implications of this if they are familiar with John 1:16.

The second connection between D&C 93:4 and the Johannine Prologue comes from the phrase "I was in the world and made flesh my tabernacle and dwelt among the sons of men." In John 1:14, to which this phrase alludes, the purpose is to demonstrate that the divine, pre-existent λόγος became fully incarnate, taking upon itself a human body without having to surrender any divinity. One of John's purposes in penning the Fourth Gospel was likely to combat docetism, which taught that Jesus only *appeared* to exist in human form but was in reality an incorporeal spirit. John, however, wants his readers to view Jesus as an incarnate deity, for "It is in his sheer humanity that he is the Revealer."[32] There is now a connection between the λόγος and humanity: "The Logos becomes part of the world of humanity, *kosmos* with all the associations of that world, earthbound, transient and perishable, part of the realm of first appearances . . . the Logos is one with the reader. He shares in the very same nature—he too is a human being."[33] Again, this unity is paramount for Joseph Smith and the theology of D&C 93, in particular verse 3, with its allusion to John 17, unified Father, Son, and humanity. The first half of D&C 93:4 more explicitly unifies Father and Son, while the second half of D&C 93:4 unifies, through reference to the incarnation, the Son and humanity. It is readily apparent that the author of D&C 93 needs readers to understand that Father, Son, and humanity, the divine and the mortal, are fully conjoined—they share a common origin, and they potentially share a common destiny.

D&C 93:5 reads best as a summary or synopsis of the preceding four verses: "I was in the world and received of my father, and the works of him were plainly manifest." The crucial points established by this statement are that 1) Jesus Christ himself was in the world. He descended to Earth and dwelt among men. This is important in establishing a connection between Jesus and humanity. Jesus was not in the heavens or on some transcendent plane where he communicated with humanity from afar through some sort of revelation. He himself was literally, physically, upon the Earth; 2) Jesus received of his Father. This establishes a connection or link between Jesus and the Father. Even though Jesus was physically upon the Earth, he is still connected to the Father. What he "received" from the Father is likely the "fulness" from D&C 93:4, although what that "fulness" entailed is not elaborated upon.[34] Finally, 3) the Father's works are plainly manifest upon Earth, for all to see. D&C 93:1–4 has so far linked Jesus to humanity and Jesus to the Father. This final verse, D&C 93:5, provides the last link, namely the Father to humanity. Jesus performs works, but they are the Father's works, and "he that hath seen me hath seen the Father" (John 14:9). This verse is the final verse of this introductory section of D&C 93.

With D&C 93:6, Smith introduces into his revelation the first reference to a "proto-Prologue" of "John."[35] For this to be an actual Johannine text, this record would have to pre-date extant copies of John 1:1–18 as well as serve as a parent text for what eventually became the Prologue of John's gospel: "and John saw and bear record of the fulness of my glory and the fulness of Johns reccord is hereafter to be reveiled." One pressing question is *which* John is being referred to in 93:6? Did Smith have John the Baptist or John the Apostle in mind? If Smith intended John the Baptist, this would imply that the current Prologue of John 1 was redacted from an earlier text penned by John the Baptist, to be "revealed" at some future point.[36] The apostle John would then have come into contact with this record through his association with the Baptist.[37] This was the view of some early Mormon writers. John Taylor quotes from D&C 93 and lists it under the title "Record of John the Baptist."[38] Orson Pratt referred to the "record of John" as being penned by "him who baptized the Lamb of God."[39] More recently, Mormon Apostle Bruce R. McConkie wrote "From latter-day revelation we learn that the material in the forepart of the gospel of John (the Apostle, Revelator, and Beloved Disciple) was written originally by John the Baptist. . . . The latter John either copied or paraphrased what the earlier prophet of the same name had written."[40] However, "all editions of the Doctrine and Covenants since 1921 imply that these were the writings of John the Apostle."[41] For clarification purposes, the "text" of John embedded in D&C 93 will be termed the "proto-Prologue" of John, while the author of the "proto-Prologue" will be distinguished from the Evangelist as "John."

With D&C 93:7, "and he bear reccord saying I saw his glory that he was in the begining before the world was" the proto-Prologue of John proper begins.[42] As Smith presents it, D&C 93:7 (and D&C 93:8) would be the "original" reading of John 1:1: "In the beginning was the Word, and the Word was with God, and the Word was God." One significant point raised by this verse is the claim by "John" that "I saw his glory that he was in the begining." This verse is an allusion to John 1:14, where John claims in a similar fashion that "we beheld his glory, the glory as of the only begotten of the Father."[43] In D&C 93:6, Smith claimed that "John" "saw and bear record of the fulness of my glory." In D&C 93:7, this witnessing of the "fulness of my glory" now includes Jesus' pre-mortal existence, since "John" additionally asserts that Jesus was "in the beginning, before the world was." Perhaps "John" is saying that he witnessed an event where he "saw his glory" and thus knew that Jesus was "in the beginning?"[44] If so, Smith may have intended this statement to refer to the baptismal scene, where John the Baptist saw "the Spirit descending from heaven like a dove, and it abode upon him" (John 1:32), or it could be a reference to the appearance of the resurrected Jesus to the disciples in John 20. The most logical example of the revealing of Jesus' "glory" would be the events of the Mount of Transfiguration, but that story is absent from the Fourth Gospel.

With D&C 93:8, Smith will begin to lay the groundwork for a Christological depiction of Jesus that will differ from that of John and in the

process introduce his "inversion." D&C 93:8 reads "therefore in the beginning the word was for he was the word even the messenger of salvation." This statement continues the line of thinking present in D&C 93:7
by placing emphasis upon the pre-earthly existence of the Word. On one
hand, this redundancy between the wording of D&C 93:7 and 8, in particular the repetition of the phrase "in the beginning" could be attributed to
the appropriation of John 1:1. But there may be a theological explanation
for the redundancy as well. One of the major themes behind D&C 93 is
the pre-mortal, eternal existence of everything. The elements "are eternal" (D&C 93:33), intelligence cannot be "created or made" (D&C
93:29).[45] It is significant for the reader to understand that Jesus Christ
existed pre-mortally as well, as Jesus will become the model for humanity
to follow—if he was "in the beginning," then we were as well.[46] Additionally, there may be a literary reason for the dual "in the beginnings" in
D&C 93:7 and 8. Some Johannine scholars believe that the first words of
John, "in the beginning was the Word," were meant to allude to the
opening words of Genesis, to demonstrate that a second creation was
about to occur with the incarnation of the λόγος.[47] By having two separate "in the beginnings," one in D&C 93:7 and one in D&C 93:8, Joseph
Smith may be following the example of John and alluding to both the
opening of Genesis and the opening of John, thus appropriating, again,
the Jewish Old Testament and the Christian New Testament.

However, one significance of D&C 93:8 comes in what it lacks. Notable by its absence in the verse is the third clause from John 1:1, καὶ θεὸς
ἦν ὁ λόγος. This clause is somewhat problematic and goes straight to the
heart of trinitarianism: Is Jesus God or is He a separate being like God?
Christian theologians have grappled with this clause from John 1:1 for
nearly two thousand years, yet Smith omits it from his "proto-Prologue."
Perhaps it was omitted merely to avoid entering into the contemporary
debates over the trinity which would distract from the message of D&C
93. In a subsequent verse, Joseph Smith will state that Jesus "received not
of the fulness but continued from grace to grace until he received a fulness" (D&C 93:13). More likely, however, is that Smith left out the Johannine claim that Jesus "was God" because it would conflict with the Christology advocated later in D&C 93, and thus readers get here their initial
glimpse at Smith's "inversion" of John, a location where the collision
between Johannine language and Joseph Smith's theology fosters dissonance.

This dissonance continues with the presence of the title "messenger of
salvation." D&C 93:8 appears to be implying that "messenger of salvation" is a comparable title for "word."[48] Much debate has arisen among
Johannine scholars over the meaning of the title λόγος,[49] translated as
"word" in John 1. Is the λόγος "the supreme revelation of God?"[50] The
female expression of divinity who may be connected with the biblical
Sophia?[51] The hypostatization of divine speech?[52] A Gnostic Redeem-

er?[53] A "divine communication"?[54] Is a title like "messenger of salvation" out of place amidst all these other attempts to define λόγος ? In some ways, no. The term λόγος derives from the Greek verb λέγω, meaning "to express oneself orally or in written form" or "to inform about/tell of something."[55] Surely the title "messenger" fits that designation. And what did the λόγος bring with him? According to Peter, "the words of eternal life" (John 6:68). However, what Joseph Smith's understanding of "Word" seems to lack is some conception of the λόγος as a divine entity or force. A "messenger" could simply refer to a missionary or an angel, while the Greek λόγος hints at something more cosmic or divine. Yet this understanding of Jesus as "messenger" rather than λόγος is actually quite consistent with the absence of the clause καὶ θεὸς ἦν ὁ λόγος from D&C 93:8. Again, this dissonance in Johannine titles likely stems from Smith's theological leanings. He has borrowed the language of John, but the theology of D&C 93 dictates a lower Christology, thus necessitating certain editorial adjustments, including a redefining of λόγος and the omission of καὶ θεὸς ἦν ὁ λόγος. In the process, Joseph Smith avoids titles or language that will promote too high of a Christology.

D&C 93:9 continues the attempts to define who and what Jesus is by assigning titles: "the light and the redeemer of the world the spirit of truth who 'came' into the world becaus the world was made by him and in him was the Life of men and the light of men." The first title, "light," is very much a Johannine term. It is used in the Prologue for the λόγος (John 1:4–5) and Jesus even refers to himself as the "light of the world" who offers the "light of life" (John 8:12). But while "light" may be a consistent Johannine title, one that a reader may expect to encounter in an "original" record of John, "redeemer" is not. While the words "redeem" and "redemption" do appear in the New Testament,[56] the noun "redeemer" is absent. Additionally, fourteen of its eighteen Old Testament usages are limited to the prophecies of Isaiah. However, this title is much more prominent in Mormon scripture, appearing over sixty times in the Book of Mormon and the Doctrine and Covenants, a trend that suggests the influence of Joseph Smith more than that of John.

As with "redeemer," there is also some dissonance with the next title "John" attributes to Jesus, the "spirit of truth." Like "light," this title is very much Johannine, one that appears only in Johannine texts (John 14:17; 15:26; 16:13; 1 John 4:6).[57] But in the Johannine context, the term "spirit of truth" referred to the Holy Spirit who would act as a "successor" of sorts once Jesus had departed. All three passages from the Fourth Gospel clearly delineate between Jesus and the Holy Spirit; while Jesus may be the παράκλητος, the Holy Spirit will function as the ἄλλον παράκλητον. Thus while "spirit of truth" may apply to the Holy Spirit, it is unlikely that the Johannine Jesus would use it of himself.[58] Yet in D&C 93:9 the title is clearly being used to describe Jesus Christ, again hinting at the separation between Smith's text and John's, even if much of the language will be identical.

After the jarring nature of the titles "redeemer" and "spirit of truth" in D&C 93:9, the verse ends with the much more Johannine "the world was made by him and in him was the Life of men and the light of men." The clause "the world was made by him" alludes nicely to John 1:3: "All things were made by him," while the complementary pair "the Life of men and the light of men" is a slight re-working of John 1:4: "In him was life; and the life was the light of men." As with much of Joseph Smith's work, this verse feels, at first glance, to be very biblical. Readers are told that these verses represent an unavailable record of John, and terms like "life" and "light" gently coax readers to see a Johannine provenance. Yet a closer investigation again reveals a slight dissonance, the presence of "redeemer" and a misapplication of "spirit of truth" remind readers that what Joseph Smith is doing is not merely recapitulation, but re-creation or reconstruction. He sets his readers up to expect one thing, and then gives them something else, forcing them to reconcile ideas and language, presenting what appears to be a deliberate misreading under the shroud of divine revelation, as if God himself desires to shift our own personal biblical paradigms.[59]

Joseph Smith continues to build his "proto-Prologue" in D&C 93:10: "the worlds were made by him men were made by him all things were made by him and through him and of him." John 1:3 states that "All things were made by him; and without him was not any thing made that was made." Joseph Smith adds two additional nuances. First, he takes "all things" and breaks it down into three separate categories: 1) "worlds," 2) "men," and 3) "all things." It appears that Smith has taken the Johannine "all things" and elaborated on it by emphasizing "worlds" and "men" as subcategories of "all things," or else he views "worlds" and "men" and "all things" as separate, perhaps considering "all things" as inanimate, non-living objects. The interesting term here is the appearance of "worlds." The word "world" only appears in one verse in the Prologue, John 1:10, and there it is clearly singular. The previous verse, D&C 93:9, also includes several uses of "world," but singular rather than plural. The presence of "worlds" rather than "world" in D&C 93:10 is again slightly dissonant. If we as readers had come upon D&C 93:10 not having read D&C 93:9, then we may have passed over "worlds" without much thought. But D&C 93:9 emphasizes "world," and then D&C 93:10 gives us "worlds," as if the intent is to highlight the latter term.

A second item of note is the clause "by him and through him and of him." This is reminiscent of language from Joseph Smith's vision in D&C 76: "that *by him and through him and of him* the worlds are made and were created and the inhabitants thereof are begotten sons and daughters unto God" (D&C 76:24). The reproduction of this clause from D&C 76:24 in D&C 93:10, along with the presence of the terms "worlds" as well as "fulness" in both, strongly hints at a connection between the two revelations. Joseph Smith has borrowed language and terminology from D&C 76 in the construction of D&C 93, which was his own literary construction, and then presented it as the "fulness" of John's record.

The subsequent verse, D&C 93:11, "and I, John bear reccord that I beheld his glory as the glory of the only begotten of the father full of grace and truth even the spirit of truth which came and dwelt in flesh and dwelt among us," again seems very Johannine at first, since it is clearly alluding to John 1:14:

> And the Word was made *flesh*, and *dwelt among us*, (and we *beheld his glory, the glory as of the only begotten of the Father*), *full of grace and truth.*

There are, however, three minor differences between the two texts. First, the use of "I" vs. "We." The proto-Prologue is attributed to one individual, identified as "John." The Gospel, on the other hand, uses the first person plural ἐθεασάμεθα. This plurality of witnesses will be a theme of the Gospel from beginning (John 1:14) to end (John 21:24). Second, "came and dwelt in flesh" vs. "was made flesh." This is a difference that comes out in the Greek of John 1:14 more so than in the English of the King James Bible. John uses the verb ἐγένετο for "was made," a verb that at its most basic level means "to become." As Ridderbos observes, this does not mean that the Word was "changed into" flesh, but it does illustrate a link between the divine and the human that goes to the heart of what the incarnation represents. Ridderbos continues: "At stake here is the Word's act of being united with the man Jesus such that in his self-revelation in words and deeds the glory of the Word of the beginning manifested itself, visibly and audibly, and is interpreted by him as such with a recurrent appeal to his Sonship and his having been sent by the Father. Thus 'became' refers to a mode of existence in which the deity of Christ can no more be abstracted from his humanity than the reverse." [60]

This paradox that John develops between the divinity and humanity of Jesus is lost to some extent in D&C 93, where Jesus "came and dwelt in the flesh." John also says that Jesus "dwelt" among us, and the verb he uses there is ἐσκήνωσεν, which literally means "to tent" or more generally "to abide or dwell in a tabernacle." It is this verb, "to tent," rather than "to become," that D&C 93 focuses on, suggesting that Jesus' body was something akin to a "shell" or "tent" and downplaying a deeper, fundamental connection between his humanity and his divinity. [61] Perhaps this tension is implied in D&C 93, but the verbal pairing of "came" and "dwelt" as a description of the paradox of the *kenosis* seems a cursory one, lacking the depth given it by the Johannine "was made" and "dwelt."

Finally, the presence of "spirit of truth." As we saw earlier, this is a Johannine title that referred to the Holy Spirit, not to Jesus himself. Its use in D&C 93:9 was surprising, especially when coupled with Redeemer. Its place in D&C 93:11 seems to be playing off of the noun "truth," as if because Jesus is "full of grace and truth" he is qualified to be called the "spirit of truth." This play on words is possible in the Greek text as well, as both John 1:14 ("full of grace and truth") and John 14:17 ("Spirit of truth") both use the genitive noun ἀληθείας. Likely this connection in D&C 93:11 can be attributed to Joseph Smith creatively connecting two Johannine usages of "truth," since it seems a stretch to see Joseph Smith going to such lengths to twice call Jesus a "spirit," especially in a verse such as D&C 93:11 that is describing his incarnation. The Christology of D&C 93, as laid out in D&C 93:8–11, seems inconsistent at times. Jesus is the "word," the "light," and the "creator," but he is also a "messenger" and a "Spirit."

To borrow a phrase from R. Alan Culpepper, D&C 93:12–14 represents the "pivot" of D&C 93: "and I John saw that he received not of the fulness at the first but received grace for grace and he received not of the fulness but continued from grace to grace until he received a fulness and thus he was called the son of God because he received not of the fulness at the first." Up until this point, D&C 93 has emphasized, largely through an assortment of titles, the eternal nature and mission of Jesus Christ. He is the eternal word, the messenger of salvation, redeemer, the Spirit of truth, the creator of "all things," and finally the "Only Begotten of the Father." Joseph Smith has constructed a Christology that is all-encompassing, with one exception—Jesus Christ is not identified in D&C 93 as "God," in direct contrast to John 1:1. Now, in D&C 93:12–14, the inversion that Joseph Smith has been subtly constructing comes into focus. According to "John," Jesus did not "receive of the fulness" at the first. He did not begin as "God" or as the "mind" of God. Rather, Jesus went through a progression, a journey of sorts that eventually led to his "receiving of a fulness," but only after continuing "grace for grace" and "grace to grace." These verses are crucial for understanding both the relationship between the Father and Jesus, as well as the relationship between the Father and humanity, as these three verses "are the first detailed indication in the Restoration scriptures of what has come to be called the principle of progression or of becoming like God."[62] The purpose of these verses will be to establish a divine paradigm, a pattern by which humanity cannot only progress in a similar fashion as Jesus but also end up like Jesus, by "receiving of a fulness." In addition to fulness, which we examined in the previous chapter, there are three phrases that need further examination.

First is the Johannine allusion "grace for grace." This phrase appears biblically only in John 1:17 and in Mormon scripture only in Helaman 12:24. As we earlier discussed, scholars differ on their interpretation of the phrase in John 1:17, with possibilities ranging from the "accumulation" of grace to a "compensatory exchange" of grace, that as we act "graciously" toward others, God acts "graciously" toward us. This idea of "grace for grace" as a "compensatory" act is also how the phrase seems to be employed in Helaman 12:14. Once we repent and turn our minds and hearts toward performing "good works," we enter into a relationship with God where he "exchanges" or bestows upon us his "grace" for the "grace" we have shown to others through our works. It is not our works that save us, rather the grace we receive by virtue of performing those works. Thus the phrase implies a reciprocal relationship between the Father and the Son, and by extension the Father and us. In the context of D&C 93:12, the presence of the phrase would indicate that Jesus progressed due to his demonstration of "grace" toward others. As Jesus prayed and acted on behalf of others, grace would be bestowed both upon the party being prayed for and upon Jesus himself.

This use of John 1:17 is crucial to D&C 93's overall theme of constructing a paradigm for salvation. In John, it is "we" who receive "grace for grace" from Jesus, who has a "fulness." In D&C 93, it is Jesus who receives "grace for grace" from the Father, who likewise has a "fulness." If either of these verses are read without attention being given to the other, the reader misses half of the equation and sees only the relationship between Jesus and the Father or humanity and Jesus. But to readers who have both verses in mind, a tripartite schema is established wherein the Father gives to Jesus, who gives to us, and wherein we need Jesus, just as Jesus needs the Father. This verse begins the paradigm by establishing a relationship between Jesus and the Father that is similar to the one mentioned in John regarding Jesus and humanity. It is not just the fulness we are meant to receive from Jesus, but his example as well, for just as he progresses "grace for grace" so also do we.

Second, the pivotal phrase "Grace to grace." D&C 93:13 reads almost identically to D&C 93:14 with the exception of this phrase "grace to grace" and the verb "continued" rather than "received." Two grammatical points assist readers in interpreting the nuanced meaning of this phrase. First, the obvious switch in prepositions from "for" to "to." The "for" reflects the implicit reciprocity, namely that you receive something "for" something else. The "to" may suggest something slightly different, something directional, something that requires movement. You go "to" somewhere or something only "from" somewhere else. This interpretation suggests that "grace to grace" implies a "progression" or a "movement toward" something else. Second, the change in verbs is also useful in understanding what this phrase means. Both "receive" and "continue" are active verbs, but the former again suggests the reciprocity implicit in "grace for grace," while "continue" suggests "movement" or "progression," the actions required to complete an as yet incomplete endeavor. Furthermore, this idea of "progression" is supported by the use of the preposition "until" as well. This is an instance of the context of a phrase providing its definition, for "grace to grace" is unique in scripture.[63]

What D&C 93:13 implies is a second dimension at work in Jesus' progression toward the "fulness." Robinson observes that "The key to this verse is the word *to*, indicating that there are levels of grace, or degrees to which one may enjoy the grace and God and act graciously toward others. Thus from birth on, we move forward in a process of learning and responding to God's grace, which process can, if we continue in it, lead us to receive a fulness of God's grace, or gifts." [64] Thus D&C 93:13 expands upon D&C 93:12. At a fundamental level, Jesus progressed "grace for grace" in that he received "grace" from the Father for his own acts of "grace." But D&C 93:13 makes clear that this exchange of grace is only continuous in that grace is exchanged, but not continuous in *how much* grace is exchanged. Apparently, there are "degrees" or "levels" of grace that must be obtained in order to allow one to progress. Perhaps one could use the example of a student who receives a grade from a teacher in exchange for work provided. This is "grace for grace." But the student, in order to progress, must continually move up, from first to second grade, from high school to college, at each point of receiving a grade in exchange for work done. This is "grace to grace." It is also highly ironic, as D&C 93 has constructed what appears to be a "theology of works" but is, quite literally, a "theology of grace."

Finally, the title "the Son of God." This title played an important role in the Christology of the Fourth Gospel, and was arguably the most important indicator of Jesus' divine status. "Son of God" appears eight times in the Fourth Gospel, and "Son" eighteen, as opposed to the three Synoptic usages of "Son." The distinction between humanity and the true "Son" of God comes across most clearly in the Gospel of John, where "there is a consistent linguistic distinction between being a son of God and a child of God. Only Christ is now υἱός. In distinction from him believers are exclusively τέκνα." [65] The Synoptics tend to reserve the references to Jesus as "Son" for highly significant moments in the narrative, such as the Lucan annunciation (Luke 1:35), Jesus' baptism (Mark 1:11), or his temptation in the wilderness (Matt. 4:3–6), whereas in the Fourth Gospel the title can occur at any time. In the words of one scholar, "There can be no doubt that we have here an essential theme of Johannine theology and Christology. The 'Father-Son' relationship is the key to the understanding of Jesus as portrayed by the evangelist, and of his words and actions as interpreted by him." [66]

The significance of the title "Son of God" and "Son" comes in the way it is used in the Gospel of John, in particular its relationship with God as "Father." In perhaps the single most striking statement in all of the Fourth Gospel, Jesus claims that "I and my Father are one" (John 10:30). When the Jews take up stones to punish him for his blasphemy, he further elaborates that "the Father is in me, and I in him" (John 10:38). There is an unmistakable claim of unity by Jesus with the Father. The Fourth Gospel goes to great lengths to establish the unity between Father and

Son. Jesus is the λόγος due to his proximity with the Father in a way that exceeds space and time. The λόγος is the mind of God—it may be able to separate itself temporally and spatially to become incarnate, but it is still God's mind, his reason; it is still a part of him. This absolute unity at the heart of the "Son" Christology is perhaps most resounding in a discourse given by Jesus to the Jews in John 5, one for which the Jews also attempt to stone him because he was "making himself equal with God" (John 5:18) In this discourse he states that "The Son can do nothing of himself, but what he seeth the Father do: for what things soever he doeth, these also doeth the Son likewise" (John 5:19). Here John emphasizes the unity of the two and the Son's absolute reliance upon the Father. This unity is again emphasized a few verses later when Jesus states that "He that honoureth not the Son honoureth not the Father which hath sent him" (John 5:23). Additionally, the Son carries the full authority of the Father, as demonstrated in John 5:22, "For the Father judgeth no man, but hath committed all judgment unto the Son," and John 6:27 "Labour not for the meat which perisheth, but for that meat which endureth unto everlasting life, which the Son of man shall give unto you: for him hath God the Father sealed."

With D&C 93:14 again takes a Johannine phrase and inverts it. Jesus is called "the son of God" not because of his absolute unity with the Father or his role as divine agent, but rather because "he received not of the fulness at first." As before, the author of D&C 93 seems to be hesitant to identify the mortal Jesus as "God." Where John uses the title "Son of God" to establish a link between the Father and Jesus, D&C 93 seems to be using the title to distance Jesus from God, as a way of explaining why Jesus is not God. The use of "thus" and "because" establish a causal link between Jesus being "son of God" and his "not receiving the fulness at the first." There is clearly a connection between "son of God" and "not receiving of the fulness at the first." The fact that Jesus is not called "God" in the Christological statement in D&C 93:8–11, combined with the wording of D&C 93:14, strongly indicates the author's intent was to downplay the divinity of the mortal Jesus prior to his resurrection. This required, once again, an "inversion" or "redefinition" of a well-known and important Johannine title, but it allowed the author to preserve one of his pivotal ideas—namely that Jesus and humanity have enough in common that Jesus can be looked to as an example of how one does become divine. To make Jesus a "God" at an earlier phase of his existence would risk negating the common ground between him and humanity.

Following the inversion of the previous three verses, D&C 93:15 returns to a more familiar description of events in a way that supplies a narrative foundation for the inversion: "and I John bear reccord and lo the heavens were opened and the holy ghost decended upon him in the form of a dove and sat upon him and there came a voice out of heaven saying this is my beloved son." The previous verses spoke of how, at

some point, Jesus did not yet have a "fulness" but that he was progressing through the accumulation of "grace" toward receiving a "fulness."
Up to this point in the revelation, the temporality of Jesus' progression
has been ambiguous—there were no markers within the text to allow
readers to know where Jesus was "in time." Pre-mortal? Mortal? Post-
mortal? Now, in D&C 93:15, readers encounter the one reference to an
earthly event—the baptism of Jesus. Prior to D&C 93:15 Jesus doesn't
possess the "fulness." Yet by D&C 93:16 he does. There are at least two
possible ways to interpret this transition. First, the explicit mention of the
baptism in D&C 93:15 is meant to indicate the actual point in time when
Jesus received the fulness, meaning that the baptism itself was the crucial
moment in which this reception occurred. Second, D&C 93:15 and D&C
93:16 are simply referring to two separate events.[67] While the baptism is
explicitly mentioned in D&C 93:15, there is a second moment in Jesus'
ministry that is alluded to in D&C 93:16 where Jesus actually receives of
the "fulness." Why D&C 93 would not reveal the event beyond "John's"
statement that it happened is unknown, although it is tantalizing to see
the Mount of Transfiguration, an episode that is, ironically enough, also
absent from John's gospel as the location of Jesus' reception of the "fulness."

Theologically, D&C 93:16 finally reveals to readers what exactly the
"fulness" is, namely the "glory of the Father." The word "glory" is an
important word in the Fourth Gospel, particularly in John 17 where Jesus
offers his intercessory prayer. First, Jesus asks: "And now, O Father, glorify thou me with thine own self with the glory which I had with thee
before the world was" (John 17:5). Here Jesus appears to speak of his pre-
mortal "glory," the state of divinity he had previously held as the one
who was once "with God" and even "God" himself. The idea that the
glory Jesus would be receiving was something he had once had but had
temporarily abandoned, something akin to the theology behind the
Christ-hymn in Philippians 2:6–11, goes against the logical flow of D&C
93, which teaches that Jesus' glory was not received "at the first." Jesus'
second statement in John 17 is, however, more in line with D&C 93's
purpose: "And the glory which thou gavest me I have given them; that
they may be one, even as we are one" (John 17:22). This verse re-estab-
lishes the connection between the Father, Son, and humanity that had
been so crucial at the beginning of the revelation: The Father gave glory
to the Son, the Son both received and gave glory, and humanity received
glory. It is this three-level relationship between Father, Son, and humanity that D&C 93 is attempting to explicate further.

The terms "fulness" and "glory" in these verses also play a notable
role. In its Johannine context, the "fulness," or πλήρωμα, seemed to be an
allusion to the phrase "full of grace and truth" of John 1:14. It was then
this "fulness" that Jesus passed on to humanity. The presence of "received," "fulness," and "grace for grace" in both John 1:17 and D&C 93:12

suggests that the author of D&C 93 intended the reader to see a link between the two verses. If so, then readers would need to explain how Jesus was, at some point in his progression, lacking "grace and truth." Is this a reference to the pre-mortal Jesus, who reached a point prior to his incarnation where he became "full of grace and truth" and was thus prepared to condescend to Earth? Or does this refer to his actual incarnation, that he received the "fulness" only upon becoming "flesh" and dwelling upon the Earth? The first correlates with the Gospel of John better than the second, as in the Fourth Gospel Jesus arrives upon earth already "full of grace and truth." However, this connection with John 1:14 may actually assist in understanding D&C 67, where the Father was curiously described as being "full of grace and truth." If readers take John 1:16 to understand "fulness" to mean "full of grace and truth," and pair it with D&C 93:16 which speaks of the "fulness of the Father," the implication is that the Father is "full of grace and truth," which is what D&C 67 explicitly states. Furthermore, now that Jesus has "received of the fulness of the glory of the Father," he, like the Father, can be described as being "full of grace and truth." Thus the statement in John 1:14 may be anachronistic, but it is correct.

D&C 93:18, with its promise that "and it shall come to pass that if you are faithful you shall receive the fulness of the reccord of John," marks the end of the record of "John" proper. This verse does present something of an irony, as readers are given a condition that "if you are faithful" then "you shall receive of the fulness." This is an example of the "grace for grace" method of worship presented in D&C 93:12, namely that if we act "graciously" then God "graces" us with a blessing, in this case the fulness of John's record. Thus God integrates the practical application of "grace for grace" within a text explicating the theory and significance of "grace for grace."

Finally, in D&C 93:19–20, Joseph Smith expounds upon the reasons behind revealing part of the record of "John:" "I give unto you these sayings that you may understand and know how to worship and know what you worship that you may come unto the father in my name and in due time receive of his fulness for if you keep my commandments you shall receive of his fulness and be glorified in me as I am glorified in the father, therefore I say unto you you shall receive grace for grace." Smith then lays out, through the voice of "the Lord," four distinct purpose clauses in order to illustrate *why* the record of "John" has been revealed. The first one, "that you may understand and know how to worship," is a little ambiguous, as it is unclear how revealing the record of John assists in helping humanity "understand and know how to worship." There are two possibilities: First, this is a reference to progression "grace for grace" and its inherent reciprocity. As we demonstrate "grace" in our words and actions toward others, we are demonstrating our love and devotion for the God who gives us life. This correlates well with one of Jesus' teachings in the Olivet discourse that "Inasmuch as ye have done it unto one of the least of these my brethren, ye have done it unto me" (Matt. 25:40). Establishing reciprocal relationships, both with each other and with God, serves as the highest form of worship, and if we cannot learn to act with "grace" toward one another we cannot be worthy of receiving "grace" from God.

A second possibility is more practical. In D&C 93:20 God lists the requirement that we "keep my commandments." This phrase alludes back to D&C 93:1, the verse that began the entire revelation: "Verily thus saith the Lord, it shall come to pass, that evry soul who forsaketh their sins and cometh unto me and calleth on my name and obeyeth my voice and keepeth all my commandments shall see my face and know that I am." Understood in the context of D&C 93:19, D&C 93:1 is laying out the methodology for true worship: the forsaking of sins; coming unto God; calling upon his name; obeying his voice; and keeping his commandments. Either way, this first point establishes a baseline for discipleship, the first step in our own progression "grace to grace."

The second purpose clause, "know what you worship," ties back to a major theme of D&C 93, namely the promise that those who follow Jesus "shall see my face and know that I am." This revelation places a great emphasis upon "knowing" God. What do readers learn about Jesus from D&C 93? Jesus is "the true light" (D&C 93:2), one who is "in the father and the father in me" (D&C 93:3). He was "in the world" and manifested the "works" of God (D&C 93:5). He had a glory "in the beginning" (D&C 93:7) and brought the good news of "salvation" (D&C 93:8). He is the "light and redeemer" and the "spirit of truth" who made not only the "world" but also the "worlds" (D&C 93:9–10). He is the "only begotten of the father" who chose to dwell "in the flesh" (D&C 93:11), to progress "grace for grace" (D&C 93:12) and "grace to grace" (D&C 93:13), finally receiving "a fulness of the glory of the father" (D&C 93:16). He stands as one who holds "all power both in heaven and on earth" (D&C 93:17), and out of "grace" he offers the same to all who follow him. It is crucial that readers realize both that Jesus holds "all power" and held glory "in the beginning" so that they feel confident placing their eternal lives in his hands. Yet they must also know that, for all his grand stature, he still had to progress through different stages of existence, the highs and the lows of the soul's journey, so that they know it can be done.

The first two purpose clauses carefully build toward the third: "that you may come unto the father in my name." As we learn how to worship through the expression of grace and or through keeping the commandments, we come to understand who Jesus is, why it can be said of him that he is "full of grace and truth." We reach a point in our progressions where we have refined ourselves spiritually, become worthy to come into the presence of God, but only by taking upon ourselves the "name" of Jesus Christ. We can get there, but only through him, for he is "the way, the truth, and the life" (John 14:6). The final purpose clause, the promise that "In due time receive of his fulness" alludes back to D&C 93:18, re-enforcing for readers the idea that obtaining the "fulness" of the Father is not just limited to Jesus Christ, but is accessible to "every soul" (D&C 93:1). It is not easily attainable; one must "keep my commandments," and even then the "fulness" will only be received "in due time."

With the final phrase, "therefore I say unto you you shall receive grace for grace," Smith makes explicit what had been implicit, namely that the purpose of the record of John was to demonstrate that Jesus was to serve as a model for humanity. He received "grace for grace" and eventually "received a fulness." Now he tells us that we are to "receive grace for grace" with the hopes of eventually "receiving a fulness" as well. He is the model, the paradigm, the pattern that all must follow. In the Fourth Gospel, Jesus stated that "No man cometh unto the Father but by me." D&C 93 expands upon this idea, explicating for readers how we come "by him." It is not merely that we listen to him or promise to do what he asks, but we endeavor to follow his example, to strive to imitate him not merely in regards to how he lived his life on earth, but how he lived his life from the beginning of his existence. Once we have done that, once we have taken this *imitatio Christi* to heart and truly striven to follow in his steps, then we shall "see my face and know that I am" (D&C 93:1).

Many interesting observations can be drawn from this intertextual reading of D&C 93. Most importantly, D&C 93 of the Doctrine and Cove-nants demonstrates a thorough "deconstruction" and "reconstruction" of the Johannine Prologue in terms of its language, its context, its basic meaning, and its theology. This re-contextualizing of John represents strong evidence that Joseph Smith viewed part of his prophetic mission as granting him the prerogative to redefine and rewrite scripture. Joseph Smith, as creative and imaginative as he was, seems to have been hesitant to merely create theology or doctrines *ex nihilo*. The Bible was crucial to his prophetic identity. Anything new, such as his three-tiered kingdom or his eventual foray into plural marriage, required a biblical source. Where there wasn't one, or where he saw one that wasn't explicit enough, he produced one, whether through a "vision" of Moses, a new "translation," or, as in this case, a "record of John." To some readers, this may appear disingenuous, a way of legitimizing his own beliefs and doctrines with a divine "stamp-of-approval," raising doubt as to whether the text present-ed anything of value. For other readers, in particular those who accept Smith's prophetic role, they may simply view it as a "more correct" or "more accurate" version of the Gospel of John and thus miss something as well. One prominent Mormon has stated that "The Joseph Smith Translation, or Inspired Version, is a thousand times over the best Bible now existing on earth."[68] While this sentiment may be true from the perspective of some believers, it promotes an attitude of dismissal and disregard for the Bible. While Joseph Smith himself may have doubted the accuracy of some of its translation, the Bible was still and always "the word of God."[69] Smith himself was constantly engaging the Bible, its language, its stories, its teachings. While much of what he brought out of the Bible may not be best described as "biblical," these ideas still had their genesis in the Bible. By integrating biblical verses into his own scriptural voice, as Smith so often does, Mormon scripture calls out to readers, begging them to engage the text on more than just a superficial level, one that gives proper due to texts both ancient and modern. A close examination of D&C 93 demonstrates that an intertextual dialogue between the Bible and Mormon scripture has value, that identifying both points of similarity and difference, points where contact is made and missed, opens up new areas of investigation, answering old questions while asking new ones.

However, the primary way to appreciate how significant the changes to the Johannine Prologue are is to recognize and understand the original meaning. D&C 93 represents the only "inverted" use of the Johannine Prologue, one where the original context needs to be understood so that the reader can identify the places where Joseph Smith has taken a verse or a *pericope*, broken it down and constructed something entirely different, wholly new, and contrary to how the source text had read. There is a certain amount of audacity not only in this type of scriptural reconstruction, but in claiming one's reconstruction is, in fact, the original construction. This type of textual claim urges its readers to compare the two texts, and while readers of D&C 93 can still gain a great amount of insight and understanding into Joseph Smith's theology without being aware of its Johannine provenance, an awareness of the original challenges readers to perform their own "deconstruction" and "reconstruction," as they examine the text, looking for points of contact and points of divergence, gleaning insights from deep within the text.

It may be that the radical nature of D&C 93 was due in large part to its nineteenth-century religious context. On one hand, some readers may note that what Joseph Smith was advocating in D&C 93 reflected many ideas popular in early nineteenth-century New England, especially among the more liberal theologians. At the heart of the "New England Theology" made popular by the successors of Jonathan Edwards was a modification of "Original Sin" and "Human Depravity" as men like Nathaniel W. Taylor and Joseph Bellamy sought to find a place within Calvinism for an increasing confidence in the ability of man to achieve his desires, and an affirmation of humanity's potential. Regeneration was not a single act fully engineered by God, but a cooperative endeavor between God and man. In a similar fashion, Unitarianism emerged built upon a platform of a lower *Christology* but a higher *anthropology*. By advocating belief in only "one God," they demoted Jesus to a lesser being, but in the process they elevated humanity by linking it with Jesus. In his 1819 Baltimore sermon, the emerging spokesman for Unitarianism William Ellery

Channing stated that "We believe that Jesus is one mind, one soul, one being, as truly one as we are, and equally distinct from the one God."[70] This distinction allows Christ to serve as a model for us: "for though so far above us he is still one of us, and is only an illustration of the capacities which we all possess."[71] Ralph Waldo Emerson would take Channing's words to their logical conclusion by humanizing Jesus and deifying humankind, a pantheistic vision that rejected the supernatural in favor of the natural, holding up the figure of Jesus as a "good man" but denouncing his miracles as "Monster."[72] The Universalist movement of John Murray and Hosea Ballou would likewise deny the divinity of Jesus Christ and a substitutionary atonement, proclaiming instead the "universal" salvation of all humankind at the hands of a loving God. One of the leading figures of the period, Horace Bushnell, would affirm the accuracy of a "moral influence" theory of atonement, which claimed that Jesus was the "best of the best" as far as humanity was concerned, and that the purpose of his ministry and sacrifice was to provide a "moral example" for humanity to follow. D&C 93 appears very much to be entering into a dialogue with these contemporary religious conversations. In this revelation, Joseph Smith seemingly reduces the divinity of Jesus as one who "received not of the fulness" at first. He elevates the divine potential of humanity, promising that they too can "receive of the fulness." He constructs a paradigm for all—not just the elect—to follow as a means of salvation.

But at the same time, Smith also seems to be pushing back against this liberal religious tide on at least two critical fronts. First, while Jesus may have at one time been without the "fulness" of the Father, he has now "received all power." The presence of so many Christological titles for Jesus in D&C 93:8–11 demonstrates the breadth and scope of Joseph Smith's Jesus, a being who is creator and redeemer, spirit and light. This vision of Jesus, a figure who is on one hand the all-powerful creator and redeemer yet on the other is also "progressing" toward a "fulness," is a paradox that D&C 93 never fully resolves, but it is clear that while the lower Christology of D&C 93:12–14 may have mirrored that of contemporary religious movements, Joseph Smith was not content to completely strip divinity from Jesus, even if it meant widening the gulf between humanity and God.

Second, Channing and others saw a divine potentiality within humanity, a "likeness to God" that could be realized through "the Perfection of Human Nature, the elevation of men into nobler being."[73] This potentiality could be obtained through human effort, seemingly negating the need for grace. The question was no longer "is grace irresistible" but "is grace necessary?" This too was further than Joseph Smith was comfortable going. Yes, humanity could reach a point where they could "receive of the fulness," but only by progressing "grace for grace" and "grace to grace." The presence of these phrases, one from the Bible and one not, but both built around "grace," suggests that Smith viewed grace as a necessity, even if his definition of "grace" differed slightly from others. It may be somewhat striking to see the word "grace" appear six times in a span of nine verses that preach the divine potential of man and describe a lower Christology (at least from a Johannine perspective) to Jesus, but it is just that tension that runs through so much of Smith's writings in a way that often attracts some while frustrating others. If certain elements of D&C 93 seemed to be in dialogue with liberal Christianity, this restoration of divinity to Jesus and an emphasis upon grace brings Smith closer to the likes of Charles Finney and the "Second Great Awakening."

It is uncanny how many of the issues that occupy Joseph Smith's writings appeared at a time when they were culturally relevant, to believers a sign of divine intention and to skeptics a sign of fraud. Alexander Campbell famously stated that the *Book of Mormon* resolves "every error and almost every truth discussed in New York for the last ten years."[74] It is not so difficult to see D&C 93 as filling a similar role, providing a synthesis of the major religious issues that were sweeping through the eastern states. Who was Jesus—Deity or sage? Who is man—Human or divine? Is grace necessary, or does humanity have inherent within themselves the capacity to rise beyond its divine assistance? But the uniqueness of Joseph Smith comes not in what answers he provides, but in how he provides the answers. Channing and Finney were great thinkers, but they provided answers to questions about the Bible from within the Bible. Joseph Smith didn't. By assuming the role of prophet, he felt empowered to take scripture from the Bible, sometimes phrases, sometimes passages, and re-image them. He could answer the great philosophical questions not because he was intelligent but because he believed himself prophetic, because when he needed an answer he believed God would provide one, whether through revelation or through ancient texts or, in the case of D&C 93, both.

NOTES

1. Gregory K. Beale, *John's Use of the Old Testament in Revelation* (Sheffield: Sheffield Academic Press, 1998), 122.

2. Beale, *John's Use of the Old Testament*, 123.

3. Truman Madsen, *Joseph Smith: The Prophet* (Salt Lake City: Deseret Book, 2008), 140–41.

4. Bushman, *Rough Stone Rolling*, 208.

5. Stephen Prothero, *American Jesus: How the Son of God Became a National Icon* (New York: Farrar, Straus and Giroux, 2003), 181.

6. Blake Ostler writes of D&C 93: "There is in these scriptures the undeniable structure of comparison between humans and Christ, demonstrating that Christ became what we are that we might become what Christ is. The focus of this revelation is clear: We are Christified to the extent we receive the glory of God or light and truth. We are deified to the extent that we keep the commandments of God because, to that same extent, we express the love that is definitive of participating in the divine na-

ture. . . . This revelation illustrates the profound sense of sonship and being like Christ that is expressed in 1 John 3:1–4. However, this revelation adds that, by participating in the light or energies of God, we are also like him in the sense that we participate in the fulness of divine knowledge and power" (Ostler, *Of God and Gods*, 369).

7. For the circumstances of the reception of D&C 93, see Gerrit John Dirkmaat, et al., *The Joseph Smith Papers: Documents, vol. 3* (Salt Lake City: The Church Historian's Press, 2014), 83–85.

8. Elizabeth Harris, *Prologue and Gospel: the Theology of the Fourth Evangelist* (London: T&T Clark, 1994), 133. Catrin H. Williams, citing specifically the use of the title in John 8:58, writes that "This pronouncement is so distinctive in its form and content that a Jewish audience cannot fail to recognize its significance as a divine self-proclamation" ("'I Am' or 'I Am He'? Self-Declaratory Pronouncements in the Fourth Gospel and Rabbinic Traditions," in *Jesus and the Johannine Tradition*, eds. Tom Thatcher and Robert T. Fortna [London: Westminster John Knox Press, 2001], 351).

9. D&C 88:3–4 promises, in a *pericope* inspired by John 14, that "Wherefore, I now send upon you another Comforter, even upon you my friends, that it may abide in your hearts, even the Holy Spirit of promise; which other Comforter is the same that I promised unto my disciples, as is recorded in the testimony of John. This Comforter is the promise which I give unto you of eternal life, even the glory of the celestial kingdom." Regarding these verses, Joseph Smith taught that "Now what is this other Comforter? It is no more or less than the *Lord Jesus Christ* himself and this is the sum and substance of the whole matter; that when any man obtains this last Comforter he will have the personage of Jesus Christ to attend him or appear unto him from time to time and even he will manifest the Father unto him and they will take up their abode with him and the visions of the heavens will be opened unto him and the Lord will teach him face to face and he may have a perfect knowledge of the mysteries of the kingdom of God" (Cook and Ehat, *The Words of Joseph Smith*, 5).

10. Keener, *The Gospel of John*, 1:405.

11. R. A. Culpepper writes "The statement that the Messiah came to 'his own' and 'his own' did not receive him (1:11) is not in and of itself anti-Jewish. . . . Nevertheless, the axiom remains valid that the more Jewish the Christology, the more it is apt to be anti-Jewish. Claims of fulfillment easily mutate into claims of replacement, that is, that apart from its fulfillment in Jesus, Judaism is no longer valid. . . . The effect of this fulfillment/replacement motif is that the Gospel declares, by means of various specific illustrations, that Judaism apart from its fulfillment in Jesus has been rendered invalid by his coming" ("Anti-Judaism as a Theological Problem," in *Anti-Judaism and the Fourth Gospel*, eds. Reimund Bieringer, Didier Pollefeyt, and Frederique Vandecasteele-Vanneuville [Louisville: Westminster John Knox Press, 2001], 72).

12. This similarity is more apparent in the Greek. The Greek word used in John 1:14 for "dwelt" is ἐσκήνωσεν, which literally means "to live, settle, take up residence." The noun ἡ σκηνή often referred to the tabernacle or sanctuary of a deity (Ex. 27:21; 29:4; Lev 1:1; Num. 1:1; cf. Heb. 9:2, 6, 7; 13:10) (*BDAG*, 928–29). Thus D&C 93's description of the physical body as "the tabernacle of God" continues the trend of adopting the language and theology of the Johannine Prologue throughout the section.

13. This idea is reinforced by the use of the adjective ἀληθινόν, which is best understood as "real," "genuine," or "authentic," and is to be distinguished from ἀληθής, which "is applied only to opinions and statements, and those who hold or make them" (Barrett, *The Gospel According to St. John*, 160).

14. Bultmann, *The Gospel of John*, 52.

15. Ridderbos states that "Here it also has a clearly exclusive meaning, referring as it does to the 'uniqueness' of Jesus" (*The Gospel of John*, 43).

16. *BDAG*, 1074.

17. Barrett, *The Gospel According to St. John*, 161.

18. Brown, *The Gospel According to John*, 1:9.

19. Ridderbos, *The Gospel of John*, 43.

20. It is interesting to note that D&C 50:40–45 shares many similarities with D&C 93:1–3, 20:"Behold ye are little Children and ye cannot bear all things now ye must *grow in grace and in the knowledge of the truth* fear not little children for you are mine and I have overcome the world and you are of them that my Father hath given me and none of them which my father hath given me shall be lost and *the father and I are one I am in the father and the father in me and in as much as ye have received me you are in me and I in you* wherefore I am in your midst and I am the good shepherd and the day cometh that you shall *hear my voice and see me and know that I am*" (D&C 50:40–45). Now compare: "Verily, thus saith the Lord, it shall come to pass, that every soul who forsaketh their sins, and cometh unto me, and calleth on my name, and *obeyeth my voice,* and keepeth all my commandments, *shall see my face and know that I am* and that I am the true light that lighteth every man who cometh into the world and *that I am in the Father, and the Father in me: And the Father and I are one.* . . . For if you keep my commandments you shall receive of his fulness, and be glorified in me, as I am glorified in the Father. Therefore, I say unto you, *you shall receive grace for grace*" (93:1–3, 20). Perhaps D&C 50:40–45 is something akin to a "proto-text" for D&C 93, providing the "seed" for the "fruit" of D&C 93, or perhaps D&C 93 presents a midrash on D&C 50.

21. Ridderbos, *The Gospel of John,* 563.

22. Bultmann interprets the unity as one of contributing to the formation of an "eschatological community" (Bultmann, *The Gospel of John,* 517), while Francis J. Maloney argues for a unity in the sense of a "oneness of love" (Maloney, *The Gospel of John,* 474). Craig Keener sees the possibility of an "ethnic unity" but states that the primary function of the unity in John 17 is one of example: "But in any case, the loving unity between the Father and the Son provides a model for believers, not necessarily a metaphysical, mystical ground for it" (Keener, *The Gospel of John,* 2:1062). Raymond Brown observes that while the exact nature of the unity remains a topic of debate, "Sooner or later most authors say that it is a union of love" (Brown, *The Gospel According to John,* 2:776).

23. John 17 plays a crucial role in Mormon arguments for deification. Blake Ostler writes that "The scripture most often cited in Mormon sources to support our shared divinity is John 17, known also as Christ's High Priestly prayer because it is a prayer of intercession. John 17 is a glimpse into the amazingly intimate prayer of Jesus as it was known in the Johannine community. The sense of intimacy is so strong that the boundaries and barriers of alienation between Father and Son are dissolved and the glory that Christ enjoyed with the Father before he became mortal is restored to him during this prayer" (Ostler, *Of God and Gods,* 420).

24. Sidney B. Sperry writes: "At any rate, there is a physical and spiritual rapport between the Father and the Son, and between them and ourselves when we receive them, that is but vaguely understood by us" (Sidney B. Sperry, *Doctrine and Covenants Compendium* [Salt Lake City: Bookcraft, 1965], 470).

25. Joseph Smith would go on to teach that ". . . God had materials to organize from—chaos—chaotic matter.—element had an existence from the time he had. The pure pure principles of element are principles that never can be destroyed—they may be organized and re organized=but not destroyed" (Cook and Ehat, *The Words of Joseph Smith,* 359). Compare Parley P. Pratt, who wrote that "God, angels and men are all of one species" (Pratt, *Key to the Science of Theology* [Liverpool: F.D. Richards, 1855]), 33. What writers like Smith and Pratt seem to be hinting at is an emerging doctrine of emanation. Pratt would write on another occasion that "the redeemed to return to the fountain, and become *part* of the great *all,* from which they emanated. Hence the propriety of calling them "GODS, even the *sons of God*" (Pratt, *Mormonism Unveiled* [Painesville, OH: 1838], 27). One revelation, dated 1833 and described only as "Sang by the gift of Tongues and Translated" records that Enoch "saw the beginning the end of man he saw the time when Adam his father was made and he saw that he was in eternity before a grain of dust in the balance was weighed he saw that he emenated and came down from God he saw what had passed and then was and is present and to

come" (Robin Scott Jensen, et al., *The Joseph Smith Papers: Revelations, vol. 1,* 509). It was presumably this idea of "emanation," that God somehow constructed all other beings out of the same matter by which he was constructed due to his "overflowing," that allowed early Mormons to overcome the ontological gap between God and man. See Givens, *Wrestling the Angel,* 264–66.

26. Although Joseph Smith doesn't include the Father explicitly in D&C 93 as someone who "received not of the fulness at first" and progressed "grace to grace," he does seem to have believed, at least by 1844, that this progression applied to the Father as well. He stated "First, God himself, who sits enthroned in yonder heavens, is a man like one of yourselves, that is the great secret. If the veil was rent today and you were to see the great God who holds this world in its orbit and upholds all things by his power, you would see him in the image and very form of a man; for Adam was created in the very fashion and image of God. He received instruction from and walked, talked, and conversed with him as one man talks and communes with another. . . . I am going to tell you how God came to be God. We have imagined that God was God from all eternity. [That he was not is an idea] incomprehensible to some. But it is the simple and first principle of the gospel—to know for a certainty the character of God, that we may converse with him as one man with another. God himself, the Father of us all, dwelt on an earth the same as Jesus Christ himself did" ("Conference Minutes," *Times and Seasons* 5 [August 15, 1844]: 613–14).

27. Samuel Morris Brown, *On Heaven as it is on Earth: Joseph Smith and the Early Mormon Conquest of Death* (Oxford: Oxford University Press, 2012), 250.

28. "Conference Minutes," *Times and Seasons* 5 (August 15, 1844): 614.

29. "Conference Minutes," *Times and Seasons* 5 (August 15, 1844): 614.

30. Ostler, *Of God and Gods,* 421.

31. It is interesting to compare how both the Bible and Mormon scripture use the title "Son of God." For the biblical writers, the key element of the title "Son of God" was the term "God," meaning that Jesus had some sort of connection with the divine. Thus the title was used to elevate Jesus to a state above mortals, similar to how the title *divi filius* was used by the Roman Emperors to designate their greater-than-mortal status. This title occurs eighteen times in the Fourth Gospel, and becomes key in viewing Jesus as the "agent" of the Father. For Mormons, however, the title became a way of linking Jesus and humanity, as the emphasis was upon "Son" rather than "God." Charles Harrell observes that "The earliest LDS teachings seem to refer to Christ as the Son of God to denote his human nature. . . . In sum, early Mormonism designates Christ as the Son because he took on the finite characteristics of humans, not because he was God's biological son" (Charles R. Harrell, *"This is My Doctrine:" The Development of Mormon Theology* [Salt Lake City: Greg Kofford Books, 2011], 161–62).

32. Barrett, *The Gospel According to St. John,* 165.

33. Philips, *The Prologue of the Fourth Gospel,* 197.

34. A fair amount of speculation has occurred within Mormonism in attempting to pin down why exactly Jesus is the being upon whom this divine status was bestowed. Has he always been a being with more divinity than other spirits, or was that status given him due to special circumstances? Usages of the title "Only Begotten Son" in the Book of Mormon and in the Doctrine and Covenants suggest that Jesus held a special status from the beginning. Rodney Turner states that "Jesus was the first and *only* spirit begotten into the Father's fulness in pre-mortality. All others are spiritually begotten *through* the Son" (Rodney Turner, "The Doctrine of the Firstborn and Only Begotten," in *The Pearl of Great Price: Revelations from God,* ed. H. Donl Peterson and Charles D. Tate Jr. [Provo: Religious Studies Center, 1989], 109–10). In an 1842 *Times and Seasons* editorial, Jesus Christ was referred to as "the anointed Son of God, from before the foundation of the World" ("Baptism," *Times and Seasons* 3 [September 1, 1842]: 905). As the Mormon doctrine of pre-mortality developed, the idea grew that Jesus Christ was literally the firstborn of all the spirit children of God. As Harrell notes, "As the emphasis on Christ being the firstborn spirit offspring of God grew

from this point, scriptural references to the Firstborn were reinterpreted to provide scriptural proof-texts for this doctrine" (Harrell, *This Is My Doctrine*, 171). By the early twentieth-century, the idea that Jesus was chosen to act as Savior due to a sort of seniority and loyalty toward the Father had become standard. James E. Talmage wrote: "Evidence is abundant that Christ was chosen and ordained to be the Redeemer of the world, even from the beginning. We read of His formost position amongst the sons of God in offering Himself as a sacrifice to carry into effect the will of the Father" (Talmage, *The Articles of Faith* [Salt Lake City: Signature Books, 2003], 195). It was thus a combination of rank (as first-born) and loyalty to the Father that enabled Jesus to receive the "fulness" and become elevated to a more divine status. Joseph Smith taught that Jesus received the "fulness of the Priesthood" upon the Mount of Transfiguration (Cook and Ehat, *The Words of Joseph Smith*, 246). Does this mean that Joseph Smith viewed "Savior" as a priesthood office, requiring keys and authority? This would not be surprising giving Smith's penchant for democratizing authority.

35. Brown calls D&C 93 "an inspired reworking of the Gospel of John" (*On Heaven as it is on Earth*, 250).

36. The theory that the original *logos* hymn was connected with John the Baptist is argued by Bultmann: "The *motive* for the insertion of vv. 6–8, 15 is clear from their polemical character. For their purpose is not only the positive one of proclaiming the Baptist as witness for Jesus; it is also polemical: to dispute the claim that the Baptist has the authority of Revealer. This authority must therefore have been attributed by the Baptist sect to their master; they saw in him the φῶς, and thus also the pre-existent Logos become flesh. This suggests that the source-text was *a hymn of the Baptist-Community*" (Bultmann, *The Gospel of John*, 17–18).

37. This theory raises some questions pertinent to the Gospel of John. Noticeable by its absence in the Fourth Gospel is the story of Jesus being baptized by John the Baptist. The Fourth gospel preserves the witness of John the Baptist that he "saw the Spirit descending from heaven like a dove, and it abode upon him" (John 1:32). But no mention is made of John the Baptist actually performing the baptism. Scholars have been puzzled by the absence of this event. One theory is that there existed some sort of "proto-Mandaean" community in the first century that was in conflict with the Johannine community, and thus the Evangelist downplayed the role of John the Baptist. Raymond Brown writes that "Verse 31 also has a role in the polemic against the Baptist sectarians. Christians did not find it easy to explain why Jesus allowed himself to be baptized with John the Baptist's baptism of repentance. . . . Thus John has removed from his account of the incident any aspects of the baptism that the sectarians might glory in" (Brown, *The Gospel According to John*, 1:65). Bultmann, while acknowledging the absence of the Baptism scene, writes "Yet it would be wrong to conclude from this that Jesus' baptism was an embarrassment for the Evangelist, so that he passes over it as quickly as possible. On the contrary he clearly refers to it without misgivings. Yet he does not give an account of it, firstly because he can assume that his readers are acquainted with the story, and secondly, because for him the mere historical fact is of no significance by comparison with the witness of the Baptist which is based on it" (Bultmann, *The Gospel of John*, 94). Additionally, nowhere in D&C 93 does it mention a baptism of Jesus by John. In fact, this "fulness" quotes from two passages in John 1, verses 32 (D&C 93:15) and 34 (D&C 93:6). For those who view D&C 93 as representing a "proto-Prologue," this reading suggests that the baptism of Jesus by John may not have even been in the original record prior to its redaction by John the Evangelist, a curious omission if in fact there was a group of "Baptist sectarians."

38. John Taylor, *The Mediation and Atonement* (Salt Lake City: Deseret News Company, 1882), 55.

39. *Journal of Discourses* (London: Latter-day Saints' Book Depot, 1854–1886), 16:58.

40. Bruce R. McConkie, *Doctrinal New Testament Commentary* (Salt Lake City: Bookcraft, 1966), 1:70–71. Robert J. Matthews agrees, stating that "Here we are informed that the 'fulness of John's record' is still to come forth, and verse 15 identifies this to be the words of John the Baptist. . . . It appears from the above revelation that he (John)

used the Baptist's written record in compiling his own gospel account" (Robert J. Matthews, *A Burning Light: The Life and Ministry of John the Baptist* [Provo: BYU Press, 1972], 79). Cf. Susan Easton Black, who wrote in a recent publication "The record of John is a record that was kept by John the Baptist (Susan Easton Black, *400 Questions and Answers about the Doctrine and Covenants* [American Fork: Covenant, 2012], 163). Black cites Pratt as a source for this claim.

41. Harper, *Making Sense of the Doctrine and Covenants*, 560. Cf. Lyndon W. Cook, *The Revelations of the Prophet Joseph Smith* (Salt Lake City: Deseret Book, 1981), 194–95. Others who argue for John the Evangelist as author of the "record of John" include Charles W. Penrose, *CR* April 1916, 19–20.

42. In order to keep identities straight, I will use John to refer to the author of the Fourth Gospel and "John" to refer to the author of D&C 93:7–17.

43. For Bultmann, this statement is key to an understanding of the entire Fourth Gospel: This passage "is the confession of those who, having overcome the offence, have perceived the divine glory in the man Jesus. Yet how can God's glory be manifested in the σὰρξ γενόμενος? The claim that it was so is the subject of the Gospel; its aim is to show how this is possible. . . . The δόξα (of the Revealer) consists in what he is as *Revealer* for men, and he possesses the δόξα *really*—as becomes clear towards the end of the Gospel—when that which he himself is has been *actualised* in the believer. Correspondingly it is those who, as believers, allow him to be for themselves what he *is*, who see his glory" (Bultmann, *The Gospel of John*, 67–69).

44. Part of the problem with interpreting this verse is the difficulty surrounding the Greek word δόξα, translated in John 1:14 as "glory" and used in both D&C 93:6 and D&C 93:7. Rudolf Bultmann notes this difficulty, writing "Δόξα . . . refers to the epiphany and the manifestation of the Godhead. The origin of this meaning, which is divergent from the normal Greek meaning of δόξα, is disputed . . ." (Bultmann, *The Gospel of John*, 67–68 fn. 2). In classical Greek δόξα meant "opinion" or "what one thinks," however "even a cursory survey of the position in the NT reveals a totally different picture. The old meaning 'opinion' has disappeared completely." Rather NT usage of δόξα denotes "'divine and heavenly radiance,' the 'loftiness and majesty' of God, and even the 'being of God' and His world" (Kittel, *Theological Dictionary*, 2:233, 237). It is equally difficult to pin down exactly how Joseph Smith is using the term in D&C 93:6–7. The term appears nearly 150 times in the revelations and is used as both a verb and a noun. When used as a noun Joseph used it both in the sense of "honor" or "fame," such as D&C 10:41, or as a sort of measuring-rod of levels of divinity, as he does in D&C 76 and 88. It is most likely the second sense that Joseph intends in D&C 93:6–7, especially since it is the "fulness" of glory that is viewed by John, meaning that Jesus possesses a "full amount" of divinity.

45. In Johannine studies of 1:1, the linking verb ἦν has drawn a great deal of attention. Keener notes that "For John, the Word was not only 'from the beginning,' but 'in the beginning.' Many commentators have laid heavy stress on the verb ἦν: in contrast to many Wisdom texts which declare that Wisdom or Torah was created 'in the beginning' or before the creation of the rest of the world, John omits Jesus' creation and merely declares that he 'was.' This verb (ἦν) may thus suggest the Word's eternal preexistence" (Keener, *The Gospel of John*, 1:369). Joseph Smith's point in D&C 93 seems to be something similar. First, note the clear, if not awkward, presence of "was" in D&C 93:8, as if the author went to pains to emphasize the "was" by altering the expected word order of John 1:1, "in the beginning was the word." If we allow the meaning of the Greek verb ἦν to be carried over to the "was" of D&C 93:8, it again re-enforces not only a pre-earthly but also an eternal existence for the Word. Note as well D&C 93:29, that "Man was also in the beginning with God." This repetition of "in the beginning" takes the reader back to verses 7 and 8 and suggests that humanity shared a similar pre-earthly existence as the Word did, by implication "eternal" rather than just "pre-earthly."

46. As John Ashton notes, "The Prologue (of John) offers a vision of eternity, stretching back to before the creation of the world and forward until after its end"

Chapter 4

(Ashton, *Understanding the Fourth Gospel*, 2nd Edition [Oxford: Oxford University Press, 2007], 503). D&C 93 represents an attempt by Joseph Smith to accomplish a similar vision.

47. Ridderbos writes "The words 'In the beginning,' with which the prologue begins, also form the beginning of the book of Genesis and hence of the entire Torah. . . . Furthermore, the words that follow in John, the pronouncements concerning the Word, echo what in Genesis 1 constitutes the foundation of God's revelation in the Old Testament and of Israelite religion: God's creation of heaven and earth" (Ridderbos, *The Gospel of John*, 23). Keener asserts, rather confidently, "That John intends an allusion to Genesis 1 may be regarded as certain" (Keener, *The Gospel of John*, 1:366). This does not mean, however, that the author of the Prologue intended it to be a midrash on Genesis 1, although that viewpoint has been argued. See Peder Borgen, "Observations on the Targumic character of the Prologue of John," *NTS* 16 (1970): 288–95.

48. Sidney Sperry makes an interesting insight in regards to this verse. He notes that there appears to be some incongruity between the JST of John 1:1, which reads "In the beginning was the gospel preached through the Son. And the gospel was the word, and the word was with the Son, and the Son was with God, and the Son was of God," and the JST of John 1:16, "For in the beginning was the Word, even the Son, who is made flesh, and sent unto us by the will of God," and D&C 93:8, which presumes to be an early record of John: "Therefore, in the beginning the Word was, for he was the Word, even the messenger of salvation." Sperry notes that there are multiple ways in which the term "word" is used in these verses, none of which correlate with the Greek context. However, he then makes the argument that "it is far more probable that John took the word out of its Greek context and used it as he saw fit. . . . From what has been said it is obvious that John (writer of the Fourth Gospel) does not attempt to use *Word* in one technical sense only" (Sperry, *Doctrine and Covenants Compendium*, 473–74). Ironically, Sperry uses John as an example of a writer who recontextualizes key terminology in order to construct a new theological statement which is the very thing Joseph Smith himself is doing in D&C 93: Joseph does to John what John has done to those authors who precede him.

49. This figure of the λόγος, while new to the Gospel writings was by no means new to the ancient world. Heraclitus had first defined the intelligible unity of being or the determinate structure of thought and gave this concept the somewhat ambiguous name λόγος. By this he seemed to mean that every man had the capacity to understand the creative order of the universe, although not everyone would take advantage of this knowledge (Heraclitus Fragments 1 and 2. See G. S. Kirk and J. E. Raven, *The Presocratic Philosophers: A Critical History with a Selection of Texts* [Cambridge: Cambridge University Press, 1984], 181–213). With the advent of Stoicism, λόγος came to mean something more akin to the rationality and order of the universe. Because Stoicism was largely concerned with explaining rationally the nature of the universe and man's role within it, λόγος was applied to humankind as well as a description or encapsulation of their proper moral attitudes. Thus λόγος could be understood as "the intelligence behind an idea, the idea itself, or the expression of the idea" (W. Robert Cook, *The Theology of John* [Chicago: Moody Press, 1979], 48). Significantly, the Stoic λόγος was not an emanation or aspect of God—but was God itself. T. W. Manson noted that "The Stoic does not have a God, one of whose attributes is *logos*. He has one God who can be called indifferently . . . many other names including *logos*" ("The Johannine Jesus as Logos" in *A Companion to John: Readings in Johannine Theology*, ed. Michael J. Taylor [Alba House, 1977], 6). During the Middle Platonic period, λόγος began to be used as a mediating figure (likely building upon the idea of the "demiurge" in Plato's *Timaeus*) who bridges the gulf between the transcendent, spiritual God and the mortal realm. This view of the λόγος became particularly well-developed in the writings of the Jewish exegete Philo, who saw a need to combine his ancestral Jewish faith with the Hellenistic world in which he lived (See Dodd, *The Interpretation of the Fourth Gospel*, 54–73). It is Philo's concept of the λόγος that likely would have been familiar to audiences contemporary with the Fourth Gospel (see Thomas Tobin

"The Prologue of John and Hellenistic Jewish Speculation," *CBQ* 52 [1990]: 252–69). Significant for our understanding of John, once the λόγος began to be connected with the transcendent God, "The divine functions of creating, sustaining and governing the world are transferred to the Logos, but he also shares in the work of salvation of men" (Schnackenburg, *The Gospel According to St. John*, 1:486).

50. Keener, *The Gospel of John*, 1:363.

51. Martin Scott, *Sophia and the Johannine Jesus* (Sheffield: Sheffield Academic Press, 1992), 106. Scott writes that Sophia's "participation and her priority at the act of creation certainly implies a special relationship between herself and Yahweh," a relationship that finds its culmination in Proverbs 8:30 where Sophia proclaims that "I was daily his delight, rejoicing always before him" (Scott, *Sophia and the Johannine Jesus*, 51).

52. Peder Borgen, "Observations on the Targumic Character of the Prologue of John," 290.

53. Bultmann, *The Gospel of John*, 25.

54. Brown, *The Gospel According to John*, 1:24.

55. *BDAG*, 588–90.

56. In the King James translation of the New Testament, "redemption" appears a total of a eleven times, the majority of those from Pauline texts and none from the Johannine writings. "Redeem" also appears eleven times, again mainly in Pauline texts, but three of those are from the Book of Revelation.

57. The title "Spirit of truth" is found outside the Bible in *Jub.* 25:14; *Community Rule* 4.21; *Joseph and Asenath* 19:11; and *Shepherd of Hermas* (Mand. 3.4). The use of "Spirit of truth" in 1 John 4:6 is slightly more ambiguous than the usages in the Fourth Gospel, but still likely refers to the Holy Spirit. See Brown, *The Epistles of John*, 501.

58. See Ridderbos, *The Gospel of John*, 502–504.

59. That Joseph Smith would adopt this mentality of shattering paradigms through his use of Johannine language is itself somewhat ironic, seeing as how the Gospel of John often attempts something similar. One writer, speaking of the presence of the term λόγος in John 1:1, makes an interesting observation: "λόγος was used in a number of contemporary contexts, which may or may not have been familiar to the Gospel's intended or real audience. None of these contexts provides a dominant use for the lexeme at the time of the Prologue's composition. λόγος represents a flux of ideas and meanings interacting with one another crossing a number of different cultural milieux. Therefore, the reader has no specific guidance on how to sort out the intertextual problems. Instead of bringing clarification, λόγος seems particularly suited to impede disambiguation: as though the author uses the word in order to further the process of making his readers suspend their decision-making process. The result of this suspension . . . may well be to encourage the development of a Johannine anti-language. Because readers cannot disambiguate, then they are forced to remain in ambiguity. This makes them question the semantic domain of the word in question and await resolution from within the text itself" (Phillips, *The Prologue of the Fourth Gospel*, 148–49).

60. Ridderbos, *The Gospel of John*, 50. Cf. also Bultmann, "It is in his sheer humanity that he is the Revealer" (Bultmann, *The Gospel of John*, 63).

61. The reason this stands out is that the author of D&C 93 relies heavily upon a connection between the divine Jesus and humanity to make the logic of his argument in D&C 93:12–20 work. By ignoring the implications of ὁ λόγος σὰρξ ἐγένετο Smith misses an idea that could have strengthened his argument.

62. Robinson and Garrett, *A Commentary on the Doctrine and Covenants* (Salt Lake City: Deseret Book, 2004), 3:181.

63. It is not, however, the invention of Joseph Smith. John Wesley also used the phrase "from grace to grace" to elaborate upon the doctrine of sanctification: "From the time of our being born again, the gradual work of sanctification takes place. . . . We go on from grace to grace, while we are careful to 'abstain from all appearance of evil, and are 'zealous of good works,' as we have opportunity, doing good to all men; while we walk in all His ordinances blameless, therein worshipping Him in spirit and in

truth; while we take up our cross, and deny ourselves every pleasure that does not lead us to God" (*The Works of the Rev. John Wesley* [London: John Mason, 1829], 6:46). Following Wesley, most, if not all, usages of the phrase prior to Joseph Smith speak of humanity's progression toward sanctification, not about Jesus Christ's progression toward Godhood. It is likely that Joseph Smith encountered the phrase from the Methodists, a group with whom both he and many of his early converts were familiar, and incorporated it into his own work. See Christopher C. Rich, "We Latter-day Saints are Methodists": The Influence of Methodism on Early Mormon Religiosity" Master's Thesis, Brigham Young University, 2009.

64. Robinson and Garrett, *A Commentary on the Doctrine and Covenants*, 3:183. John A. Widtsoe elaborates on what this growth may entail: "In any case, the operation of the will, under normal conditions, adds power to man; and by the use of the intelligent will in a world of matter and energy, the increasingly complex man grows in power and strength towards perfection, in an increasingly interesting world. . . . This law of progression is the great law of the universe, without beginning and without end, to which all other laws contribute. By adherence to this law the willing, intelligent beings have risen to their present splendid state of manhood, and by further compliance with this law they will advance to a future God-like state of perfection" (*Rational Theology* [Salt Lake City: Signature Books, 2007], 20–22).

65. Kittel, *Theological Dictionary*, 5:653. It is possible that the use of "Son of God" in D&C 93:14 is more of an allusion to John 1:12 than a replication of the Christological title. Perhaps Smith is attempting to expand on the "power" that allows humanity to become the "sons of God." This "power" would be the "fulness," or "glory of the Father," and would mean that Jesus is "Son of God" both in his Christological role as divine agent of the Father, in accordance with the Fourth Gospel, but also "Son of God" in the sense of John 1:12, that a spiritual change has occurred within Jesus, a move that would allow the paradigm of D&C 93 to remain intact as we too can follow the model of Jesus and become "Sons" and "Daughters" of God. If this were the case, the use of "Son of God" in D&C 93:14 is both quite creative and quite ironical, as the reader would need to be familiar both with the Christological title and the theology of John 1:12 to grasp the full implications of the verse.

66. Schnackenburg, *The Gospel According to St. John*, 2:172.

67. From the perspective of the Fourth Gospel, this would be a curious claim on the part of "John." Robert Kysar writes: "In the place where the synoptics narrate the origin of the eucharist stands the account of the foot washing (13:1–10). The last meal Jesus celebrates with his disciples before his passion is not a Passover meal at all. Thus one of the basic features of the institution scenes in the synoptics is missing. Furthermore, there is no account of the baptism of Jesus, and there is confusion about whether or not Jesus practiced baptism (compare 3:22 and 4:2). Water baptism is treated critically and assigned strictly to the Baptizer in contrast with Spirit baptism (1:26, 31, 33). One is left with the impression that the sacraments of baptism and eucharist did not figure in the theology of the fourth evangelist" (Robert Kysar, "The Gospel of John," in *The Anchor Bible Dictionary*, ed. David Noel Freedman [New York: Doubleday, 1993], 3:929).

68. Bruce R. McConkie, *Doctrines of the Restoration: Sermons and Writings of Bruce R. McConkie*, ed. Mark L. McConkie (Salt Lake City: Bookcraft, 1989), 289.

69. Joseph Smith wrote in 1842 that "We believe the Bible to be the word of God, as far as it is translated correctly" (Joseph Smith, "Church History," *Times and Seasons* 3 [March 1, 1842]: 709).

70. William Ellery Channing, "Unitarian Christianity," in *The Complete Works of William Ellery Channing* (London & New York: Routledge and Sons, 1884), 282.

71. William Ellery Channing, "Imitableness of Christ's Character," in *The Complete Works of William Ellery Channing* (London & New York: Routledge and Sons, 1884), 244.

72. Ralph Waldo Emerson, "The Divinity School Address," in *The Spiritual Emerson*, ed. David M. Robinson (Boston: Beacon Press, 2003), 70.

73. William Ellery Channing, "The Essence of the Christian Religion," in *The Complete Works of William Ellery Channing*, 47.

74. Alexander Campbell, "The Mormonites," *Millennial Harbinger* 2 (January 1831): 93.

Epilogue

The purpose of this study was to perform an in-depth examination of three crucial contentions: First, that Mormon scripture employs the rhetoric of allusivity as a means of juxtaposition with the Bible in order to procure literary authority with a nineteenth-century audience. Second, that through the rhetoric of allusivity, which resulted in a remarkable deconstruction and reconstruction of the Bible, Joseph Smith initiated a lengthy and complex discourse between the Prologue of John and Mormon scripture. Third, that four different strata or levels of discourse within this larger Johannine discourse can be identified and analyzed. To explore how every verse in the Bible contributes to these contentions would be quite laborious and, quite frankly, unrealistic for a single lifetime, let alone a single monograph. In order to provide the necessary minute examination this type of intertextual study requires, the eighteen verses that comprise the Prologue of the Gospel of John were employed as a means of exploring these contentions.

As to the first point, namely that Joseph Smith infused Mormon scripture with allusions to the Bible as a way of gaining acceptance in nineteenth-century America, the examination of Johannine echo in Mormon scripture perhaps addresses this contention most clearly. In the case of the Book of Mormon, the use of biblical language (such as Alpha and Omega) that would have made little sense to a proposed Nephite audience suggests that a primary purpose for its inclusion was to provide a nineteenth-century audience with a text that sounded or read as biblical. The Doctrine and Covenants, with its own frequent allusions to the Prologue of John's gospel, simply repeated the pattern of allusion established successfully by the Book of Mormon. In his study of how early converts to Mormonism viewed the Book of Mormon, Steven C. Harper wrote that "Those who became Mormons were almost always first contemplative Bible believers who were skeptical of false prophets. They considered it reasonable that signs would follow true believers, and they held out for empirical confirmation. Dozens of primary accounts of early Mormon conversions emphasize this pattern."[1] By providing texts that echoed the Bible, specifically texts that were Johannine, to "contemplative Bible believers," Smith found a means of turning aside this skepticism.

As for the second point, that through the rhetoric of allusivity which resulted in a remarkable deconstruction and reconstruction of the Bible

Joseph Smith initiated a lengthy and complex discourse between the Prologue of John and Mormon scripture, the second and third categories we
have examined, Johannine allusion and Johannine expansion, demonstrate how much the meaning and context of the Johannine text mattered
to Joseph Smith. He possessed the ability to weave Johannine phrases
into a larger, pseudo-biblical tapestry in which not just the recognition of
the source of the allusion, but the context of the allusion mattered. In the
case of Johannine allusion, readers encounter phrases such as "Only Begotten Son" or "He came unto his own" and can apply the context of the
subtext to the intertext, using a Johannine lens to bring in the interpretation of Mormon scripture into focus. That Joseph Smith rarely, if ever,
acknowledged the biblical sources from which he drew should not be
understood as ignorance of his source text.[2] On the contrary, not only
was Smith adept at reading and synthesizing the Bible, he apparently
placed a similar expectation upon his audience. On the process of biblical
allusion, Pheme Perkins has written: "Central to the enterprise is the
subtle introduction of single words or phrases *whose provenance and context the reader must recognize* in order to understand the argument of a
particular text. *Such facility presumes an audience that can hear such allusions
easily.*"[3]

This dialogic process between John and Joseph Smith deepens with
Johannine expansion and inversion. The burden upon readers increases
as they must not only recognize the context of the subtext but also how
the intertext has expanded upon (or inverted) that context if they are to
tease out the additional meanings added by Smith. This expansion can be
most clearly seen in how Smith appropriates Johannine phrases such as
"full of grace and truth" or "of his fulness have all we received" and
expands both lexically ("full of grace, *mercy*, and truth") and circumstan-
tially (such as D&C 76), while inversion can be seen in Smith's reconstruction of John's prologue in D&C 93. It is with this expansion and
inversion that Joseph Smith comes closest to fitting David G. Meade's
image of a *Vergegenwartigung*, a pseudepigrapic author who relies upon
"their participation in an ongoing revelation and their dependence on
previous revelation" as a means of establishing a text where "previous
revelation was actualized to meet the needs of a new generation."[4] That
Joseph Smith understood himself in this fashion, as one more link in a
biblical chain, appears likely based upon the extensive use of scripture
explored in this work.[5] The myriad of ways in which Smith used the
language of the Bible mirrored that of writers such as the author of Deuteronomy, Second and Third Isaiah, Matthew and Paul, men who relied
upon the language of the established past to construct a realized present
and a hopeful future.

The third contention, namely that four different strata or levels can be
identified and analyzed through an examination of how the Prologue is
used in Mormon scripture, is perhaps most difficult to assess. That Smith

employed scripture in different ways is clear, but the assignment of certain passages from Mormon scripture to specific categories is not an exact science. Others may argue that "full of grace, equity, and truth" works better as an inversion, or that D&C 93 is better understood as expansion. Perhaps even the choice of categories could be called into question by some, feeling that too little exists to separate allusion and echo, or inversion and expansion. After having carefully studied each of the passages under consideration, these are the categories that made the most sense and appeared the most accurate. But this study does not attempt to be the final word on how the Bible functioned in Smith's corpus. Far from it. By its very existence Mormon scripture asks to be interpreted and understood through the lens of the Bible. There are 31,102 verses in the Bible. This study analyzed only eighteen of them. In order to truly understand and categorize the function of the Bible in Mormon scripture, the number contributing to an analysis must be nearer the former than the latter.

NOTES

1. Harper, "Infallible Proofs," 104.
2. "Lack of citation formulae hardly signals lack of interest" (Perkins, "Gnosticism and the Christian Bible," in *The Canon Debate,* 365).
3. Perkins, "Gnosticism and the Christian Bible," 365. Italics added.
4. Meade, *Pseudonymity and Canon,* 42–43.
5. "In Joseph's revelations, figures from the Bible return to bestow their powers on the Church, joining past and present. The past in Enoch's narrative breaks into the present in order to complete the scriptural story. More than restoring the New Testament church, the early Mormons believed they were resuming the biblical narrative in their own time. Linking the "latter-day" church to an ancient sacred history was to become a hallmark of Joseph's prophesying" (Bushman, *Rough Stone Rolling,* 142).

Bibliography

Alexander, Thomas G. *Mormonism in Transition: A History of the Latter-day Saints, 1890–1930*. Chicago: University of Illinois Press, 1986.

Ashton, John. *Understanding the Fourth Gospel*. 2nd edition. Oxford: Oxford University Press, 2007.

Bakhtin, M. M. *The Dialogic Imagination: Four Essays by M. M. Bakhtin*. Edited by Michael Holquist. Austin and London: Universiy of Texas Press, 1981.

Balz, Horst, and Gerhard Schneider. *Exegetical Dictionary of the New Testament*. 3 vols. Grand Rapids: William B. Eerdmans Publishing Company, 1982.

Barlow, Philip. *Mormons and the Bible: The Place of the Latter-day Saints in American Religion*. 2nd edition. Oxford: Oxford University Press, 2013.

Barrett, C. K. *The Gospel According to St. John, Second Edition: An Introduction with Commentary and Notes on the Greek Text*. Philadelphia: The Westminster Press, 1978.

Barthes, Roland. "The Death of the Author." In *Image-Music-Text*. Translated by Stephen Heath. London: Fontana, 1977

Bauer, Walter. *A Greek-English Lexicon of the New Testament and Other Early Christian Literature*. 3rd edition. Revised and edited by Frederick W. Danker. Chicago/London: University of Chicago Press, 2000.

Baugh, Alexander L. "Parting the Veil: Joseph Smith's Seventy-Six Documented Visionary Experiences." In *Opening the Heavens: Accounts of Divine Manifestations 1820–1844*. Edited by John W. Welch, 265–326. Provo: Brigham Young University Press, 2005.

Beale, G. K. *The Book of Revelation: A Commentary on the Greek Text*. Grand Rapids: William B. Eerdmans Publishing Company, 1998.

———. *Handbook on the New Testament Use of the Old Testament*. Grand Rapids: Baker Academic Press, 2012.

———. *John's Use of the Old Testament in Revelation*. JSNTSup 166. Sheffield: Sheffield Academic Press, 1998.

Beale, G. K., and D. A. Carson. *Commentary on the New Testament Use of the Old Testament*. Grand Rapids: Baker Academic Press, 2007.

Beetham, Christopher. *Echoes of Scripture in the Letter of Paul to the Colossians*. BIS 96. Leiden: E. J. Brill, 2008.

Ben-Porat, Ziva. "The Poetics of Literary Allusion." *PTL: A Journal for Descriptive Poetics and Theory of Literature* 1 (1976): 105–28.

Bernstein, Moshe J. "Pseudepigraphy in the Qumran Scrolls: Categories and Functions." In *Pseudepigraphic Perspectives: The Apocrypha and Pseudepigrapha in Light of the Dead Sea Scrolls*. Edited by Esther G. Chazon and Michael Stone, 126. STDJ 28. Leiden: E. J. Brill, 1999.

Bethel, Christopher. *A General View of the Doctrine of Regeneration in Baptism*. London: J. G. & F. Rivington, 1836.

Black, Susan Easton. *400 Questions and Answers about the Doctrine and Covenants*. American Fork: Covenant Communications, 2012.

Bokovoy, David. *Authoring the Old Testament: Genesis-Deuteronomy*. Salt Lake City: Greg Kofford Books, 2014.

Borgen, Peder. "Logos was the True Light: Contributions to the Interpretation of the Gospel of John." *NovT* 14 (1972): 115–30.

———. "Observations on the Targumic Character of the Prologue of John." *NTS* 16 (1970): 288–95.

Boyarin, Daniel. *Intertextuality and Midrash*. Bloomington: Indiana University Press, 1990.

Brant, Jo-Ann A. *John*. Grand Rapids: Baker Academic Press, 2011.

Brawley, Robert L. *Text to Text Pours Forth Speech: Voices of Scripture in Luke-Acts*. Bloomington: Indiana University Press, 1995.

Brodie, Fawn M. *No Man Knows My History: The Life of Joseph Smith*. New York: Vintage Books, 1995.

Brodie, Thomas L. *The Gospel According to John: A Literary and Theological Commentary*. Oxford: Oxford University Press, 1997.

Brooke, George J. "Between Authority and Canon: The Significance of Reworking the Bible for Understanding the Canonical Process." In *Reworking the Bible: Apocryphal and Related Texts at Qumran*. Edited by Esther G. Chazon, Devorah Dimant, and Ruth A. Clements, 85–104. Leiden: E. J. Brill, 2005.

Brown, Gillian, and George Yule. *Discourse Analysis*. London: Cambridge University Press, 1983.

Brown Raymond B. *An Introduction to New Testament Christology*. Mahwah: Paulist Press, 1994.

———. *The Epistles of John*. Anchor Bible Series. New York: Doubleday, 1982.

———. *The Gospel According to John I-XII*. Anchor Bible Series. Garden City: Doubleday and Co., 1966.

———. *The Gospel According to John XIII-XXI*. Anchor Bible Series. Garden City: Doubleday and Co., 1966.

Brown, Samuel Morris. *On Heaven as it is on Earth: Joseph Smith and the Early Mormon Conquest of Death*. Oxford: Oxford University Press, 2012.

Bruce, F. F. *The Book of the Acts*. Grand Rapids: William B. Eerdmans Publishing Company, 1988.

———. *The Gospel of John*. Grand Rapids: William B. Eerdmans Publishing Company, 1994.

———. *New Testament Development of Old Testament Themes*. Grand Rapids: William B. Eerdmans Publishing Company, 1968.

Bultmann, Rudolf. *The Gospel of John: A Commentary*. Philadelphia: The Westminster Press, 1971.

Bushman, Richard Lyman. *Joseph Smith: Rough Stone Rolling*. New York: Alfred A. Knopf, 2005.

———. "The 'Little, Narrow Prison' of Language: The Rhetoric of Revelation." In *Believing History: Latter-day Saint Essays*. Edited by Reid L. Neilson and Jed Woodworth, 248–61. New York: Columbia University Press, 2004.

Campbell, Alexander. "The Mormonites." *Millennial Harbinger* 2 (January 1831): n.p.

Carey, Chris, ed. *Aeschines*. Austin: University of Texas Press, 2000.

Channing, William Ellery. *The Complete Works of William Ellery Channing*. London and New York: Routledge and Sons, 1884.

Charlesworth, James H. "Intertextuality: Isaiah 40.3 and the Serek Ha-Yahad." In *The Quest for Context and Meaning: Studies in Biblical Intertextuality in Honor of James A. Sanders*. Edited by Craig A. Evans and Shemaryahu Talmon, 197–224. Leiden: E. J. Brill, 1997.

———. "In the Crucible: The Pseudepigrapha as Biblical Interpretation." In *The Pseudepigrapha and Early Biblical Interpretation*. Edited by James H. Charlesworth and Craig A. Evans, 20–43. JSPSup 14. Sheffield: Sheffield Academic Press, 1993.

Cherry, Conrad. *God's New Israel: Religious Interpretations of American Destiny*. Chapel Hill: University of North Carolina Press, 1998.

Clarke, Adam. *The Holy Bible, with a Comm. and Critical Notes*. New York: T. Mason & G. Lane, 1837.

———. *The New Testament of Our Lord and Savior Jesus Christ, Containing the Text Taken from the Most Correct Copies of the Authorised Translation, Including the Marginal Readings and Parallel Texts, with a Commentary and Critical Notes*. 3 vols. London: J. Butterworth & Son, 1817.

Clayton, Jay, and Eric Rothstein. "Figures in the Corpus: Theories of Influence and Intertextuality." In *Influence and Intertextuality in Literary History*. Edited by Jay C. Clayton and Eric Rothstein, 2–36. Madison: University of Wisconsin Press, 1991.

Collins, John J. "Changing Scripture." In *Changes in Scripture: Rewriting and Interpreting Authoritative Traditions in the Second Temple Period*. Edited by Hanne von Weissenberg, Juha Pakkala, and Marko Marttila. Berlin: Walter de Gruyter, 2011.

Cook, Lyndon W., ed. *David Whitmer Interviews: A Restoration Witness*. Orem: Grandin Book Co., 1991.

———. *The Revelations of the Prophet Joseph Smith*. Salt Lake City: Deseret Book, 1981.

———, and Andrew F. Ehat. *The Words of Joseph Smith*. 2nd rev. edition. Orem: Grandin Book Co., 1991.

Cook, W. Robert. *The Theology of John*. Chicago: Moody Press, 1979.

Culler, Jonathan. *The Pursuit of Signs: Semiotics, Literature, Deconstruction*. Ithaca: Cornell University Press, 1981.

Culpepper, R. A. *Anatomy of the Fourth Gospel*. Philadelphia: Fortress Press, 1983.

———. "Anti-Judaism as a Theological Problem." In *Anti-Judaism and the Fourth Gospel*. Edited by Reimund Bieringer, Didier Pollefeyt, and Frederique Vandecasteele-Vanneuville, 61–82. Louisville: Westminster John Knox Press, 2001.

———. "The Pivot of John's Prologue." *NTS* 27 (1980–1981): 1–31.

Dabala, Jacek. *Mystery and Suspense in Creative Writing*. International Studies in Hermeneutics and Phenomonology, vol. 7. LIT Verlag: Munster, 2012.

Davidson, Karen Lynn, David J. Whittaker, Mark Ashurst-McGee, Richard L. Jensen, eds. *The Joseph Smith Papers: Histories, volume 1*. Salt Lake City: The Church Historian's Press, 2012.

———, Richard L. Jensen, and David J. Whittaker, eds. *The Joseph Smith Papers: Histories, vol. 2*. Salt Lake City: The Church Historian's Press, 2012.

De Chasca, Edmund. "Toward a Redefinition of Epic Formula in the Light of the Cantar de Mio Cid." *Hispanic Review* 38.3 (1970): 251–63.

Dirkmaat, Gerrit John, Brent M. Rogers, Grant Underwood, Robert J. Woodford, and William G. Hartley, eds. *The Joseph Smith Papers: Documents, vol. 3*. Salt Lake City: The Church Historian's Press, 2014.

Dodd, C. H. *According to Scriptures: The Sub-Structure of New Testament Theology*. London: Nisbet, 1952.

———. *The Interpretation of the Fourth Gospel*. Cambridge: Cambridge University Press, 1958.

Draisma, Sipke. *Intertextuality in Biblical Writings*. Kampen, Netherlands: Uitgeversmaatschappij J. H. Kok, 1989.

Draper, Richard. "Light, Truth, and Grace: Three Interrelated Salvation Themes in Doctrine and Covenants 93." In *Doctrines for Exaltation*. Edited by H. Dean Garrett, 22–41. Salt Lake City: Deseret Book, 1989.

Eagleton, Terry. *Literary Theory*. Oxford: Blackwell, 1983.

Edenburg, Cynthia. "Intertextuality, Literary Competence and the Question of Readership: Some Preliminary Observations." *JSOT* 35.2 (2010), 131–48.

Edwards, Ruth. "χάριν ἀντὶ χάριτος (John 1:16): Grace and Law in the Johannine Prologue." *JSNT* 32 (1989): 3–15.

Ellis, Bruce. *America's Prophet: Moses and the American Story*. New York: HarperCollins, 2009.

Ellis, E. Earle. *St. Paul's Use of the Old Testament*. London: Oliver and Body, 1957.

Emerson, Ralph Waldo. "The Divinity School Address." In *The Spiritual Emerson*. Edited by David M. Robinson. Boston: Beacon Press, 2003, 65–82.

Emory, John, ed. *The Works of Reverend John Wesley*. 7 vols. New York: J. Emory and B. Waugh, 1831.

The Evangelists Manual: Or a Guide to Trinitarian Universalists. Charleston: A. F. Cunningham, 1829.

Evans, Craig A. *Noncanonical Writings and New Testament Interpretation*. Peabody: Hendrickson, 1992.

Farkas, John R. and David A. Reed, *Mormons Answered Verse-by-Verse*. Grand Rapids: Baker Books, 1992.

Faulring, Scott H., Kent P. Jackson, and Robert J. Matthews, eds. *Joseph Smith's New Translation of the Bible: Original Manuscripts*. Provo: Religious Studies Center, 2004.

Fee, Gordon. *The First Epistle to the Corinthians*. Grand Rapids: William B. Eerdmans Publishing Company, 1987.

Fennema, D. A. "John 1:18: 'God the only son.'" *NTS* 31 (1985), 124–35.

Ferguson, Everett. "Factors Leading to the Selection and Closure of the New Testament Canon." In *The Canon Debate*. Edited by Lee Martin McDonald and James A. Sanders, 295–320. Peabody: Hendrickson Publishers, 2002.

Fishbane, Michael. *Biblical Interpretation in Ancient Israel*. Oxford: Clarendon Press, 1985.

Fiorenza, Elisabeth Schüssler. *The Book of Revelation: Justice and Judgment*. Minneapolis: Fortress Press, 1998.

Flake, Lawrence R. "A Shaker View of a Mormon Mission." *BYU Studies*, 20, no. 1. (Fall 1979): 94–99.

Forde, J. Massyngberde. *Revelation: A New Translation*. Anchor Bible Series. Garden City: Doubleday, 1975.

Foucault, Michel. *The Archaeology of Knowledge and the Discourse on Language*. Translated by A. M. S. Smith. New York: Pantheon, 1972.

Fowl, Stephen. "The Use of Scripture in Philippians." In *Paul and Scripture: Extending the Conversation*. Edited by Christopher D. Stanley, 163–84. Atlanta: Society of Biblical Literature, 2012.

Freedman, David Noel, ed., *The Anchor Bible Dictionary*. 6 vols. New York: Doubleday, 1993.

Gamble, Harry Y. "The New Testament Canon: Recent Research and the Status Quaestionis." In *The Canon Debate*. Edited by Lee Martin McDonald and James A. Sanders, 267–94. Peabody: Hendrickson Publishers, 2002.

Gardner, Brant. *Analytical and Contextual Commentary on the Book of Mormon*. 6 vols. Salt Lake City: Greg Kofford Books, 2007–2011.

———. *The Gift and Power of God: Translating the Book of Mormon*. Salt Lake City: Greg Kofford Books, 2011.

Genette, Gerard. *The Architext: An Introduction*. Translated by Jane E. Lewin. Berkeley: University of California Press, 1992.

Givens, Terryl L. *The Book of Mormon: A Very Short Introduction*. Oxford: Oxford University Press, 2009.

———. *By the Hand of Mormon: The American Scripture that Launched a New World Religion*. Oxford: Oxford University Press, 2002.

———. *Wrestling the Angel*. Oxford: Oxford University Press, 2014.

Godfrey, Matthew C., Mark Ashurst-McGee, Grant Underwood, Robert J. Woodford, and William G. Hartley, eds. *The Joseph Smith Papers: Documents, vol. 2*. Salt Lake City: Church Historians Press, 2013.

Gutjar, Paul C. *The Book of Mormon: A Biography*. Princeton: Princeton University Press, 2012.

Harding, Mark. "Disputed and Undisputed Letters of Paul." In *The Pauline Canon*. Edited by Stanley E. Porter, 129–68. Leiden: E. J. Brill, 2004.

Hardy, Grant. *Understanding the Book of Mormon: A Reader's Guide*. New York: Oxford University Press, 2010.

Harker, W. John. "Framing the Text: The Year 2000 in British Columbia." *Canadian Journal of Education* 17:1 (1992): 1–11.

Harper, Steven C. "'Infallible Proofs, Both Human and Divine:' The Persuasiveness of Mormonism for Early Converts." *RAC* 10.1 (Winter 2000): 105–108.

———. *Making Sense of the Doctrine and Covenants: A Guided Tour through Modern Revelations*. Salt Lake City: Deseret Book, 2008.

Harper, Steven C., Robin Scott Jensen, and Robert J. Woodford, eds. *The Joseph Smith Papers: Revelations and Translations: Manuscript Revelation Book.* Salt Lake City: The Church Historian's Press, 2009.

Harrell, Charles R. *"This is My Doctrine:" The Development of Mormon Theology.* Salt Lake City: Greg Kofford Books, 2011.

Harris, Elizabeth. *Prologue and Gospel: The Theology of the Fourth Evangelist.* London: T& T Clark, 1994.

Harris, J. Rendel. *Testimonies.* 2 vols. Cambridge: Cambridge University Press, 1916–1920.

Hays, Richard B. *The Conversion of the Imagination: Paul as Interpreter of Israel's Scripture.* Grand Rapids: William B. Eerdmans Publishing Company, 2005.

———. *Echoes of Scripture in the Letters of Paul.* New Haven: Yale University Press, 1989.

Hickman, Edward, ed. *The Works of Jonathan Edwards.* 2 vols. London: Paternoster Row, 1839.

Hicks, Michael. "Joseph Smith, W. W. Phelps, and the Poetic Paraphrase of 'The Vision.'" *Journal of Mormon History* 20.2 (1994): 63–84.

Holland, David. *Sacred Borders: Continuing Revelation and Canonical Restraint in Early America.* Oxford: Oxford University Press, 2011.

Hyde, Orson. "A Diagram of the Kingdom of God." *Millennial Star 9* (15 January 1847): 23–24.

Hylen, Susan. *Allusion and Meaning in John 6.* Berlin: Walter de Gruyter, 2005.

Jensen, Robin Scott, Robert J. Woodford, and Steven C. Harper, eds. *The Joseph Smith Papers: Revelations and Translations, vol. 1: Manuscript Revelation Books.* Salt Lake City: The Church Historian's Press, 2009.

Journal of Discourses. 26 vols. London: Latter-day Saints' Book Depot, 1854–1886.

Käsemann, Ernst. *The Testament of Jesus According to John 17.* Philadelphia: Fortress Press, 1968.

Keener, Craig. *The Gospel of John: A Commentary.* 2 vols. Peabody: Hendrickson Publishers, 2003.

Kim, Mitchell. "Respect for Context and Authorial Intention: Setting the Epistemological Bar." In *Paul and Scripture: Extending the Conversation.* Edited by Christopher D. Stanley, 115–29. Atlanta: Society of Biblical Literature, 2012.

King, J. S. "The Prologue to the Fourth Gospel: Some Unresolved Problems." *The Expository Times* (1986): 372–75.

Kirk, G. S., and Raven, J. E. *The Presocratic Philosophers: A Critical History with a Selection of Texts.* Cambridge: Cambridge University Press, 1984.

Kittel, Gerhard and Gerhard Friedrich. *Theological Dictionary of the New Testament.* 10 vols. Grand Rapids: William B. Eerdmans Publishing Company, 1972.

Koester, Craig R. *Symbolism in the Fourth Gospel: Meaning, Mystery, Community.* Minneapolis: Fortress Press, 2003.

Köstenberger, Andreas J. *John.* Grand Rapids: Baker Academic Press, 2004.

Kristeva, Julia. *Desire in Language: A Semiotic Approach to Literature and Art.* Edited by Leon S. Roudiez. New York: Columbia University Press, 1980.

———. *Semiotike: Recherchés pour une semanalyse.* Collections Tel Quel. Paris: Le Seuil, 1969.

———. "Word, Dialog and Novel." In *The Kristeva Reader.* Edited by Toril Moi, 34–61. New York: Columbia University Press, 1986.

Kugel, James. "On the Interpolations in the Book of Jubilees." *RevQ* 24 (2009): 215–72.

Kysar Robert. "John, The Gospel of." In *The Anchor Bible Dictionary.* Edited by David Noel Freedman, 912–31. New York: Doubleday, 1993.

———. *John: The Maverick Gospel.* London: Westminster John Knox Press, 1993.

Leppä, Outi. *The Making of Colossians: A Study on the Formation and Purpose of a Deutero-Pauline Letter.* Vandenhoeck & Ruprecht in Göttingen: The Finnish Exegetical Society, 2003.

Levinson, Bernard M. *Deuteronomy and the Hermeneutics of Legal Innovation*. Oxford: Oxford University Press, 1997.

Lindars, Barnabas. *New Testament Apologetic: The Doctrinal Significance of the Old Testament Quotations*. London: SCM Press Ltd., 1961.

Lioy, Dan. *The Search for Ultimate Reality: Intertextuality Between the Genesis and Johannine Prologues*. New York: Peter Lang Publishing, 2005.

Lord, Alfred. *The Singer of Tales*. Cambridge: Cambridge University Press, 2000.

MacKay, Michael Hubbard, Gerrit J. Dirkmaat, Grant Underwood, Robert J. Woodford, and William G. Hartley, eds. *The Joseph Smith Papers: Documents, vol. 1: July 1828–June 1831*. Salt Lake City: Church Historian's Press, 2013.

Madsen, Truman. *Joseph Smith: The Prophet*. Salt Lake City: Deseret Book, 2008.

Maloney, Francis J. *The Gospel of John*. Sacra Pagina Series. Collegeville: The Liturgical Press, 1998.

Manson, T. W. "The Johannine Jesus as Logos." In *A Companion to John: Readings in Johannine Theology*. Edited by Michael J. Taylor, 33–58. New York: Alba House, 1977.

Marquardt, H. Michael. *The Joseph Smith Revelations: Text and Commentary*. Salt Lake City: Signature Books, 1999.

Matthews, Robert J. *A Burning Light: The Life and Ministry of John the Baptist*. Provo: Brigham Young University Press, 1972.

Mathewson, David. *A New Heaven and a New Earth: The Meaning and Function of the Old Testament in Revelation 21.1–22.5*. JSNTSup 238. Sheffield: Sheffield Academic Press, 2003.

McClellin, William E. "Revelations." *Ensign of Liberty, of the Church of Christ* (Kirtland, Ohio), 1, no. 7 (August 1849): 98–99.

McConkie, Bruce R. *Doctrinal New Testament Commentary*. 3 vols. Salt Lake City: Bookcraft, 1966.

———. *Doctrines of the Restoration: Sermons and Writings of Bruce R. McConkie*. Edited by Mark L. McConkie. Salt Lake City: Bookcraft, 1989.

McConkie, Joseph Fielding, and Robert L. Millet. *Doctrinal Commentary on the Book of Mormon*. 4 vols. Salt Lake City: Deseret Book, 1988.

Meade, David G. *Pseudonymity and Canon: An Investigation into the Relationship of Authorship and Authority in Jewish and Earliest Christian Tradition*. Grand Rapids: William B. Eerdmans Publishing Company, 1986.

Meek, Russell L. "Intertextuality, Inner-Biblical Exegesis, and Inner-Biblical Allusion: The Ethics of a Methodology." *Biblica* 95.2 (2014): 280–91.

Merz, Annette. "The Fictitious Self-Exposition of Paul: How Might Intertextual Theory Suggest a Reformulation of the Hermeneutics of Pseudepigraphy?" In *The Intertextuality of the Epistles: Explorations of Theory and Practice*. Edited by Thomas L. Brodie, Dennis R. MacDonald, and Stanley E. Porter, 113–32. Sheffield: Sheffield University Press, 2006.

Metcalfe, Brent Lee, and Dan Vogel. *American Apocrypha: Essays on the Book of Mormon*. Salt Lake City: Signature Books, 2002.

Michaels, J. Ramsey. *The Gospel of John*. Grand Rapids: William B. Eerdmans Publishing Company, 2010.

Miller, Ed L. "The Johannine Origins of the Johannine Logos." *JBL* 112 (1993): 445–57.

Miller, Geoffrey D. "Intertextuality in Old Testament Research." *Currents in Biblical Research* 9.283 (2011): 283–309.

Morris, Leon. *The Gospel According to John*. Grand Rapids: William B. Eerdmans Publishing Company, 1995.

Moyise, Steve. "Does Paul Respect the Context of His Quotations." In *Paul and Scripture: Extending the Conversation*. Edited by Christopher D. Stanley, 97–114. Atlanta: Society of Biblical Literature, 2012.

———. *The Old Testament in the Book of Revelation*. JSNTSup 115. Sheffield: Sheffield Academic Press, 1995.

Noble Paul R. "Esau, Tamer, and Joseph: Criteria for Identifying Inner-Biblical Allusions." *VT* 52.2 (Apr. 2002): 219–52.

Nyman, Monte S. "The Designations Jesus Gives Himself in 3 Nephi." In *3 Nephi: This Is My Gospel*. Edited by Monte S. Nyman and Charles D. Tate, 41–58. Provo: Religious Studies Center, 1993.

Ostler,Blake T. *Exploring Mormon Thought*. 3 vols. Salt Lake City: Greg Kofford Books, 2001–2006.

Ostling, Richard and Joan K. Ostling. *Mormon America: The Power and the Promise*. New York: HarperCollins, 1999.

Paden, William E. *Religious Worlds: The Comparative Study of Religion*. Boston: Beacon Press, 1988.

Parry, Milman. *The Making of Homeric Verse: The Collected Papers of Milman Parry*. Oxford: Oxford University Press, 1991.

Perkins, Pheme. "Gnosticism and the Christian Bible." In *The Canon Debate*. Edited by Lee Martin McDonald and James A. Sanders, 355–71. Peabody: Hendrickson Publishers, 2002.

Peterson, D. L. "Zechariah 9–14: Methodological Reflections." In *Bringing out the Treasure: Inner Biblical Allusion in Zechariah 9–14*. Edited by Mark J. Boda and Michael Floyd, 210–24. JSOTSup 370. London: Sheffield Academic Press, 2003.

Phillips, Peter M. *The Prologue of the Fourth Gospel: A Sequential Reading*. New York: T&T Clark, 2006.

Porter, Stanley E. and Christopher D. Stanley, eds. *As it is Written: Studying Paul's Use of Scripture*. Atlanta: Society of Biblical Literature, 2008.

Pratt, Parley P. *Autobiography of Parley P. Pratt*. Salt Lake City: Deseret Book, 1994.

———. *Key to the Science of Theology*. Liverpool: F. D. Richards, 1855.

———. *Mormonism Unveiled*. Pamphlet. New York, 1838.

Price, Robert M. "Joseph Smith: Inspired Author of the Book of Mormon." In *American Apocrypha: Essays on the Book of Mormon*. Edited by Dan Vogel and Brent Lee Metcalfe, 321–66. Salt Lake City: Signature Books, 2002.

Prothero, Stephen. *American Jesus: How the Son of God Became a National Icon*. New York: Farrar, Straus and Giroux, 2003.

Putnam, Michael C. J. "The Lyric Genius of the 'Aeneid.'" *Arion: A Journal of Humanities and the Classics* 3.2/3 (Fall 1995–Winter 1996): 81–101.

Quinn, D. Michael. *Early Mormonism and the Magic World View*. Salt Lake City: Signature Books, 1988.

Rasmussen, Ellis J. "Textual Parallels to the Doctrine and Covenants and Book of Commandments as Found in the Bible." Master's Thesis. Brigham Young University, 1951.

Remini, Robert V. *Joseph Smith*. New York: Viking/Penguin Putnam, Inc., 2002.

Rich, Christopher C. "'We Latter-day Saints are Methodists': The Influence of Methodism on Early Mormon Religiosity." Master's Thesis. Brigham Young University, 2009.

Ridderbos, Herman. *The Gospel of John: A Theological Commentary*. Grand Rapids: William B. Eerdmans Publishing Company, 1997.

Robinson, David M. *The Spiritual Emerson*. Boston: Beacon Press, 2003.

Robinson, J. A. T. "The Relation of the Prologue to the Gospel of St. John." *NTS* 9 (1963): 120– 29.

Robinson, Stephen E., and H. Dean Garrett. *A Commentary on the Doctrine and Covenants*. 4 vols. Salt Lake City: Deseret Book, 2004.

Rothschild, Clare K. *Hebrews as Pseudepigraphon: The History and Significance of the Pauline Attribution of Hebrews*. Tübingen: Mohr Siebeck, 2009.

Rust, Richard. *Feasting on the Word: The Literary Testimony of the Book of Mormon*. Salt Lake City: Deseret Book, 1997.

Sanders, James A. "Intertextuality and Dialogue: New Approaches to the Scriptural Canon." In *Canon vs. Culture: Reflections on the Current Debate*. Edited by Jan Gorak, 175–90. New York: Garland Publishing, Inc., 2001.

———. "Why the Pseudepigrapha?" In *The Pseudepigrapha and Early Biblical Interpretation*. Edited by James H. Charlesworth and Craig A. Evans, 13–19. JSPSup 14. Sheffield: Sheffield Academic Press, 1993.

Sandmel, Samuel. "Parallelomania." *JBL* 81 (1962): 2–13.

Schendl, Herbet. "Morphologocial Variation and Change in Early Modern English: my/mine, thy/thine." In *Language History and Linguistic Modelling: A Festschrift for Jacek Fisiak on His 60th Birthday*. Edited by Raymond Hickey and Stanisław Puppel, 179–91. Berlin: Walter de Gruyter, 1997.

Schnackenburg, Rudolf. *The Gospel According to St. John.* 3 vols. New York: Crossroad, 1969/80, 1979/81, 1982.

Scott, Martin. *Sophia and the Johannine Jesus.* JSNTSup 71. Sheffield: Sheffield Academic Press, 1992.

Scott, Walter. *The Messiahship, or, Great Demonstration, Written for the Union of Christians, on Christian Principles, as Plead for in the Current Reformation.* Cincinnati: H. S. Bosworth, 1859.

Searle, Ambrose. *The Church of God: or, Essays on Various Names and Titles Given to the Church, in the Holy Scriptures: To which are Added, Some Papers on Other Subjects.* London: H. D. Symonds, and M. Jones, Paternoster-Row, 1806.

Sedgwick, Obadiah. *The Bowels of Tender Mercy Sealed in the Everlasting Covenant.* London, 1660.

Segal, Michael. "Between Bible and Rewritten Bible." In *Biblical Interpretation at Qumran*. Edited by Matthias Henze, 10–28. Grand Rapids: William B. Eerdmans Publishing Company, 2005.

Shalev, Eran. "Written in the Style of Antiquity: Pseudo-Biblicism and the Early American Republic, 1770–1830." *Church History* 79.4 (December 2010): 800–26.

Shipps, Jan. *Mormonism: The Story of a New Religious Tradition.* Chicago: University of Illinois Press, 1987.

———. "The Prophet Puzzle: Suggestions Leading Toward a More-Comprehensive Interpretation of Joseph Smith." *Journal of Mormon History* 1 (1974): 3–20.

Skousen, Royal, ed., *Analysis of Textual Variants of the Book of Mormon.* 6 vols. Provo: Foundation for Ancient Research and Mormon Studies, 2004–2009.

———. *The Book of Mormon: The Earliest Text.* Yale: Yale University Press, 2009.

———. "Translating the Book of Mormon: Evidence from the Original Manuscript." In *Book of Mormon Authorship Revisited: The Evidence for Ancient Origins*. Edited by Noel B. Reynolds, 61–93. Provo: Foundation for Ancient Research and Mormon Studies, 1997.

Smith, Dwight Moody. "God's Only Son: The Translation of John 3:16 in the Revised Standard Version." *JBL* 72 (1953): 213–29.

Smith, Joseph. "The Answer." *Times and Seasons* 4 (February 1, 1843): 82–85.

———. "Baptism." *Times and Seasons* 3 (September 1, 1842): 903–905.

———. "Church History." *Times and Seasons* 3 (March 1, 1842): 706–10.

———. "Conference Minutes." *Times and Seasons* 5 (August 15, 1844): 612–17.

Smith, Lucy Mack. *History, 1844–1845.* The Joseph Smith Papers. Accessed 11 Mar. 2016. josephsmithpapers.org/paperSummary/lucy-mack-smith-history-1844-1845.

Smith, Timothy L. "The Book of Mormon in a Biblical Culture." *JMH* 7 (1980): 3–21.

Smutz, Lois Jean. "Textual Parallels to the Doctrine and Covenants (Sections 65–133) as Found in the Bible." Master's Thesis. Brigham Young University, 1971.

Sommer, Benjamin D. *A Prophet Reads Scripture: Allusion in Isaiah 40–66.* Stanford: Stanford University Press, 1998.

Spencer, Joseph M. and Jenny Webb. *Reading Nephi Reading Isaiah: Reading 2 Nephi 26–27.* Salem: Salt Press, 2011.

Sperry, Sidney B. *Doctrine and Covenants Compendium.* Salt Lake City: Bookcraft, 1965.

Staker, Mark Lyman. *Hearken, O Ye People: The Historical Setting of Joseph Smith's Ohio Revelations.* Salt Lake City: Greg Kofford Books, 2009.

Stanley, Christopher D. *Arguing with Scripture: The Rhetoric of Quotations in the Letters of Paul.* New York: T&T Clark International, 2004.

———. *Paul and Scripture: Extending the Conversation.* Atlanta: Society of Biblical Literature, 2012.

———. "'Pearls Before Swine': Did Paul's Audience Understand his Biblical Quotations?" *NovT* 41 (1999): 122–44.

Stendahl, Krister. *The School of St. Matthew and Its Use of the Old Testament.* Philadelphia: Fortress Press, 1968.

———. "The Sermon on the Mount and Third Nephi." In *Reflections on Mormonism.* Edited by Truman G. Madsen, 139–54. Salt Lake City: Bookcraft, 1978.

Talmage, James E. *The Articles of Faith.* Salt Lake City: Signature Books, 2003.

Talmon, Shemaryahu. "The Textual Study of the Bible—A New Outlook." In *Qumran and the History of the Biblical Text.* Edited by F. M. Cross and S. Talmon, 321–400. Cambridge, MA: Harvard University Press, 1975.

Taylor, John. *The Mediation and Atonement.* Salt Lake City: Deseret News Company, 1882.

Thompson, Michael. *Clothed with Christ: The Example and Teaching of Jesus in Romans.* JSNTSup 59. Sheffield: JSOT Press, 1991.

Tobin, Thomas. "The Prologue of John and Hellenistic Jewish Speculation." *CBQ* 52 (1990): 252–69.

Trumbower, Jeffrey A. *Born From Above: The Anthropology of the Gospel of John.* Tubingen: J. C. B. Mohr, 1992.

Turner, Rodney. "The Doctrine of the Firstborn and Only Begotten." In *The Pearl of Great Price: Revelations from God.* Edited by H. Donl Peterson and Charles D. Tate Jr., 91–118. Provo: Religious Studies Center, 1989.

Tvedtnes, John A, "The Hebrew Background of the Book of Mormon." In *Rediscovering the Book of Mormon.* Edited by John L. Sorenson and Melvin J. Thorne, 77–91. Salt Lake City and Provo: Deseret Book and Foundation for Ancient Research and Mormon Studies, 1991.

Underwood, Grant. *The Millenarian World of Early Mormonism.* Champaign: University of Illinois Press, 1993.

van Wolde, Ellen. "Trendy Intertextuality?" In *Intertextuality in Biblical Writings: Essays in Honour of Bas van Iersel.* Edited by Sipke Draisma, 43–49. Kapen, Netherlands: Uitgeversmaatschappij J. H. Kok, 1989.

VanderKam, James. "Moses Trumping Moses: Making the Book of Jubilees." In *The Dead Sea Scrolls: Transmission of Traditions and Production of Texts.* Edited by Sarianna Metso, Hindy Najman, and Eileen Schuller. Leiden: E. J. Brill, 2010.

Vogel, Dan. *Joseph Smith: The Making of a Prophet.* Salt Lake City: Signature Books, 2004.

———, ed. *Early Mormon Documents.* 5 vols. Salt Lake City: Signature Books, 1996.

Wayment, Thomas A. "The Logos Incarnate and the Journey of the Soul: A New Paradigm for Interpreting the Prologue of John." Ph.D. Dissertation. Claremont Graduate University, 2000.

Welch, John W. "The Miraculous Translation of the Book of Mormon." In *Opening the Heavens: Accounts of Divine Manifestations, 1820–1844.* Edited by John W. Welch with Erick B. Carlson, 82–98. Provo and Salt Lake City: Brigham Young University Press and Deseret Book, 2005.

Weyde, Karl William. "Inner-Biblical Interpretation: Methodological Reflections on the Relationship between Texts in the Hebrew Bible." *SEA* 70 (2005): 287–300.

Widtsoe, John A. *Rational Theology.* Salt Lake City: Signature Books, 2007.

Williams, Catrin H. "'I Am' or 'I Am He'? Self-Declaratory Pronouncements in the Fourth Gospel and Rabbinic Traditions." In *Jesus and the Johannine Tradition.* Edited by Robert T. Fortna and Tom Thatcher, 343–52. London: Westminster John Knox Press, 2001.

Witherington III, Ben. *John's Wisdom.* Louisville: Westminster John Knox Press, 1995.

Woodford, Robert J. "Joseph Smith and the Revelations: From Manuscripts to Publication." *MHS* (Fall 2005): 135–44.

Wright, David P. "In Plain Terms that We May Understand: Joseph Smith's Transformation of Hebrews in Alma 12–13." In *New Approaches to the Book of Mormon.* Edited by Brent Lee Metcalfe, 165–229. Salt Lake City: Signature Books, 1993.

Index

Abinadi, 22, 24

Acts, Book of, 71, 89n40

Adam, fall of, 36

afterlife, 77–80; celestial marriage and, 79

"aggadic exegesis," 57

allusion, Johannine, xix, 131; biblical language and, 24, 25, 87n9; children of God, 28; convergence of Bible and Book of Mormon through, 40, 131; defined, 21, 22; directional meaning through, 21, 22; enablement, 27; exegesis *versus*, 48n2, 50n36; Greek language and, 6, 17n17, 42, 62, 88n11; high Christology and, 40, 54n59; Jesus as light and life of the world, 22–25, 49n12; Jesus as only begotten son of God, 32–39; Jesus born of God, 26–32, 50n33, 51n37; Joseph Smiths' revelations regarding "light shineth in darkness . . . ," 39–47; nineteenth century audience and, 25; spiritual birth, 28–32

allusivity, xii, xiii, xvi–xix, xxxn23, xxxin42; in Christian texts, xv, xvi; defined, xiv–xv; of Mormon Scripture to Prologue of John, xxii–xxiii, 5–6; motivations for, xv; rhetoric of, 2, 5–6, 131. *See also* echo, Johannine; expansion, Johannine; inversion, Johannine

Alma the Younger: allusion and, 26, 27, 29, 30–32, 35, 51n37; expansion and, 58–61, 63

atonement, 8; moral influence theory of, 118

audience, Book of Mormon, 6, 7, 25

authority, claim to, 1, 15, 16n11

Bahktin, Mikhail, xxii, 2

baptism, 9, 18n24, 124n37

Barlow, Philip, xxvii, 2

Barrett, C. K., 9, 29, 62, 69, 99

Barthes, Roland, xxii

Beale, G. K., xxi, 95

Bellamy, Joseph, 118

Ben-Porat, Ziva, 1, 21

Bernstein, Moshe J., xiii

Bible, the, xi; allusivity. *See* allusivity; convergence with Book of Mormon, 11, 18n30, 40, 47, 131, 132, 133n5; Greek language and, 6, 17n17, 42, 62, 88n11; intertexuality, xxi, xxii, xxxivn61, 117; Joseph Smith and, xi, xvii, 86, 87n9, 96, 131, 133n5; King James, xxvii, xxviiin10, xxixn15, 42; law and prophets, 70; light of Jesus, 85; phrases in the Book of Mormon, xxxviin90, 17n13; pseudo-biblical literature and, xvii

Biblical Interpretation in Ancient Israel, xxii

bi-directional reading, 87n3

birth, spiritual, 28–32

Book of Commandments, 74–76

Book of Mormon, xi, xxiii; allusivity in, xvii, 5, 6; atonement process in, 8; authoritative discourse, 2; baptism in, 9, 18n24; biblical lanuguage in, xxxviin90, 4, 7, 8, 17n13, 24, 25, 42, 47, 59, 60; convergence with the Bible, 11, 18n30, 40, 47, 131, 132, 133n5; early converts and, 1; intertextuality, 47, 55n74; Jacob, son of Lehi in, 8; likening of scripture, 57, 58; Moroni as final author of, 7; nineteenth-century audience of, 6, 7, 25; only begotten son phrase, 34, 35; organization of, xi; "other sheep,"

About the Author

Nicholas J. Frederick holds a PhD in the History of Christianity with an emphasis in Mormon Studies from Claremont Graduate University. He received a BA in Classics and an MA in Comparative Studies from Brigham Young University. He is married to the former Julie Parker and is the father of four children, Miranda, Samuel, Kassandra, and Madelyn. He is currently assistant professor of Ancient Scripture in the Department of Religion at Brigham Young University.